THE WORKHOUSE COOKBOOK

The women's dining hall at St Pancras workhouse in 1897. On the serving table at the rear are some scales – any inmate could request that their portion be weighed out in front of witnesses if they suspected it was a short measure.

A view of what lies behind the far wall in the above picture. Two enormous steamers dominate the centre of St Pancras workhouse kitchen, which produced meals for more than 1,500 inmates.

THE WORKHOUSE COOKBOOK

PETER HIGGINBOTHAM

The History Press

First published 2008

The History Press Ltd
The Mill, Brimscombe Port
Stroud, Gloucestershire, GL5 2QG
www.thehistorypress.co.uk

British Library Cataloguing in Publication Data.
A catalogue record for this book is available from the British
Library.

ISBN 978 0 7524 4730 8

Typesetting and origination by The History Press Ltd.
Printed in Great Britain

Contents

Weights, Measures, and Money

Below is a list of some of the older weights, measures, and monetary units that may be encountered in this book, together with their approximate metric or decimal currency equivalents. Common abbreviations are given in brackets.

Weight

1 drachm (drm)		1.8 grams (gm)
1 ounce (oz)	16 drachms	28.4 grams
1 pound (lb)	16 ounces	450 grams
1 stone	14 pounds	6.3 kilograms
1 hundredweight (cwt)	112 pounds	50 kilograms

Volume

1 fluid drachm (or dram)		3.55 cubic centimetres (cc or ml)
1 fluid ounce	8 fluid drachms	28.4 cubic centimetres
1 gill (or noggin)	5 fluid ounces	143 cubic centimetres
1 pint	20 fluid ounces	570 cubic centimetres
1 quart	2 pints	1.1 litres
1 gallon	8 pints	4.5 litres
1 peck	2 gallons	9 litres
1 bushel	8 gallons	36 litres
1 hogshead (of beer etc)	51 or 54 gallons	235 or 245 litres

Length

1 inch (in)		2.5 centimetres (cm)
1 foot (ft)	12 inches	30 centimetres
1 yard (yd)	3 feet	90 centimetres
1 mile	1,760 yards	1.6 kilometres (km)

Money

1 farthing	
1 penny (d)	4 farthings
1 shilling (s)	12 pennies
1 pound (£ or l)	20 shillings

In terms of its purchasing power, £1 in the year 1750 would now be worth around £133. £1 in 1850 would now be worth around £80.

Introduction

The evening arrived; the boys took their places. The master, in his cook's uniform, stationed himself at the copper; his pauper assistants ranged themselves behind him; the gruel was served out; and a long grace was said over the short commons. The gruel disappeared; the boys whispered each other, and winked at Oliver; while his next neighbours nudged him. Child as he was, he was desperate with hunger, and reckless with misery. He rose from the table; and advancing to the master, basin and spoon in hand, said, somewhat alarmed at his own temerity: 'Please, sir, I want some more'.

Charles Dickens has a lot to answer for. Oliver Twist's famous words, and the gruel he wanted more of, have come to epitomise most people's image of the workhouse and the food that was served to its inmates. However, as we shall see, the picture it paints is a severe distortion of the truth – it is rather like basing our entire view of the English criminal justice system on the behaviour of Mr Fang, the loathsome magistrate before whom Oliver is later brought.

Workhouses – publicly funded establishments where the destitute could be housed, clothed and fed in exchange for the performance of work – can trace their roots back to at least the early 1600s. They evolved within the broad framework of what became known as the Old Poor Law, a system of parish-based poor relief financed out of the poor rate, a local property tax.

The popularity of the parish workhouse waxed and waned over the following two centuries, and it was up to individual parishes whether they operated a workhouse and how it was run. Throughout this period, however, most of the poor rate was spent on relieving the poor in their own homes through 'out-relief' – individual handouts in the form of money, bread, fuel, clothing, and so on. In order to deter able-bodied claimants from sponging off the poor rate, parishes also acquired the power to withdraw out-relief and instead offer a place in the workhouse as the only form of assistance for the destitute. Those entering the house were presented with a routine characterised by hard work, strict rules, and a diet that varied from the meagre to the munificent. Being prepared to accept this regime was in itself viewed as a sufficient test of whether an applicant was truly in need.

In 1834, the old parish-based system was swept away. It was replaced by a national and uniform framework of poor relief – the New Poor Law – based on a new administrative unit called the Poor Law Union. A union typically consisted of twenty to thirty parishes centred on a market town and was managed by a Board of Guardians elected annually by the local ratepayers. Each union had to provide a central workhouse, whose regime included the strict segregation of males and females, old and young, infirm and able-bodied. There was also a strictly regulated 'dietary' where – at the outset at least – workhouse inmates received little else but stringently controlled portions of bread and cheese, suet pudding, gruel or broth.

Oliver Twist – subtitled *The Parish Boy's Progress* – made its first appearance in 1837 in the monthly magazine *Bentley's Miscellany*, although it may have been evolving in Dickens' mind since as early as 1833.[1] Its conception and publication came at a particularly significant point in the history of the workhouse – the transition between the old and the new relief systems. Though highly topical in its day, it straddles the two eras slightly awkwardly. For example, Mr Bumble, a prominent character in Dickens' workhouse, was a beadle, or parish constable. Despite the impression given by Dickens, the beadle had no place in the running of a union workhouse.

Dickens' story does, however, clearly reflect some of the fierce opposition that the new workhouse provoked, particularly in regard to the privations to which its inmates were supposedly subjected – most notably the food with which they were provided. The gruel scene, in its original illustration by George Cruikshank, shows a scrawny boy fearfully presenting a tiny bowl to the bulging-eyed workhouse master, in the forlorn hope of receiving another portion of watery porridge.

But exactly how accurate was that image? And, more importantly, does it tell the whole story? Were paupers in the workhouse invariably half-starved wretches, barely surviving on meagre portions of insipid gruel? Or could they be fed on an ample and varied diet which included such

'Oliver Asks for More' – one of George Cruikshank's original illustrations for Dickens' *Oliver Twist*.

treats as fish pie, shepherd's pie, pasties, haricot soup, fruit pudding, and roley-poley pudding? Was alcohol banned, or did beer and other alcoholic beverages form a regular part of the daily rations? What about tea – was it a strictly forbidden luxury or on tap from a giant urn? Was uneaten food endlessly re-served at successive mealtimes, or given to the pigs, or just thrown away? Were nettles ever on the workhouse menu? Or chocolate? Or cheesecake? Was raw sewage from the inmates' privies really used to fertilise vegetables in the workhouse gardens? Did convicted criminals in prison receive better food than people living in workhouses? Did workhouse inmates ever die of overeating, or have drunken outings to the seaside? And is it true that a workhouse boy once fell into a vat of soup and ended up being unwittingly eaten by the other inmates? In fact, as we shall see, all of these (well, maybe except for the boy in the soup!) were true at different times and at different places in the long and varied history of the workhouse and its culinary fare.

From its seventeenth-century roots until its official demise in 1930, the institution of the workhouse evolved considerably. This is especially true of the diet it provided for its inmates. Monotony certainly was a feature of workhouse food at times in its history, with the dreaded bowl of gruel indeed being a staple component of some inmates' diet. However, at other periods it featured a varied menu which included dishes such as frumenty, lobscouse, hasty pudding, and colcannon – period recipes for all of these are included in this book.

The union workhouse system was extended to Ireland in 1838. As well as looking at food in the Irish workhouse, a section is also included on the impact of the famine in Ireland which began in 1845. 1845 also saw the establishment of a new and separate poor-relief system in Scotland. Although the Scottish system was distinct from that operating in the rest of Britain, it did include some use of poorhouses – the usual terminology for workhouse-style establishments in that country. The diets of poorhouse inmates will be examined, with recipes for such dishes as sago soup and scrap bread pudding.

By the end of the nineteenth century, the majority of workhouse residents were not the idle or the work-shy for whom the union workhouse had initially been envisaged. Instead, the inmates largely comprised the elderly, the lame, the chronic sick, those with varying degrees of mental illness or disability, orphaned or abandoned children, and women who were unmarried and pregnant, or whose husbands had deserted them. For such people, an unvarying ration of bread, cheese and gruel, was physically and emotionally debilitating. In many cases it was also literally inedible and the central authorities received increasing complaints about the large amounts being thrown in the bin.

In 1900, in a major overhaul of workhouse food, the local government Board compiled a list of around fifty varied dishes from which workhouses were now free to choose their own weekly menus. The following year, the National Training School of Cookery was commissioned to prepare a cookery manual, to be issued to all workhouses, giving simple standard recipes for the new range of dishes, together with advice on the most economical cooking methods. Despite this momentous step forward in workhouse cuisine, a recipe for making gruel still featured in the new manual. *The Manual of Workhouse Cookery* makes fascinating reading and is reproduced in full as part of this book.

Today, around eighty years since its official demise, the workhouse is an establishment whose shadow still haunts the British national psyche. Some older people can still recall being told as children, 'behave or you'll end up in the workhouse.' Many of the younger generation who have been charting their family history have, at some point, discovered an ancestor who was born, who lived, or who died in the workhouse, and are eager to know what life was really like in these grim establishments. Whatever your interest in reading this book, I hope it will indeed give you the true flavour of the workhouse.

one

The Origins of the Workhouse

Until the sixteenth century, the relief of the nation's poor was not a matter in which the state was much involved. However, this was a situation that was to change dramatically. A combination of factors such as rising population, the conversion of arable land to grazing pasture, migration from the countryside to towns, and price inflation together resulted in a lowering of wages and higher unemployment. The result was an increase in poverty and destitution.

People in financial distress had traditionally received assistance through the alms-giving of individuals and from established bodies such as monasteries, hospitals, and guilds. For the 'impotent poor' – the elderly, the chronically sick, orphans and so on – this was accepted as all well and good. There was, however, a rising tide of able-bodied vagabonds and 'sturdy beggars' roaming around the countryside who refused to work and supported themselves through begging and intimidation. Such was the scale of the problem that by the 1530s, during the reign of Henry VIII, it began to be seen as a serious threat to the country's economic and social stability.

The problem of how to provide help for the deserving poor, while denying it to idlers and beggars, was one that was to preoccupy legislators for the next four centuries (and still does). The solution proposed in a parliamentary Act of 1536[2] had two lines of attack. First, beggars and vagabonds were to be whipped, with repeat offenders having part of their ear cut off, and persistent offenders facing a threat of execution. Second, direct alms-giving was to be forbidden and instead replaced by the collection of alms in church in a 'common box'. Although the 1536 Act was short-lived, the same year saw the beginning of a process that was to have rather more far-reaching consequences, namely Henry's Dissolution of the Monasteries and other charitable institutions with religious connections.

In the 1550s, voluntary alms-giving was replaced by the collection of a compulsory poor-tax in London, Cambridge, Colchester, Ipswich, Norwich, and York. This principle was adopted nationally in 1572 with the introduction of a local property tax, the poor rate, which was assessed by local Justices of the Peace and administered by parish overseers. The money raised was to be used to relieve 'aged, poor, impotent, and decayed persons'. In 1576, an Act For Setting the Poor on Work provided that stocks of materials such as wool, hemp, and flax should be bought and premises hired in which to employ the able-bodied poor.

In London, parish collections also helped fund the Royal Hospitals which had been closed after the Dissolution but which were gradually restored during the reign of Edward VI. St Bartholomew's (reopened in 1546) and St Thomas' (1551) provided care for the sick and aged, while Christ's Hospital (1553) housed and educated orphans. The Bethlem (or Bethlehem) Hospital, also known as 'Bedlam', operated as an asylum for the poor who were mentally ill. A new institution, Bridewell, occupied Henry VIII's former palace on the banks of the River

A seventeenth-century poor box from a church in Buckinghamshire; it was originally used to collect poor relief contributions.

A view of London's Bridewell as it was in around 1660. Most of the building was demolished in 1863. The Bridewell theatre now stands on part of the site.

Fleet at Blackfriars. From 1555, it provided punishment and hard labour for idlers, vagrants and prostitutes, and those of its inmates who were classed as sturdy (i.e. able-bodied) beggars received a 'thin diet onely sufficing to sustaine them in health'. Despite its prison-like character, Bridewell was also partly used for lodging the poor and sick.

A number of similar hospital establishments were set up outside London. In Ipswich – one of the first towns to impose a compulsory poor rate – Christ's Hospital offered a refuge for the old and sick, and training for orphans, and also functioned as a 'house of correction' for the work-shy. Similar institutions, occupying property confiscated during the Dissolution, existed at Reading, Norwich, King's Lynn, and York. Reading's hospital, which housed twenty-one children and fourteen old people, was funded by parish collections, private donations, and income generated from the work of the poor themselves. At King's Lynn, St James's church was converted into a house for the poor who were then provided with employment.

HOUSES OF CORRECTION

Another provision of the 1576 Poor Act was the establishment of a House of Correction in each county to deal with the able-bodied poor who refused to work. Although Houses of Correction (also known as 'Bridewells' after the original Blackfriars establishment) are the forerunner of the modern prison, prior to the English Civil War they often housed children, the elderly and the sick.

The rules of discipline and diet published in 1588 for the House of Correction at Bury in Suffolk portray it as a very severe establishment. At admission, every 'strong or sturdy rogue' was given twelve lashes and then manacled. All inmates rose at 4 a.m. in summer (5 a.m. in winter) then after communal prayers worked until 7 p.m. except for meal breaks. On 'flesh days', dinner and supper comprised 8oz of rye bread, a pint of porridge, a quarter of a pound of flesh, and a pint of beer. On 'fish days', meat was replaced by milk or peas, a third of a pound of cheese, or 'one good herring, or two white or red'.[3]

A 1794 view of the Middlesex House of Correction at Clerkenwell, later known as Cold Bath Prison and then as Clerkenwell Gaol. The Post Office's Mount Pleasant sorting office now occupies the site.

RED HERRINGS

The general observance of fish days (when the eating of flesh was prohibited) was taken very seriously – defying the ban was punishable by a £3 fine or three months in prison. In 1562, Elizabeth I added Wednesday to the existing fish days of Friday and Saturday. Although the prohibition may have been portrayed as a religious devotion, its rather more practical purpose was to aid an ailing fishing industry and to conserve meat stocks.

For the poor, herrings were often the most affordable fish. However, they went off very quickly and so were usually eaten preserved, either as white herrings (pickled in brine) or red herrings (smoked). The metaphorical use of the term 'red herring' – meaning a distraction or diversion – originally came from the phrase 'to draw a red herring across the track'. This dates from the second half of the seventeenth century when a malodorous object such as a dead cat or fox, or a red herring, was dragged along a trail to train hunting dogs to follow a scent. A farmer wishing to avoid his fields being trampled by a fox hunt could take advantage of this by trailing a red herring around his fields to divert the hounds.

THE 1601 POOR RELIEF ACT

Various strands of sixteenth-century legislation were consolidated in the 1601 Act for the Relief of the Poor. This Act, which formed the foundation of what became known as the Old Poor Law, clearly defined the parish as the body with responsibility for relieving the destitute. The system was administered locally by the Vestry – the parish's governing body. (The Vestry derived its name from its usual meeting place – the room in a church building where the priest put on his vestments.) The Vestry's membership comprised a chairman (the minister of the parish), the churchwardens, and a number of respected householders of the parish. Each householder was levied in relation to the value of their property – this was the origin of the 'rates', a local tax which survived in England and Wales until 1990 when it was replaced by the community charge.

The poor rates were collected by the overseers, of which a parish had between two and four, depending on its size. The funds were then dispensed to provide 'necessary relief of the lame, impotent, old, blind, and such other among them being poor, and not able to work'. Relief was most commonly dispensed as 'out-relief' – individual weekly handouts in the form of bread, clothing, fuel, the payment of rent, or money. The poor rates could also be used for erecting 'houses of dwelling' for the impotent poor, the employment or apprenticeship of poor children, and for buying a stock of materials such as flax, hemp and wool to provide work for the able-bodied poor. Any able-bodied pauper who refused to work was liable to be placed in a House of Correction.

The 1601 Act was originally passed as a temporary measure until 'the end of the next session of Parliament'. In fact, it became so deeply rooted at the heart of the English poor-relief system that its final vestiges were only repealed in 1967.

THE FIRST WORKHOUSES

Although the 1601 Act talked about 'work' and 'houses', it made no mention of the word 'workhouse' – a term which seems to have come into general use in the 1620s. At Sheffield, accounts from 1628 onwards record that the town council spent £200 on the erection of a workhouse together with a stock of raw materials for providing employment; 8s was spent on 'the carpenters charges going to Newarke to see their workhouse'. In 1631, the mayor of Abingdon in Berkshire reported that 'wee haue erected wthn our borough a workehouse to sett poore people to worke.' In the following ten years, workhouses appeared at places such as Taunton, Halifax, Exeter, Plymouth, and Cambridge.

The workhouses set up in the early 1600s were generally non-residential establishments where work, often related to the production of textiles, was provided for the willing able-bodied.

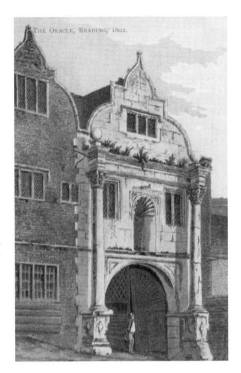

Above left: An 1802 view of Reading's Oracle workhouse – the name possibly deriving from 'orchal', a violet dye obtained from lichen. The building was demolished in 1840, but its ornate wooden gates are preserved at Reading museum. The site is now occupied by a shopping centre also known as The Oracle.

Above right: Newbury's 1627 workhouse – one of the oldest surviving workhouse buildings in Britain. This block, now housing a museum, only originally formed one side of a square courtyard.

In 1624, the towns of Reading and Newbury in Berkshire each received a substantial bequest from John Kendrick, a wealthy London draper, to establish a workhouse and provide work for unemployed clothiers. At Reading, where Kendrick had been born, the town Corporation spent £2,000 on a site on Minster Street and in 1628 opened an impressive building which became known as The Oracle. It consisted of rows of workshops around a central courtyard accessed through an ornate Dutch-gabled stone gateway. Newbury used its share of Kendrick's bequest to buy a property known as The Castle and an adjoining meadow in Cheap Street. The new workhouse was again arranged around a central courtyard.

Apart from a few supervisory staff who had accommodation on the premises, the Reading and Newbury workhouses were more like workshops than workhouses in character, with their workers living elsewhere. Newbury's workhouse account book from 1628-33 shows that almost all the outgoings relate to the purchase of materials or the paying of wages, with virtually no reference to domestic or household expenses.[4] The main exception to this is the regular purchase of oats, presumably used to make porridge or some similar dish.

London's first workhouses were set up by the Corporation of the Poor, a body created by Parliament in 1647, to administer poor relief in the capital. The Corporation was given two confiscated royal properties – Heydon House in the Minories, and the Wardrobe Building in Vintry – in which it established workhouses. By 1655, up to 100 children and 1,000 adults were receiving relief, although residence was not a prerequisite. Adults could perform out-work in their own homes, or carry it out each day at one of the workhouses. As well as basic literacy, children in Corporation care were taught singing. A verse of one of their songs paints a very rosy picture of their treatment:

In filthy rags we clothed were;
in good warm Raiment now appear.
From Dunghill to King's Palace transferred,
where education, wholesome food,
meat, drink and lodging, all that[s] good
for soul and body, are so well prepared.[5]

The Corporation's activities ended with the Restoration in 1660, when Charles II reclaimed his confiscated properties.

SETTLEMENT AND REMOVAL

In 1662, the passing of 'An Act for the Better Relief of the Poor', better known as 'The Settlement Act', was to have a far-reaching effect on the poor-relief system. It stated that a parish was required to give poor relief only to established or 'settled' residents. Any new arrival who the local justices deemed 'likely to be chargeable' to the parish poor rates could be forcibly removed back to his own parish unless he was able to rent a property for £10 a year or more.

A child's settlement at birth was taken to be the same as that of its father. At marriage, a woman took on the same settlement as her husband. Illegitimate children were granted settlement in the place they were born – this often led parish overseers to try and get rid of an unmarried pregnant woman before her child was born, for example by forcibly transporting her to another parish just before the birth, or by paying a man from another parish to marry her.

The 1662 Settlement Act was the first parliamentary Act to use the term 'workhouse'. It included a provision for Corporations to be created in the City of London, Westminster, and parts of Middlesex and Surrey. The new Corporations were empowered to erect workhouses, and in 1664, Middlesex spent £5,000 on setting one up in Clerkenwell at the corner of Corporation Lane (now Corporation Row) and Bridewell Walk (now Northampton Road). The workhouse supplied materials for the poor to work with in their own homes and was also used for 'the reception and breeding up of poor fatherless or motherless infants.' The Middlesex workhouse was not a success and closed in 1672.

SETTING THE POOR TO WORK

The last quarter of the seventeenth century was an era of experimentation in how best to provide useful work for the indigent poor and a number of schemes were put forward. The Chief Justice, Sir Matthew Hale, proposed that small groups of parishes should combine to establish premises where the poor could be supplied with materials for work and where children could be taught a trade. The chairman of the East India Co., Sir Joshua Child, suggested a similar scheme across the whole of London run by a body which he proposed calling 'The Fathers of the Poor'.

A different approach was taken by philanthropist Thomas Firmin who, in 1676, set up a workhouse at Little Britain near Smithfield. More than 1,700 carders, combers, spinners, and weavers were employed to manufacture linen from flax, much of which was done in their own homes. The establishment 'was at once school and factory, wholesale warehouse and retail shop'.[6] The workforce were treated well and their wages supplemented by handouts of coal. Children were admitted from the age of three and taught to read and spin. However, the scheme, which was financed from Firmin's own pocket, lost upwards of £200 each year.

A similar approach was adopted in 1680 by the Society of Friends, or Quakers. Stocks of flax were bought and given to the Quaker poor to spin up at home or in prison. The scheme's treasurer, John Bellers, later developed plans for a 'College of Industry' – a co-operative, self-sufficient, humanitarian community where up to 200 labourers and 100 of the impotent poor would live and work together. The College building was planned to consist of four wings: one for married people, one for single young men and boys, one for single women and girls, and one for sick and invalid members. The College was also to have a library, a 'physick-garden', and laboratories for the preparation of medicines.[7]

THE QUAKER WORKHOUSE, CLERKENWELL

Although Bellers' utopian plans were never implemented, their influence can be seen in the workhouse and school opened by the Quakers in 1702 at Clerkenwell. The establishment occupied the former Middlesex County workhouse premises and housed up to fifty-six 'decayed friends and orphans'.[8] The elderly occupied one section of the house, with the children in another where they were employed in spinning mop-yarn. The girls also made and mended the inmates' clothing, while the boys learnt to read, write and cast accounts. Cold baths were on offer to the inmates 'for their health or cleanliness'. The inmates brewed their own beer, and the children helped in preparing the food. The weekly menu is shown below.[9]

Days	Breakfast and Supper	Dinner
1st Day	4Oz of Bread 2Oz of Cheese 1Oz of Butter 1 Pint of Beer	8Oz of Roast Meat without Bones 4Oz of Bread 1 Pint of Beer
2nd Day	The same as the 1st Day	1 Pint of Milk 4Oz of Bread and Beer if desired
3rd Day	The same	8Oz of Boyl'd Meat without Bones 4Oz of Bread and 1 Pint of Beer
4th Day	1 Pint of Broth 4Oz of Bread 1 Pint of Beer	1 Pint of Frumety or Rice-Milk 4Oz of Bread and 1 Pint of Beer
5th Day	The same as the 1st Day	8Oz of Boyl'd Meat without Bones 4Oz of Bread 1 Pint of Beer
6th Day	The same as the 4th Day	1lb of Plumb or Plain pudding 1 Pint of Beer
7th Day	The same as the 1st Day	1 Pint of Milk Porridge 4Oz of Bread or 1 Pint of Pease-Pottage 1Oz Butter and 1 Pint of Beer

Children received the same diet but with reduced portions. The meals could also be varied when foods such as peas, beans, mackerel, herring, salt fish, etc were in season.

The Quaker workhouse was not set up as a punitive or deterrent establishment and although bread and cheese accounted for around half of the meals, the inclusion of butter, three meat dinners a week, and up to three pints of beer a day, made the menu far from Spartan. The beer, as we shall see later, was likely to have been a rather low-strength brew, widely consumed at virtually any meal in preference to the variable quality water supplies available.

The menu also included broth which was a basic item in many pauper diets. A typical recipe for its production was given by Hannah Glasse in her 1747 *Art of Cookery, Made Plain and Easy*:

Strong Broth for Soops or Gravy

Take a Leg of beef, chop it to pieces, set it on the Fire in four Gallons of Water, scum it clean, season it with black and white Pepper three or four ounces, a few Cloves, and a bundle of Sweet Herbs. Let it boil till two Parts is wasted, then season it with Salt, let it boil a little while, then strain it off, and keep it for Use.

A picture of life in the Quaker workhouse is provided by the remarkable survival of a notebook kept by Richard Hutton, the workhouse steward from 1711 to 1737. Early on in his notes, Hutton records that, after he took over, he improved the quality of various dishes on the workhouse menu. For example, the ingredients of a batch of frumenty, previously 12 quarts of milk, 12d worth of wheat, and 2½lb of sugar, were changed to include 15 quarts of milk. Similarly, the plum pudding, which formerly used 12 quarts of milk, 6lb of suet, and 4lb of plums, now comprised 15 quarts of milk, 10lb of suet, and 10lb of plums.[10]

Frumenty (numerous alternative spellings include frumety, frumity, furmenty and furmety) gets its name from *frumentum* – the Latin word for 'grain'. It was a porridge-like dish made by boiling up milk and hulled wheat, i.e. wheat grains with the husks removed. It could be sweetened with sugar or honey and enriched by the addition of eggs, cream, saffron or dried fruit. Here is a recipe from 1726 in John Nott's *Cooks and Confectioners Dictionary*:

Frumety

Take two Quarts of hull'd boil'd Wheat, a Gallon of Milk, two Quarts of Cream, and boil them 'till they become pretty thick; then put in Sugar the Yolks of eight or ten Eggs well-beaten, three Pound of Currants plump'd by being gently boil'd in Water; put these into the Furmety, give them a few Walms [spells of boiling], and it will be done.

(Modern version: boil then gently simmer 100gm of bulgar wheat in 350ml of water for 15 minutes. Stand for 15 minutes. Add 150ml of milk, boil, then remove from heat. Optionally, stir in a beaten egg yolk and cook gently until the egg begins to set. Stand for five minutes. Serve with salt or with brown sugar, raisins etc).

Anyone who was sick in the Quaker workhouse appears to have been looked after rather well. Hutton records that the diet of one inmate, John Wilson, over a six month period of being sick or weak, regularly included such mouth-watering items as: a pint of claret, half a pint of wine, fish, oysters, cheesecake, a ¼lb of chocolate, ½lb of double-refined sugar, ¼lb of biscuits, and conserve of roses with juleps.

When reports were spread that another young inmate, a sickly child named William Brady, had been starved whilst in the house, Hutton's notebook provided evidence to the contrary. He recorded that the child had always eaten well, and had regularly consumed mutton, veal, pork, and roast beef – the latter two of which he had been particularly fond. His breakfast had generally been ½ pint of chocolate with 4oz of toasted bread, and sometimes rice milk, milk pottage or mutton broth. When new-laid eggs were available, he had eaten them poached. On occasion he also consumed milk thickened with eggs or flour, bread pudding, fresh fish or anything else which would encourage him to eat.

THE BISHOPSGATE WORKHOUSE, LONDON

Another new workhouse was opened in 1699 by the City of London Corporation at the west side of Bishopsgate Street, where Liverpool Street Station now stands. It was set up 'for the confinement, maintaining and employing of great numbers of vagrants, idle and disorderly persons, and distressed children, found in the public streets and passages of this city.' Like the Quaker workhouse, it was influenced by the ideas of Thomas Firmin and his contemporaries.

The building ran back 400ft from the road and was divided into two portions: the steward's side, nearest to Bishopsgate Street, and the keeper's side, at the western end. The steward's side housed up to 400 poor children from a number of London parishes who paid a weekly maintenance charge for each child, originally 2s 6d. Private benefactors could also sponsor individual children at a cost of £25 a head. The children were fed, clothed, and had a surgeon and an apothecary to minister to their medical needs. They received a religious education which also included reading, writing, and casting accounts, and were also employed in spinning wool or flax, or in sewing and knitting. At a later date, the boys also wove nets for British fisheries. A boy could typically produce 25 yards of netting a week, which was sold for 1s 10½d, of which – by way of encouragement – he was allowed to keep one penny.

The Bishopsgate Street entrance of the City of London workhouse in 1819.

The keeper's side was for vagabonds, sturdy beggars, pilferers, and lewd, idle or disorderly persons. Men were given hard labour to perform, while the women were employed in beating hemp and also in the washing of linen for the children on the steward's side.

A sizeable staff was needed to run the workhouse. In 1742, it comprised:

Four physicians, who attend alternately monthly, gratis, a secretary, or clerk, a steward, minister, surgeon, writing-master, keeper, porter, messenger, master of the work, school-mistress, nine teachers, first and second matron, the cook and under-cook, eleven nurses, singing master, two hemp dressers, shoemaker, and taylor.[11]

In 1725, the diet provided for the inmates was as follows:[12]

Days	Breakfast	Dinner	Supper
Sunday	Bread and Beer	Beef and Broth	Bread and Butter or Cheese
Monday	Beef-Broth	Pease-Porridge	Ditto
Tuesday	Bread and Butter or Cheese	Rice-Milk	Ditto
Wednesday	Ditto	Plumb Dumplin'	Ditto
Thursday	Ditto	Beef and Broth	Ditto
Friday	Beef-Broth	Barley-Broth	Ditto
Saturday	Bread and Butter or Cheese	Milk-Porridge	Ditto
In Summertime, pease beans greens, and roots, are allow'd as the season affords them.			

Pease-porridge, also known as pease-pottage, was what we would now refer to as pea-soup. ('Pease' – from *pisa*, the Latin for peas – was originally a singular noun, but mistakenly came to be treated as a plural from which a new singular form of 'pea' was then derived.) Although versions of the dish using fresh peas can be found, it was most commonly made with dried peas, which made it a popular dish for seafarers. Here is a recipe from the 1708 edition of Henry Howard's *England's Newest Way in All Sorts of Cookery*:

Pease Pottage

Take two Quarts of Pease, put them into three Quarts of Water, season it pretty high with Pepper and Salt, boil them until they are enough, mix a spoonful of Flour with Water, and put in a little Mint, a Leek, two Handfuls of Spinage all cut small; put in Half a pound of Butter, boil it and dish it.

THE BRISTOL WORKHOUSE

One other notable workhouse enterprise from this period began life in 1696, when eighteen parishes in Bristol promoted a local Act of Parliament to create the Bristol Corporation of the Poor. The Act enabled the Corporation to manage poor relief across the whole city, including the setting-up of workhouses and the appointment of paid officers. The scheme's main instigator was John Cary who, in 1700, published a glowing account of its success.[13]

In 1698, the Corporation rented a building as a workhouse for 100 pauper girls who were taught to spin under the charge of four 'tutresses'. Initially, paid servants did the cooking and washing, but these were soon dispensed with and the work was done by the older girls.

On arrival, new inmates were stripped and washed by the matron and given a set of new clothes. Their diet included 'Beef, Pease, Potatoes, Broath [broth], Pease-Porridge, Milk-Porridge, Bread and Cheese, good Bear [beer], Cabage, Turnips etc.' Prayers were said twice daily with a church service on Sunday. In good weather the girls were allowed to walk on the hills with their tutresses. Sickness amongst the inmates was common, with around twenty ill at any one time, suffering from measles, smallpox and 'other distempers'.

The girls worked at their spinning for ten and a half hours a day in summer, a little less in winter. After their initial training, they were hired out to local manufacturers. However, the coarseness of the yarn they produced soon resulted in complaints and low payment rates.

The following year, the Corporation purchased a second workhouse to house the elderly, boys, and young children. The building had recently been occupied by the Treasury and so became known as the Mint Workhouse. In August 1699, 100 boys were moved in. They were occupied in 'spinning cotten wool, and weaving fustians' for which they were able to generate the creditable income of £6 per week. The boys were also taught to read and (unlike the girls) to write. Next, elderly inmates were admitted. They were clothed and given 'such employments as were fit for their ages and strengths.' Finally, young children were taken in and put in the care of nurses.

The Bristol scheme was not without its critics. In 1711, an anonymous pamphlet alleged that the workhouse was 'crowded with idle, lazy and lewd People' and that the running costs amounted to almost half the city's annual poor rate for the benefit of only 170 inmates.

Despite such complaints, the Bristol scheme helped to consolidate the emerging idea of the workhouse as a strictly run residential establishment, clearly distinct from a prison, and where the inmates were housed, clothed and fed, in return for their labour.

Bristol Mint workhouse later became St Peter's Hospital which was destroyed by bombing during the Second World War.

two

The Parish Workhouse Era

By the 1720s, workhouses run by individual parishes had started to appear. This was partly as a result of the efforts of men such as Matthew Marryott, a workhouse manager and entrepreneur from Buckinghamshire, who opened his first establishment at Olney in 1714. Marryott demonstrated that the deterrent effect of strictly run residential workhouse could save a parish money. Withdrawing all out-relief and instead offering only the workhouse would discourage all except those in real need, a principle which became known as the 'workhouse test'. As well as saving on out-relief, a parish could also contract out the burdensome business of running the workhouse to individuals such as Marryott who were paid so much per inmate per week to 'farm' the poor. Apart from his capitation fee from the parish, a contractor could also generate income from hiring out the inmates' labour to local employers.

In 1723, the principles of the workhouse test and farming the poor were incorporated into what is often known as the 'Workhouse Test Act'. In many respects, the Act formalised what had become increasingly common practice over the previous decade. It was, however, a 'permissive' Act, giving parishes a free choice as to whether or not they made use of its provisions.

For a parish and its ratepayers, the workhouse could now offer a means of reducing expenditure on relieving the poor. The replacement of weekly out-relief by the workhouse test could encourage poor relief claimants to try and provide for themselves or to seek support elsewhere. The cost of maintaining those who did take up the offer of the workhouse could also be reduced. This was partly through the economies of scale in supporting just one household and kitchen, rather than many separate individuals in their own homes. In addition, competitive tendering for contracts to farm the poor could also cut costs.

Further encouragement for parishes to set up a workhouse came from a perhaps unexpected quarter. The Society for Promoting Christian Knowledge (SPCK) was a small but influential London-based organisation which, amongst its other activities, promoted the use of charity schools and workhouses. The SPCK published a variety of resources such as handbooks for masters, guides to rules and diets, and so on. One of the Society's most influential publications was *An Account of Several Work-Houses for Employing and Maintaining the Poor, Setting Forth the Rules by Which They Are Governed* which first appeared in 1725. The *Account* was in the form of a directory of more than 100 workhouses then in operation, together with descriptions of their setting up and operation, and examples of the impressive financial savings they had achieved. For example, at St Martin's parish in Leicester:

> The Charge of maintaining the Poor us'd to be about £250 or £300 a year. The Charge this Year in cloathing the Poor, upon placing them in the Workhouse, and buying Utensils, &c. is much greater

An early parish workhouse erected at Witham in Essex in 1714.

than can be in future Years; and yet the Overseer assures me, that he is confident the Parish will even this Year save £100.

The deterrent effect of the strictly run workhouse was also frequently highlighted, for example at Ashton-under-Lyne:

> The Dread of what is called Confinement, having spurr'd on several of our Poor to labour for a Livelihood, which they would never have endeavoured, as long as they could have been relieved by the Parish-Rate, or by an Alms at our Doors.

It was a rather different story at Southwark. Here, conditions inside the workhouse were apparently sufficiently attractive as to entice paupers to apply for admission, as the *Account* reported:

> It is remarkable, that all the Parishes in Southwark, except St. Thomas's, have set up large Workhouses, for the Reception of their numerous Poor, which are so well regulated, that as fast as there is any Vacancy, interest is made by the poor themselves to be admitted.

The *Account's* entry for Romford, dated March 1725, gives a good idea of the operation of the workhouse there:

> It will conveniently lodge about 48 People, two in a Bed; and there is a small Infirmary built on the Backside of the House, but the People are generally in so good Health, that there has been hitherto little Occasion to use it.
>
> The Number of Poor now in the House is 4 old Men and 10 old Women from 50 to 80 Years of Age; 3 Boys and 3 Girls from 4 to 7 Years of Age. Their Employment is picking Ockam, at which they earn altogether about £20 per Annum; the Materials for this Sort of Work being pieces of old cable, or Junk (as it is called), are bought of two Merchants, one at Rotherhith, near Three Mariners Stairs, and the other at Cuckold's Point, and cost 7s per hundred Weight; which is sold again in Ockam for 10s per hundred. Or in spun yarn at 2d ½ per pound. Or in rope yarn at 2d per pound, or 16s 8d per C.Wt. For all these are made out of old Cable.

The title page of the 1732 edition of *An Account of Several Work-houses for Employing and Maintaining the Poor* – an early workhouse directory published by the Society for Promoting Christian Knowledge.

The Women knit, and mend Stockings for the whole Family, make Beds, and keep the House clean, and sometimes pick Ockam.

The Steward and his Wife have the Government of the Family; he buys all the Necessaries for Food at the Market, and she takes Care for dressing it.

London's first new parish workhouse following the Workhouse Test Act was set up in 1724 by St Giles, Cripplegate, near Bunhill Fields. In 1732, it housed 110 old men and fifty-three boys and girls. The inmates were chiefly employed in knitting, spinning, and picking 'ockam' or oakum – an onerous task in which old ropes were separated into their raw fibres.[14]

The parish workhouse movement did have its detractors, however. In 1731, an illustrated pamphlet entitled *The Workhouse Cruelty; Workhouses Turn'd Gaols; and Gaolers Executioners* was published under the pseudonym of 'Christian Love Poor'. It accused Marryott or his associates of vicious cruelty at the St Giles-in-the-Fields workhouse. Inmates punished by being placed in the 'Dark Hole' were said to have been starved to death, while the corpse of a woman who had died during childbirth was mutilated with her finger cut off and her eyes gouged out.

Nonetheless, the number of parish workhouses grew steadily over the next century. A parliamentary survey of national poor relief expenditure published in 1776-7 listed almost 2,000 parish workhouses in operation in England and Wales – approximately one parish in seven employing one. These institutions had a total capacity of over 90,000 – an average of around forty-five places each – but they varied considerably in size. The smallest (Hougham in Kent) provided a single place, while the largest (St George, Hanover Square, and St Martin in the Fields, both in Westminster) could each house 700. Outside London, Liverpool operated the largest workhouse with room for 600. Workhouse provision in Wales was almost non-existent although, curiously, Pembrokeshire had more workhouses than the rest of Wales put together.

Cudham parish workhouse in Kent was erected in 1731 during the workhouse boom that came in the wake of Knatchbull's Workhouse Test Act of 1723.

Despite the rise in the popularity of setting up workhouses, the majority of expenditure on the poor was still in the form of out-relief. The national survey of 1776-7 reported that the total expenditure on poor relief in England and Wales in the year ending at Easter 1776 was just over £1.55 million, of which only £80,000 (about five per cent) was spent on the provision of workhouses. Even where parish workhouses were successfully adopted, their use often lapsed after a few years. This could be due to difficulties in finding contractors to run them, or the initial financial savings not being maintained.

POORHOUSE OR WORKHOUSE

Parish records often contain references to 'poorhouses' rather than workhouses. Although the terms are often used more or less interchangeably, there was sometimes a difference.

In a workhouse, labour would be required from those inmates capable of doing it, the diet would be restricted and plain, and there would be a strict set of rules enforced by a resident master or mistress.

A parish poorhouse was generally a rather informally run affair. It typically consisted of one or more cottages or adjoining tenements where the elderly of the parish were given free lodging, or where the sick or disabled were housed. It might also be used as a temporary residence for paupers about to be removed to other parishes.

In 1834, a Poor Law inquiry reviewing the operation of poorhouses commented that 'No regular provision for the diet is made, and little order or discipline is maintained in them. Some of the paupers who are placed there work for private employers and maintain themselves; others receive pay from the parish and also provide their own food. Houses of this description appeared in general to be dirty and disorderly.'[15] The inquiry also heard that the population of a large poorhouse typically comprised:

A dozen or more neglected children, twenty or thirty able-bodied adults of both sexes and probably an equal number of aged and impotent persons who are proper objects of relief. Among these the mothers of bastard children and prostitutes live without shame, and associate freely with the youth, who also have the example and conversation of the inmates of the county gaol, the poacher, the vagrant, the decayed beggar, and other characters of the worst description. To these may be added a solitary blind person, one or two idiots, and not infrequently are heard, from among the rest, the incessant ravings of some neglected lunatic.

The interior of the St James, Poland Street workhouse in Westminster. It was drawn in around 1809 by the artist and caricaturist Thomas Rowlandson. The scene appears to be a women's day room – some of the inmates are sewing.

Workhouses and poorhouses were also distinct from almshouses, which were charitably endowed establishments providing permanent accommodation for the elderly of good character.

PARISH WORKHOUSE RULES AND DISCIPLINE

From the outset, most parish workhouses were run according to a strict set of rules and regulations. A typical regime was operating at the Aylesbury parish workhouse in 1831:

Every Person in health shall rise by six o'Clock the summer half year, and by seven the winter half year, and shall be employed in such labour as their respective age and ability will admit… any one refusing to work, shall for the first offence go without their next meal, and for the second offence be reported to the Overseers, that they may otherwise be punished.

That all the poor in the house go to bed by eight o'Clock the summer half year, and by seven o'Clock the winter half year, and that all candles be put out by that time.

That the poor shall have their provisions in a clean and wholesome manner, their breakfast by eight, their dinner at twelve, and their supper at six o'Clock; that no waste be made, nor any provisions carried away; and that Grace shall be said before and after dinner, and none may depart until Grace is said; and their dinner three times a week to be hot meat and vegetables properly cooked.

That the House be swept from top to bottom every morning and cleaned all over once a week, or so often as the Master and Mistress think necessary; and the windows be opened daily.

No person shall be permitted to bring spirituous liquors into the House, or smoke in any part of the premises, except the hall. Those found transgressing, shall lose their next meal, or be otherwise punished.

Workers shall be allowed 2d in every shilling they earn; Cook 4d per week; Doctor's Nurse from 1s; Washerwomen half a pint of ale each per day, and tea in the afternoon.

For inmates who broke the rules, the consequences often involved the loss of one or more meals. At Chichester, in 1756, the workhouse rules stipulated that anyone found guilty of lying would be:

Sett upon a stool during Dinner in the most public place in the Dining Room with a paper fixed on his or her breast whereon shall be wrote in capital letters *Infamous Lyar* and shall also lose that meal and for the second offence be put into the stock or wear the Pillory for two hours.

Idlers get their comeuppance at the Hamburg workhouse in 1777.

Interestingly, a similar approach seems to have been used at the Hamburg poorhouse in Germany in 1777 where the idle were punished by being suspended in a basket above the dining table at mealtimes while the more industrious inmates dined below.[16]

EDEN'S STATE OF THE POOR

Sir Frederic Eden published his pioneering work of social investigation, *The State of the Poor*, in 1797. The massive three-volume text, begun during a period of severe grain shortage in 1794-5, included reports from over 170 parishes across the country, detailing such matters as local food prices, labourers' wages, rents, and the poor relief customs. Where a workhouse was in operation, Eden itemized the number of inmates and often included illuminating details of the workhouse's operation. At Shrewsbury, for example, clean sheets were provided for the beds once a month, or more often if necessary, and clean linen for the inmates once a week. The 'decent and orderly' inmates were separated from the 'profligate and debauched'. No work was required on Sundays, Good Friday, Christmas Day and the two following days, Monday and Tuesday in Easter and Whitsun weeks, on Shrewsbury Show day, and on Saturday afternoons after 3 o'clock.

Some workhouses surveyed by Eden appeared to offer a fairly comfortable home, at least for some of their inmates. For example, the elderly at the Liverpool workhouse were:

Provided with lodging in a most judicious manner. Each apartment consists of three small rooms, in which are the fire-place and 4 beds, and is inhabited by 8 or 10 persons. These habitations are furnished with beds, chairs, and other little articles of domestic use that the inmates may possess, who being thus detached from the rest of the Poor, may consider themselves as comfortably lodged as in a secluded cottage, and thus enjoy, even in a Workhouse, in some degree, the comfort of a private fireside. The most infirm live on the ground floor; others are distributed through the upper storeys. They all dine together in a large room, which occasionally serves as a chapel.

three

Food in the Parish Workhouse

Publications such as *An Account of Several Work-houses* and Eden's *The State of the Poor* provide many examples of the diet on offer to inmates of the eighteenth-century workhouse. A typical menu is the 1724 'Bill of Fare' for the workhouse at Bury-King (Barking) in Essex. The food was served out in 'messes', with four persons sharing each mess. On most days, supper consisted of the leftovers from dinner-time – what happened if there were no left-overs is not revealed!

Days	Breakfast	Dinner	Supper
Sunday	Sheep's Head Broth	Beef, Pudding, and Broth	What's left at Noon
Monday	Beef Broth	Oatmeal Hasty Pudding with a quarter of a Pound of Butter to a Mess	Bread and Butter or Cheese
Tuesday	Hasty Pudding	Three bak'd Ox Cheeks	What's left at Dinner
Wednesday	Ox Cheek Broth	Pease Porridge	Bread, Cheese and Butter
Thursday	Hot Pease Porridge	Beef and Broth	What's left at Dinner
Friday	Beef Broth	Milk Porridge	Bread and Cheese
Saturday	Milk Porridge	Sheep's Head for each Mess	What's left at Dinner
Bread and Beer are allowed without Limitation. They have roast beef at the three great festivals, and plum pudding at Christmas			

Hasty pudding was usually made from flour stirred into boiling milk or water until it had the consistency of a thick batter. It could perhaps be the dish referred to in the children's nursery rhyme 'Girls and Boys Come Out to Play', which includes the lines: 'You find the milk and I'll find the flour / And we'll have pudding in half an hour'. Here is a recipe from *Collection for the Improvement of Husbandry and Trade* by John Houghton and Richard Bradley published in 1727:

Hasty Pudding

Take one quart of milk, the grated crumbs of a penny loaf; set all over the fire to boil, then sift in half a pound of flower dried before the fire, with a little salt stir in also some butter and some add quarter of a pound of currants. Some love it best with undried flower that will make lumps.

(Modern version: stir 60gm of sifted plain flour into 500ml milk and bring to the boil stirring all the time. Optionally add sugar, butter, raisins etc. to taste).

Hasty pudding could be enriched by the addition of eggs or cream. It could also be made with ground oatmeal, as was the practice in 1725 at Romford workhouse. Here is Hannah Glasse's recipe from 1747:

Oatmeal Hasty Pudding

Take a quart of water, set it on to boil, put in a piece of butter and some salt; when it boils, stir in the oatmeal till it is of a good thickness. Let it boil for a few minutes, pour it in your dish, and stick pieces of butter in it; or eat with wine and sugar or ale and sugar, or cream or new milk. This is best made with Scotch oatmeal.

Exactly when gruel began its well-known association with the workhouse is a little unclear. *An Account of Several Work-houses*, first published in 1725, made no mention of a dish by that name. One of the first references to gruel on a workhouse menu is in the 1742 bill of fare at the St Margaret's workhouse in Westminster:[17]

Days	Breakfast	Dinner	Supper
Sunday	Bread and Beer	Meat and Broth	Bread and Cheese
Monday	Bread and Broth	Peas Pottage	Bread and Butter
Tuesday	Bread and Gruel	Meat and Broth	Bread and Cheese
Wednesday	Bread and Broth	Hasty Pudding	Bread and Butter
Thursday	Bread and Gruel	Meat and Broth	Bread and Cheese
Friday	Bread and Broth	Barley Broth	Bread and Butter
Saturday	Bread and Gruel	Baked Puddings	Bread and Cheese
There is always Beer at Noon and Night; and the indispos'd are allow'd Mutton Four-times a Week.			

Gruel, or water gruel, contained a little oatmeal and a lot of water boiled up together. Here is Hannah Glasse's recipe from her 1747 *Art of Cookery, Made Plain and Easy*:

> **Water Gruel**
>
> You must take a Pint of Water, and a large Spoonful of Oatmeal, then stir it together, and let it boil up three or four Times, stirring it often. Don't let it boil over, then strain it through a Sieve, salt it to your Palate, put in a good Piece of fresh Butter brue [mix] it with a Spoon till the Butter is all melted, then it will be fine and smooth, and very good. Some love a little Pepper in it.

Gruel was notably absent from the rather more generous diet that was served up to the inmates of the Hunslet workhouse near Leeds, which opened on in May 1761:

Days	To Breakfast	To Dinner	To Supper
Friday	Milk porridge	Pudding or dumplins with treakle sauce, with a small piece of bread and butter or occasionally a pye of broaken meat	Milk Porridge
Saturday	Milk porridge	Drink porridge and bread	Milk porridge
Sunday	Milk porridge	Boyld beef or mutton with bread and beer, pottatoes or greens, broth served first	Broth
Monday	Broth or milk porridge	Rice milk and broaken meat with drink	Milk Porridge
Tuesday	Milk porridge	Bread, cheese and drink. N.B. – Instead of the above, two calves' hearts, boyld with two pounds bacon	Milk Porridge
Wednesday	Milk porridge	Dumplins with sauce and old milk	Milk Porridge
Thursday	Water porridge	Beef or mutton boyled with pottatoes or greens	Milk Porridge

Interestingly, the Hunslet fare included 'milk porridge', 'water porridge' and 'drink porridge'. Since oatmeal porridge has associations with Scotland and the North of England, it is tempting to view these terms simply as regional variations on hasty pudding, perhaps with 'drink porridge' being equivalent to gruel. However, things are not that simple because the 1724 menu at Barking presented earlier included milk porridge in addition to hasty pudding and oatmeal hasty pudding. Use of the simple term 'porridge' in its usual modern sense of oatmeal boiled in water seems to have begun during the nineteenth century.

The rice milk served at Hunslet had, as its name suggests, rice and milk as its main ingredients. Here is a 1797 recipe from *The Universal Cook, and City and Country Housekeeper* by Francis Collingwood, and John Woollams:

> **Rice Milk**
>
> Put half a pound of rice into a quart of water, with a little cinnamon and let it boil till the water is wasted; but take care that it does not burn. Then add three pints of milk and the yolk of an egg beat up. Keep stirring it, and when it boils, take it up and sweeten it.

Evidently, the diet allowed by the Hunslet Workhouse Committee did not meet with the approval of all the inmates. It was ordered that if Elizabeth Walker, an old woman of seventy-two, 'will not sup no broth of mutton at night it be kept till the next morning for breakfast.'

As at Hunslet, milk porridge featured on the breakfast menu at Shrewsbury, where a 'House of Industry' had opened in 1784. Eden reported that the bill of fare included four meat days where inmates were also served 'garden stuff' – perhaps what we would now term 'seasonal vegetables':

Breakfast – Sunday, Thursday, broth; other days, milk porridge. Dinner – Sunday, Thursday, butcher's meat and garden stuff; Monday, hasty pudding with butter and treacle sauce; Tuesday, Saturday, stewed meat with potatoes or other garden stuff; Wednesday, bread and cheese; Friday, yeast dumplins. Supper – Sunday, Wednesday, Thursday, Saturday, broth; Monday, Friday, mashed potatoes; Tuesday, pease soup.

Beyond the confines of the workhouse, Eden noted some interesting regional differences in the general diet of the poor at large. In the south of England, the poorest labourers had a fairly unvarying diet of bread and cheese accompanied by tea. Some might have the luxury of meat once a week, which would probably be roasted or baked. Cheese also featured prominently in the diet of the workhouse at Tiverton in Devon:

Breakfast – Sunday – Bread and cheese; Monday, Thursday, Saturday – Bread and broth; rest of week – Bread, broth and cheese. Dinner – Sunday – Pease and beer; Monday, Saturday – Cheese and pudding; Tuesday – Bread, cheese and beer; Wednesday, Friday – Bread, flesh, bowl of vegetables; Thursday – Cheese, pease and beer. Supper – Sunday, Monday, Thursday, Saturday – Bread and milk; Tuesday, Friday – Bread and cheese; Wednesday – Beer, bread and milk.

Although the Tiverton inmates only ate meat once a week, it was more usual for it to appear three or four times. Fairly typical was the 1790s' dietary at the Portsea workhouse in Hampshire:

Either meat broth or a sort of gruel called flour broth, made of flour and water, is their common breakfast. Dinner, 3 days in the week, consists of meat, and on the other 4 days, bread and cheese. Suppers are bread and cheese. Beer is allowed at bread and cheese meals only. Each adult person has 1lb of bread a day, and 8oz of meat on meat days.

At nearby Southampton, the inmates started most days with a bowl of onion broth. There were also three meat days each week, plus a liberal daily ration of beer:

Breakfast – every day except Monday, onion broth; Monday, bread and butter. Dinner – Sunday, beef and vegetables; Monday, broth and bread; Tuesday, pork and vegetables; Wednesday, Friday, bread and butter; Thursday, salt beef and vegetables; Saturday, bread and cheese. Supper – every day, bread and cheese or butter. Two cups of beer (near 3 pints) are allowed to grown persons, and a proportionate quantity to children.

Eden characterised the diet of the labouring class living in Northern England, Scotland, and Wales as rather more varied and including some dishes he regarded as little known in the south, such as:

Hasty Pudding
Eden's recipe consisted of 13oz of oatmeal gradually added to a quart of salted boiling water and stirred for a further two or three minutes. This quantity made a meal sufficient for two labourers. It was typically eaten with a little milk or beer poured on, or with some cold butter put in the middle, or a little treacle.

Crowdie
Although less common than hasty pudding, crowdie was popular with Northern labourers, especially miners. It was typically made by pouring boiling water onto oatmeal and then stirring. It could be eaten with milk or butter, or with a piece of fat from the broth pot.

Frumenty or Barley Milk
As made in the North, this contained barley with the husks taken off boiled in water for up to two hours then mixed with skimmed milk or sugar. In Cumberland, it was generally eaten with barley bread.

Boiled Milk
Three pints of milk were boiled and a handful of oatmeal added. It was taken off the heat soon afterwards and eaten with barley bread for breakfast or supper.

Pease-kail
Peas were boiled until soft, the water poured off and milk added. Eden's verdict was that this dish was not much to be commended.

Sowens or Flummery
The husks and siftings from grinding oatmeal were soaked for several days, then the liquor was strained and boiled to produce a smooth blancmange-like pudding.

Lobscouse
This dish that provid the main use for potatoes, which were not particularly good in the North. The potatoes were peeled or scraped, then chopped and boiled together with a small amount of meat cut into very small pieces. The mixture was then formed into a hash with onions, salt, and pepper. Lobscouse, now shortened to scouse, has become an informal name for natives of Liverpool.

The most distinctive feature of the diet of the labourer in the North of England was the great variety of cheap and savoury soups that it contained. The ready availability of barley and barley bread contributed to this, as did the cheapness of fuel in the North.

A typical Northern workhouse diet was provided by Eden's report from South Shields:

> Breakfast – every day, hasty pudding; Dinner – Sunday and Wednesday, beef, etc.; Monday, Thursday, pease soup; Tuesday, Saturday, barley boiled in milk; Friday, suet dumplings. Supper – Sunday, Wednesday, broth and bread; Monday, Thursday, boiled milk; Tuesday, Saturday, bread and milk; Friday, cold milk.

A similar mix was found on the menu at Stokesley in North Yorkshire. However, Saturday dinners here were enlivened by the appearance of salt fish:

Breakfast – every day, milk and oatmeal. Dinner – Sunday, beef, roots and dumplins; Monday, hasty pudding, oatmeal; Tuesday, frumenty French barley; Wednesday, beef broth and bread; Thursday, frumenty; Friday, fry and potatoes; Saturday, potatoes and butter and salt fish. Supper – every day, milk and oatmeal.

A typical soup or broth recipe from Northumberland or Cumberland contained meat, oatmeal, barley, onions, and herbs such as chives, parsley or thyme:

Broth

A pound of good beef, or mutton, 6 quarts of water, and 3oz of barley, are boiled till the liquor is reduced to about 3 quarts: one ounce of oatmeal, which has previously been mixed up with a little cold water, and a handful, or more, of herbs, are added after the broth has boiled for some time. A pint, or a pint and a half of the broth, with 8oz of barley bread, makes a very good supper. The day the broth is made, the dinner usually is broth, with part of the meat, bread, and potatoes, chopped and boiled: and the supper is broth and bread: the next day, the dinner is cold meat from the broth, warm potatoes, broth and bread; and the supper, bread and broth warmed up, but not boiled again. The broth will keep good three days, if kept cool, and may be heated if wanted.

BREAD

In the seventeenth and eighteenth centuries, a wide variety of different types of bread were made. These reflected different grades of flour used in their baking, and also differing regional preferences and availability of various types of grain and flour. Bread made from wheat flour predominated in the south of England. The finest type of white bread, made from finely sieved flour, was known as 'manchet'. Manchets were usually made as small loaves or folded over to form a 'roll'. A more coarsely sifted flour was used to produce cheat-bread, light brown in colour, and produced in several grades ('seconds' and 'thirds') with ravelled cheat being the heaviest and having the most bran. The term 'brown bread' was used for the most inferior, coarsest, and most branny wheat bread.

Rye-based bread was the most common variety eaten in the east of England, particularly Norfolk. In areas where wheat was also grown, maslin bread was made from a mixture of rye and wheat, sometimes sown as a mixed crop.

In the south-west of England, Wales, and parts of the north and west, there was a strong tradition of eating barley bread. In Cornwall, the barley flour was sometimes mixed with scalded skimmed milk and extra yeast to give the bread a wheat-like character. Here, and also in Wales, cooking was often carried out on a hearth under an upturned metal pot covered with hot ash. In Cumberland, barley bread was the norm, either baked into flat unleavened cakes, twelve inches across by half an inch thick or, more usually, leavened and made into twelve-pound loaves. Such bread was said to keep for up to three weeks in summer, and five weeks in winter. Some parts of Northumberland and Durham used flour made from a mixture of barley and peas.

In the south of England, oats were usually given only to horses. In much of the North, they constituted the staple cereal. Varieties of oat bread included:

Hearth-cakes
There were also known as thar-cakes, hard-cakes, or (in Scotland) bannocks – thick cakes of unleavened bread made with oatmeal and water and baked on a hearth.

Clap-bread

These were thin, hard, unleavened oat-cakes beaten out by hand on a round and slightly concave 'clap-board' and baked in an oven. In Lancashire and Westmorland, the mix was rolled out into a 20in diameter cake and baked over a fire on a griddle.

Kitcheness bread

These were thin oat-cakes made of thin batter.

Riddle-cakes

These were thick sour cakes baked on a griddle.

The bread eaten by workhouse inmates generally reflected what was eaten locally. Some larger workhouses operated their own bakehouses while others bought in bread from local suppliers. A workhouse could also make its own dough which was then baked in the ovens of a local baker.

MILK CHEESE AND BUTTER

Milk, according to Edward Smith, a Poor Law medical official in the 1860s, was 'probably the most important food that has been placed at the service of man.' This was not, however, a view that had always existed. In the seventeenth century, milk from any source was considered as suitable only for young children and very elderly people. For others, it was seen as positively unhealthy – in young men it was said to cause sore eyes, headaches, agues, palsies and stones or other obstructions. Even the elderly and invalids were considered at risk since it was not uncommon for them to be provided with a wet nurse.[18]

From medieval times and before, milk was thought to consist of three distinct substances: cream, curds (or 'cruds'), and whey. In modern terms, these correspond to three of the most important constituents of milk, namely fat, water-soluble elements, and the protein casein. Not all milk was equal, however, and milk from asses and goats was widely held to be the most nourishing alternative to women's milk, with cow's milk the least nutritious.

By the eighteenth century, the supply of milk in towns had a very bad reputation, something that did not improve substantially until the late 1800s. Urban cows were often kept in cramped, dark and dirty sheds and badly fed. The milk they produced was often watered down. As a result, in some parts of London, it became popular to buy milk direct from cows being driven around the streets. Rural production of milk was largely used to produce butter and cheese which could then be sold in towns.

Milk could be provided in various forms: fresh full-fat milk (often referred to as 'new' milk); skimmed milk (after most of the fat has been removed to make butter); buttermilk (the liquid remaining after producing butter from cream); whey (the liquid left over after milk has been curdled and strained in cheese-making).

In rural areas, buttermilk and whey were often used for feeding pigs. In London, however, they were once popular drinks sold on the streets. Londoners, too, devoured large amounts of butter, much of which came from Yorkshire and East Anglia, and cheese, particularly that from Cheshire and transported by ship from Liverpool to London.

For workhouse inmates, where cost was invariably the main consideration, the milk consumed would usually be skimmed milk or buttermilk, both of which were substantially cheaper than new milk.

A FAR CRY FROM GRUEL

Although most workhouses provided a fairly basic diet, both as part of a deterrent regimen, and also to keep the running costs down, there were occasional instances of generous or even extravagant expenditure on food.

One of the most profligate institutions was the Norwich workhouse where, in 1784, according to Eden, the daily serving of cooked beef was as much 19½oz for every man, woman, and child. This was partly accounted for by the inmates taking heaped plates away to eat on their own beds rather than using a communal dining-room. The cost was such that it would have been cheaper for the inmates to dine at a cook's shop or public house. Eventually, changes were introduced to the dinner menu and beer was bought in rather than being brewed in the workhouse – this resulted in a saving of almost £6,000 over a three year period. Sunday dinner for 171 persons (which had formerly consisted of 1,768oz of boiled beef at a cost of 55s) was replaced by an economical soup made up of:

	s	d
70lb of cheeks at 2s the stone	10	0
43 gallons of water		
2 pecks of old pease at 1s	2	0
4½lb onions at 1d	0	4½
4¾ pints of oatmeal at 1½d	0	7
3¾oz pepper at 1½d	0	5½
5 crusts of loaves burnt	0	1¾
1¾lb salt	0	2
Thyme	0	1
Total cost	13s	9¾

A report in 1834 found that the Brighthelmstone (Brighton) workhouse, which then housed 336 inmates, provided three meals a day with no limits on quantity. Men received two pints of beer a day, children one pint, and women a pint of beer and a pint of tea. There were six meat dinners in the week and the inmates were served at table with the governor carving for the men and boys, and the matron for the women and girls. The full diet is shown below.[18]

BRIGHTHELMSTONE 1834 PARISH WORKHOUSE DIET TABLE	
Breakfast	Women: One pint of tea, with bread and butter. Men, boys and girls: Bread and gruel (of flour and oatmeal excepting some old men, who are allowed a pint of tea, with bread and butter)
Dinner	Monday: Pease soup, herbs, &c. with bread; men and women a pint of table-beer; boys about half a pint. Tuesday: Beef and mutton puddings, with vegetables; the beer, &c., same as Monday. Wednesday: Boiled beef and mutton (sometimes pork with it), hard puddings, bread, vegetables, &c.; beer same as before. Thursday: Mutton and beef-suet puddings; beer same as before. Friday: Beef and mutton puddings, with vegetables; beer same as before. Saturday: Irish stew-meat, potatoes, herbs, &c.; beer same as before. Sunday: Boiled beef and mutton (sometimes pork with it), hard puddings bread, vegetables, &c.; beer same as before.

Supper	Women: One pint of tea, with bread and butter or cheese. Men and boys: Bread and butter or cheese; men, one pint of beer or tea each; boys, about half a pint. Girls and small children: Bread and butter drink, milk and water.

There was equally generous provision at Chester workhouse, where a hot dinner was served every day. On five days, this consisted of 6oz of boiled beef with mashed potatoes, or stew with boiled potatoes. On the other two days, it comprised oatmeal 'sturrow', with either treacle or buttermilk. Although beer was rationed to half a pint a day, some inmates were allowed gin. Men aged over fifty were allowed half an ounce of tobacco or snuff a week while the women were each given ½oz of tea with a ¼lb of sugar.[20]

ALCOHOL

As we have already seen, beer formed a regular part of the parish workhouse diet, even for children. The Leeds workhouse dietary from 1788 was typical:

Breakfast	Every day	Milk pottage and bread
Dinner	Sunday	Mutton and broth, bread and beer
	Monday	Rice milk, bread and beer
	Tuesday	Dumplings and beer
	Wednesday	Bread, cheese and beer
	Thursday	Beef and broth, bread and beer
	Friday	Rice milk, bread and beer
	Saturday	Drink pottage and bread
Supper	Sunday and Thursday	Bread and broth or broth and beer
	Other days	Milk pottage and bread

Prior to the opening of the Hunslet workhouse in 1761, provisions ordered to be purchased for the new establishment included ten twelve-gallon casks of beer. Beer was subsequently brewed on the premises, as an 'iron pott for brewing and washing' was also purchased.[21]

As well as being provided at mealtimes, extra rations of beer were often given to inmates engaged in heavy labour. At one time, the pauper washerwomen of Bulcamp workhouse in Suffolk were allowed eight pints of beer per day each.[22]

Many workhouses brewed their beer on site and their brewhouses contained all the paraphernalia associated with beer-making. In 1859, when the contents of the old Oxford Incorporation workhouse were sold off, the auctioneer's catalogue entry for the brewhouse listed the following items:

Mash tub, underback, four brewing tubs, five coolers, five buckets, skip, tun bowl, tap tub, bushel, spout, malt mill, copper strainer, two pumps, brewing copper, three square coolers, with supports, spout, &c. Large working tub, two others, beer stands, three lanterns, & c., three casks, and strainer.

During the parish workhouse era, beer was part of most people's everyday diet. Apart the attractions of its flavour, it could provide a safe alternative in localities where the water supply was of dubious quality. Beer came in two main forms, strong ale and small beer. Small beer was usually half the strength of strong ale and was a standard accompaniment for meals. Here is Elizabethe Cleland's recipe for brewing beer from her 1759 book, *A New and Easy Method of Cookery*. Amazingly it was claimed to have a shelf life of two years or more!

Strong Ale and Small Beer

Boil the Water, and put some of the Malt in the Vat, and stir it and the boiling Water very well together; then put in more Malt and more Water mashed pretty thin; then cover the Vat, and let it stand three Hours; then let some of the Wort run, and throw it up again once or twice till it is clear; strew some dry Malt on the Top of the Vat; put your Hops in the Tub that the Wort runs in, and then put them in the brewing pan on the fire with the Wort; let it boil till it curdles and then clears; put boiling Water on the Vat by Degrees. Twenty English Bushels of Malt will make two Hogsheads of strong ale, and four Hogsheads of small beer, but it will take ten Pounds of Hops. This Ale will keep two or three Years; when it is almost as cold as Water, barm it, but strain the Hops out of it when it is Warm, and boil them in the small Beer. Let it work three Days, then skim it and barrel it, and when it is done working stop it up close, but keep the Barrel always filling while it is working. October or March is the best Time to brew.

Although beer was a staple item in many workhouses, spirits were generally prohibited. At the Croydon workhouse, opened in 1727, the rules forbade any 'Distilled Liquors to come into the House' – the latter probably aimed at the new habit of gin-drinking which was sweeping England at around this time. Although the sale of ale and beer were tightly controlled, this did not apply to spirits such as gin (originally imported from Holland and known as genever). Furthermore, the level of duty on spirits was only 2d a gallon, making them extremely cheap. In some parts of London, hundreds of backstreet gin-shops sprang up selling illicit gin, which was made from virtually anything that would ferment. Between 1700 and 1735, the sales of 'real' gin – on which duty had been paid and which was more or less drinkable – rose from half a million gallons to more than five million gallons.[23] The rising consumption of illicit and impure 'gin', whose contents might include anything from turpentine to sulphuric acid, led to widespread ill-health and death, particularly among the poor – much of whose out-relief might end up crossing a gin-house counter.

Brandy, too, appears to have been in a similar situation. The 1725 edition of *An Account of Several Work-houses* notes in its entry for St Mary Whitechapel that some of the parish's poor rejected the offer of the workhouse and 'chose to struggle with their Necessities, and to continue in a starving Condition, with the Liberty of haunting the Brandy-Shops, and such like Houses, rather than submit to live regularly in Plenty.'

Gin consumption reached record levels in 1750-51, resulting in increased taxation and the suppression of the illegal production and sale of spirits. Despite these measures, the problem continued. A Royal Commission in 1834 was told by the overseers for the London parish of St Sepulchre that intemperance was a major cause of pauperism: 'After relief has been received at our board, a great many of them proceed with the money to the palaces of gin shops, which abound in the neighbourhood.'[24]

Although the imbibing of spirits by workhouse inmates was usually prohibited, items such as wine, brandy and rum were often prescribed for medicinal purposes because of their supposed stimulant properties. The accounts for the Bristol workhouse in 1787 record the expenditure of £2 19s 7½d on 'wine, brandy, and ale for the sick'. At the Lincoln workhouse, in the winter of 1799-1800, colds and other ailments were so prevalent that the clerk was instructed by the Board to purchase two gallons of rum 'for the use of the House'. Surprisingly, gin still occasionally features in workhouse expenditure – the 1833 accounts for the Abingdon parish workhouse include an entry for two pints of gin, although the precise use to which this was to be put is not revealed.

TOBACCO

Tobacco, a native plant of the American continent, is said to have been introduced into England in the 1560s by Admiral Sir John Hawkins, but until the 1580s was used chiefly by sailors. Its use became widespread in the early seventeenth century despite attempts by physicians to make it obtainable only under prescription, and the raising by James I of the import duty on tobacco from 2d per lb to 6s 10d per lb in 1604. By 1614, however, it was suggested that there were '7,000 shops, in and about London, that doth vent Tobacco'.[25] Although tobacco is not mentioned by Shakespeare, it does feature in the 1599 play *Every Man Out of His Humour* by Ben Jonson.

During this period, tobacco would have been smoked in a pipe, sniffed in the form of snuff, or chewed – cigarettes did not come into widespread use in England until the second half of the nineteenth century.

As with spirits, the use of tobacco by workhouse inmates was frequently banned or severely restricted. In 1725, *An Account of Several Work-houses* recorded that at the St Giles's Cripplegate workhouse in London none of the inmates was to 'smoak Tobacco in their Lodgings, or the Work-house'. Some establishments were a little more tolerant, however. At the Portsea workhouse in 1795, those who used tobacco were each given a weekly allowance of 2oz. Some workhouses gave tobacco allowances only to those who were well behaved – at Stone in Staffordshire, in 1810, such inmates could receive up to an ounce a week.

Where the use of tobacco was allowed in a workhouse, there were often restrictions on where or when smoking could take place. Smoking in bed, a great fire hazard, was often specifically prohibited – the rules for Hackney parish workhouse stipulated that 'no person of either sex be allowed to smoke in Bed, or in any bed-chamber of the house'. At the Kendal workhouse in 1793, anyone caught smoking in their bed or in their room could be put in the dungeon for six hours. At Lacock in Wiltshire in the 1770s, smoking was forbidden in the workhouse except in the workrooms. Anticipating present-day trends in this matter, smoking was often restricted to outdoors areas. Leeds workhouse placed a ban on smoking after 7 p.m. in winter and 8 p.m. in summer.

At Manchester in the 1790s, no tobacco was to be brought into the workhouse unless ordered by the workhouse surgeon or weekly Board meeting. Such prescriptions were apparently issued reasonably often – in 1792-3, the workhouse spent a total of £39 10s 6d on snuff and tobacco.

Snuff was usually treated in much the same way as tobacco except presumably for the restrictions on where it could be used. At Halifax workhouse, tobacco users and snuff users were each allowed 8oz a month of their preferred pleasure.

TEA

Tea from China was introduced to Britain in the mid-1600s. Originally very expensive, by the 1740s its price had fallen to the level where it was affordable by all and rapidly became a staple item of many people's diet. Tea was drunk without milk but with sugar (whose price by the mid-1700s had come down to around 6d a pound). Tea could be drunk with every meal, or might substitute as a meal in itself, most often at breakfast time.

Eden's *State of the Poor* includes many examples of the regular expenditure of labourers and their families in the 1790s. In many instances, tea and sugar form a substantial part of the annual outgoings: for example, at St Nicholas parish in Durham, one family spent £2 12s a year on these two items, out of a total layout of £26 8s 8d. However, tea was often still viewed as a luxury which the poor should do without. *An Account of Several Work-houses* recorded that, in 1729, in the parish of Westham in Essex, 'many of those pensioners who before spent the alms of the parish in tea, and other entertainments, now live without it, and turn themselves to labour in their own houses, to avoid being sent to the workhouse.'

As with tobacco, there were great variations in the restrictions placed on the consumption of tea. In the 1790s at the Ealing parish workhouse, only the sick were given tea and sugar. At the St Mary parish workhouse in Reading, the elderly were allowed tea with bread and butter for breakfast. At the Bulcamp workhouse in Suffolk, tea was allowed to be drunk only on Sundays. At Chichester, in 1765, the 'pernicious and scandalous practice' of drinking tea was banned entirely from the workhouse following the scalding of two children.

Eden also highlights how women often seem to have been particularly associated with tea drinking. Breakfast for women inmates at the Empingham workhouse in Rutland comprised tea and bread and butter, while the men were given milk or broth. At Hampton in Middlesex, it was said that the female inmates 'would be riotous without tea every morning: this, however, is not allowed them by the master.' At Kendal, Eden noted that 'the women live much on tea but have, of late, discontinued the use of sugar.'

As recently as 1899, W. Penney, a senior official of the Scottish Local Government Board, was convinced that 'excessive tea-drinking by women accounts largely for the number of pauper lunatics'. Another inspector pronounced that 'tea-drinking, when carried to excess, may also produce… hyper-excitability, sleeplessness, and nervousness'. Penney concluded that 'when these stages are reached by a poorly-nourished, confirmed tea-drinker, the boundary line of insanity is easily crossed.'

Then, as now, the preparation of tea was a subject that aroused strong views. In 1840, assistant Poor Law Commissioner, Mr Parker complained about the practice of allowing inmates rations of dry tea, sugar, and their own teapots, cups and saucers. A day ward in one workhouse he visited had three separate fires lit to heat the same number of kettles. He proposed that tea would be more efficiently prepared in a communal tea-urn which would also improve its quality.

But how to make the perfect brew? In 1866, the Poor Law Board's medical offer Dr Edward Smith, presumably not a tea drinker, offered the scientific view:

Tea

Tea should not be boiled, but placed in boiling water, and the water kept quite hot for about ten or fifteen minutes. Carbonate of soda should be added to the water (and particularly if the water is hard). The tea should either be thrown loose into the boiling water, and the whole occasionally stirred, or it should be enclosed in very coarse muslin or strainering, with plenty of space allowed in the bag and be well moved about, and at the end of the operation the bag should be well squeezed. As the quantity of tea allowed is small, a better infusion will be obtained if the leaves are thrown in loosely than if enclosed in a bag, and after they have been stirred round they will for the most part fall to the bottom of the vessel, and not inconvenience the distribution of the tea. The sugar should not be boiled in the tea, as it loses a part of its sweetening properties when kept at a boiling temperature, but added after the boiling has ceased.[26]

four

The Victorian Workhouse Age

THE NEW POOR LAW

By 1832, the escalating national cost of poor relief, coupled with rising criticisms of how it was administered, led to the appointment of a Royal Commission to review the whole poor relief system. Their report resulted in the 1834 Poor Law Amendment Act which formed the basis of what became known as the New Poor Law. The Act created a uniform national system of poor relief based on the workhouse test – the belief that only those truly in need would be prepared to enter a strictly run workhouse. Out-relief, at least to the able-bodied, was to cease.

The new workhouse system was run by a central Poor Law Commission (PLC) and operated locally through a new administrative area called the Poor Law Union – a group of parishes, typically twenty or thirty in number, centred around a market town. Each union was run by a Board of Guardians elected annually by the rate-payers in each member parish. Each union was required to provide a central workhouse for its paupers.

CLASSIFICATION AND SEGREGATION

The 1832 Royal Commission had originally proposed that each union should operate separate workhouses for different categories of pauper inmate: 'At least four classes are necessary: 1. The aged and really impotent; 2. The children; 3. The able-bodied females; 4. The able-bodied males.' Apart from providing different types of accommodation to suit the particular needs of different groups, separate establishments would also have allowed many former parish workhouses to be reused under the new system. However, running four or more institutions for unpredictable numbers of inmates soon began to look expensive and difficult, especially when it came to dispersing and reuniting families entering or leaving the workhouse. Thus, most unions adopted the 'general mixed workhouse' as the single establishment for the whole union.

The PLC devised a sevenfold classification of workhouse inmates (revised slightly by 1842), each of which was to be housed separately:

1. Aged or infirm men.
2. Able-bodied men, and youths above thirteen.
3. Youths and boys above seven years old and under thirteen.
4. Aged or infirm women.
5. Able-bodied women and girls above sixteen.
6. Girls above seven years old and under sixteen.
7. Children under seven years of age.

Seperate accommodation was provided in the workhouse for each category, with no contact between them. If an able-bodied man entered the worhouse, he had to take his whole family with him, the family being split up as soon as they were admitted.

In fact, there were some exceptions to the segregation rule. Children under seven could be placed in the female quarters and, from 1842, their mothers could have access to them 'at all reasonable times'. Parents could also have an 'interview' with their children 'at some time in each day'. From 1847, married couples over the age of sixty could request a shared bedroom, although not all unions provided this facility.

ENTERING THE WORKHOUSE

The workhouse was not a prison and entry into it was essentially a voluntary process. People were not 'thrown' or 'sent' into the workhouse, rather they resigned themselves to it, albeit often as a last resort when all other options had been exhausted.

The first step to entering a workhouse was most often through a union official called the relieving officer. Each relieving officer was responsible for a certain number of parishes which he visited at regular times during the week to interview relief applicants. In some circumstances, the relieving officer could issue an order for out-relief, for example in cases of illness. If an applicant was given, and accepted, the offer of the workhouse, they would be issued with an admission order and then made their way with their family to the workhouse.

On arrival at the workhouse, each new applicant entered a male or female receiving ward where their details were recorded in the admissions register. They would then be searched for prohibited items such as alcohol, bathed, and issued with the workhouse uniform. Children, but not adults, could be required to have their hair cut. An applicant's own clothing would be fumigated and put into store until they left the workhouse. Each new arrival was examined by the workhouse medical officer to assign them to the appropriate dietary class and to check for any medical condition that would require treatment or isolation.

An admission 'ticket' for the St Marylebone workhouse, c. 1902.

An 1844 illustration from
Frances Trollope's *Jessie Phillips*
– Jessie undergoes a terrifying
inquisition by the Board of
Guardians.

Entry into the main workhouse required the formal approval of the union's Board of Guardians at one of their regular (usually weekly) meetings. This was usually a formality, although in some cases an applicant might be summoned before the guardians to state their case – often a very intimidating experience.

WORKHOUSE UNIFORM

Originally, the Poor Law Commissioners expected that workhouse inmates would make their own clothes and shoes, providing a useful work task and a cost saving. However, they probably failed to realise the level of skill required to perform this and uniforms were often bought-in. Uniforms were generally made from fairly coarse materials with the emphasis on them being hard-wearing rather than on their comfort and fitting.

In 1837, the guardians of Hereford Union advertised for the supply of inmates' clothing. For the men this consisted of jackets of strong 'fernought' cloth, breeches or trousers, striped cotton shirts, cloth cap and shoes. For women and girls, there were strong 'grogram' gowns, calico shifts, petticoats of linsey-woolsey material, gingham dresses, day caps, worsted stockings and woven slippers. ('Fernought' or 'Fearnought' was a stout woollen cloth, mainly used on ships as outside clothing for bad weather. Linsey-woolsey was a fabric with a linen, or sometimes cotton, warp and a wool weft – its name came from the village of Linsey in Sussex. Grogram was a coarse fabric of silk, or of mohair and wool, or of a mixture of all these, often stiffened with gum.)

By 1900, male inmates were usually kitted out in jacket, trousers and waistcoat. Instead of a cap, the bowler or billycock hat had become the standard issue for male inmates in some unions.

The uniform for able-bodied women was generally a shapeless, waistless, blue-and-white-striped frock reaching to the ankles, with a smock over. Old women wore a bonnet or mop-cap, shawl, and apron over. The daughter of the matron of Ongar workhouse in the early 1900s recalls that:

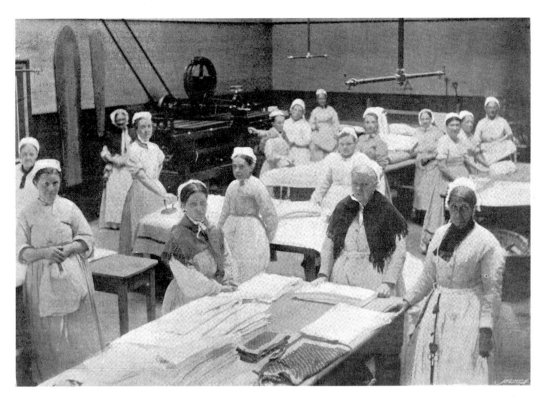

Female inmates at work in the laundry at the Mitcham workhouse in 1896.

My mother made all the women's dresses, I think. They were blue and white striped cotton material, lined. Some wore white aprons and some did not. I think the ones who worked wore caps, and the dear grannies who did not work, bonnets. They had woollen material shawls to wear, and red flannel petticoats tied around the waist, thick black stockings and black shoes or boots. The men wore thick corduroy trousers, thick black jackets and black hats, grey flannel shirts, black thick socks and hobnailed boots.

THE WORKHOUSE ROUTINE

Daily life in a union workhouse was conducted to a strick timetable, punctuated by the ringing of the workhouse bell. On Sundays, no work was performed except for essential domestic chores. The standard routine for able-bodied inmates is shown below.

	Rise	Breakfast	Start work	Dinner	End work	Supper	Bedtime
25 March to 29 September	6 a.m.	6.30-7 a.m.	7 a.m.	12-1 p.m.	6 p.m.	6-7 p.m.	8 p.m.
29 September to 25 March	7 a.m.	7.30-8 a.m.	8 a.m.	12-1 p.m.	6 p.m.	6-7 p.m.	8 p.m.

Communal prayers were read before breakfast and after supper every day and Divine Service performed on Sunday, Good Friday, and Christmas Day.

WORK

The type of work demanded from the able-bodied inmates was largely at the discretion of the local guardians. Some workhouses set up workshops for sewing, spinning and weaving or other local trades. Others had their own vegetable gardens where the inmates worked to provide food for the workhouse. Women performed the domestic tasks of cooking, cleaning, and the workhouse laundry. Men were generally given heavy manual work which in the 1830s and 1840s could include: stone-breaking – the results were saleable for road-making; grinding corn – heavy mill-stones were rotated by four or more men turning a capstan (the resulting flour was usually of very poor quality); crushing Gypsum – for use in plaster-making; picking oakum – teasing out the fibres from old hemp ropes; Bone-crushing – old animal bones were pulverised to produce fertiliser.

The type of work done by workhouse inmates gradually changed over time, with some unions introducing forms of labour which were both more useful, and able to be performed by the older or less able inmates who by now formed the majority of the workhouse population. In 1896, the work performed by inmates of the Holborn Union workhouse at Mitcham included farm cultivation, grinding corn, chopping firewood, tailoring, bricklaying, painting, plumbing, basket and mat-making, and gas-making in the union's own gas works.

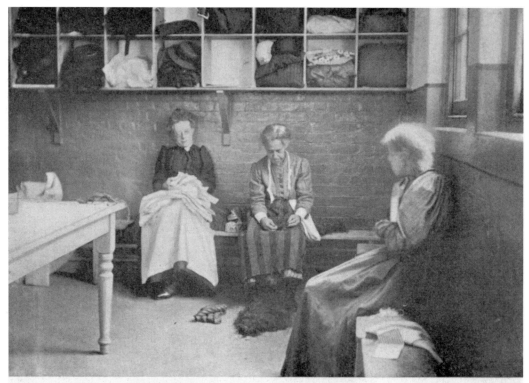

OLD WOMAN PICKING OAKUM IN A CASUAL WARD.

Female workhouse inmates picking oakum in around 1906.

The grounds of the Aylsham workhouse in Norfolk, where crops are being cultivated by one of the inmates.

Inmates at work in the shoemaking shop at the Mitcham workhouse.

A large workhouse could provide a surprisingly wide range of tasks to occupy its residents. At Macclesfield in 1886, the jobs assigned to the able-bodied females included: twenty-one washers, twenty-two sewers and knitters, twelve scrubbers, twelve assisting women, four in the kitchen, four in the nursery, and four stocking darners. On the men's side there were two joiners, one slater, one upholsterer, one blacksmith, three assisting the porter with the tramps, six men attending the boilers, three attending the stoneshed men, four whitewashers, four attending the pigs, two looking after sanitary matters, one regulating the coal supply, eighteen potato peelers, one messenger, twenty-six ward men, two doorkeepers. There were twelve boys at work in the tailor's shop.

LEAVING THE WORKHOUSE – OR NOT

A workhouse inmate could, in principle, discharge himself at any time. However, he could not just walk out of the door since he would then be guilty of the serious offence of stealing union property – his uniform. 'Reasonable notice' – typically three hours – had to be given for an inmate's own clothes to be retrieved.

If an adult inmate had their spouse or family in the workhouse, the whole family had to leave together – a husband could not abandon his wife and family in the workhouse to be supported by the union. Temporary leave could, however, be granted for an able-bodied inmate to go and seek work.

Although some people were in the workhouse for relatively short periods, for example during times of high unemployment, many stayed for years. A survey in 1906-7 found that 30 per cent of workhouse inmates were there for less than four weeks, while a further 18.5 per cent stayed less than thirteen weeks. Just over a quarter were there for the whole year.[27]

In 1861, a parliamentary survey recorded the inmates at each workhouse who had been in continuous residence for five years or more. Of a total workhouse population (excluding vagrants) of 67,800, the total falling into this category numbered 14,216, or almost 21 per cent. Just over half of these long-term inmates (7,771) had been resident for between five and ten years. Thirty-one inmates were recorded as being resident for fifty years or more.[28] The reasons given for inmates' inability to maintain themselves were categorised as:

Old age and infirmity	5,932
Mental disease (e.g. idiot, imbecile, lunatic, weak mind)	4,989
Bodily disease (e.g. asthma, ulcerated legs, rheumatism)	924
Bodily defects (e.g. cripple, blind, lame, deaf and dumb)	1,619
Moral defects (e.g. females having bastard children, prostitute)	182
Other causes (e.g. widow, orphan, deserted by husband, laziness)	570

THE 'INS' AND 'OUTS'

Despite, or perhaps because of, the workhouse's uncongenial conditions some paupers entered and then discharged themselves with surprising frequency, treating the establishment almost

Charlie Chaplin, who spent some of his childhood in the Lambeth workhouse and at the poor law district school in Hanwell.

like a free lodging-house. Such people became known as the 'ins and outs' and, because of the lengthy procedure that was required on the occasion of each admission, became the bane of the workhouse staff's life. Finally, in 1899, officers were given powers to delay the discharge of such inmates: a pauper who had discharged himself in the previous month could be detained for forty-eight hours, while one who was considered to have discharged himself frequently and without sufficient reason, could be detained for up to a week.

Some inmates, no doubt, found that they could put up with the privations of the workhouse only for so long, after which, escaping for a few days provided a welcome respite, even if they ended up returning soon afterwards. When seven-year-old Charlie Chaplin, his half-brother, Sydney, and their mother, Hannah, entered the Lambeth workhouse in 1896, the two boys were soon packed off to the Poor Law district school at Hanwell. Two months later, the children were returned to the workhouse where they were met at the gate by Hannah, dressed in her own clothes. In desperation to see them, she had discharged herself from the workhouse, along with the children. After a day spent playing in Kennington Park and visiting a coffee shop, they returned to the workhouse and had to go through the whole admissions procedure once more, with the children again staying there for a probationary period before returning to Hanwell.

Another example of inmates 'playing the system' is given by the anonymous author of *Indoor Paupers* – purportedly an insider's account of workhouse life, published in 1885. The writer reports how – despite the strict segregation – male and female inmates were able to pursue 'flirtations', often aided by secret notes passed between each other by covert means. Eventually, a couple might arrange an assignation:

The enamoured pair discharge themselves on the same morning, and go out to spend twelve to forty-eight hours together, according to the amount of money at their disposal. This is at once the consummation of the love-fit and its close. They resume their places in the house completely cured of it.

A survey of a sample of workhouse admissions in 1906-7 recorded that 83.7 per cent of inmates had entered once during the year, 13.5 per cent entered on between two and four occasions, and 2.8 per cent were admitted five or more times. It was also noted that during 1901, one eighty-one-year-old woman named Julia Blumsun had recorded 163 separate admissions to the City of London workhouse, while a forty-year-old man in the Poplar workhouse had been in and out 593 times over the period since 1884.[29]

OUT-RELIEF

It is easy to form the impression that, after 1834, all poor relief was administered through the union workhouse. However, this is a long way from the truth. Although the 1834 Act had been intended to remove the option of out-relief for the able-bodied, especially men, this failed to happen. Between 1840 and 1930, the proportion of the population residing in workhouses stayed fairly steady at around 0.7 per cent of the population. The numbers on outdoor relief varied between roughly 1 per cent and 4 per cent. Expenditure on indoor and outdoor relief tells a similar story. Prior to 1900, the total national cost of workhouse relief was always less than that of out-relief.[30]

On purely economic grounds, many unions took the view that it was cheaper to try and maintain a family in its own home through out-relief than to house and feed them all in the workhouse. Since medical out-relief was still permissible, the head of a destitute family could be declared 'sick' for a few weeks and given support. Resistance to the withdrawal of out-relief, particularly in the North of England, also led the central authorities to gradually widen the circumstances under which it could be offered.

Out-relief could be administered either as money or in kind, for example as bread. Some unions issued bread tokens which could only be exchanged at a local bakery rather then being spent on anything less nutritious such as alcohol.

Those who, because of illness or injury, were considered to be long-term paupers often went for years without being reassessed by the relieving officer. This could sometimes lead to relief continuing to be given to those who no longer had need of it. The Local Government Board's annual report in 1874 recounts the example of an officer of the Guildford Union, engaged shortly after his appointment in looking up his cases. He came upon a pauper of long standing, at work in the well-stocked garden of his cottage. The following dialogue ensued:

'You have got a nice bit of garden here?'
'Yes, it is pretty good.'
'And are those your pigs in the sty there?'
'Yes, they be mine.'
'And there is a horse and cart, is that yours, too?'
'Oh yes, that is what I goes to market with. And who be you, Sir?'
'Well, I am the new relieving officer, and I think you had better come up and see the guardians next Board day.'

SOME CASES OF OPPOSITION TO THE NEW POOR LAW

The implementation of the New Poor Law began in earnest on 1 January 1835, when the first new Poor Law Union was formally created at Abingdon in Berkshire. Throughout 1835 and 1836, matters proceeded remarkably smoothly as a growing team of Assistant Poor Law Commissioners rolled out the system to East Anglia, the south-west of England, Wales, and up towards the North of England.

There were occasional short-lived local incidents of resistance. At the end of April 1835, in the new Milton Union in Kent, the introduction of the new poor relief policy led to a disturbance at the village of Bapchild when a guardian and relieving officer were assaulted. At Milton, guardians leaving a Board meeting were stoned. A week later, guardians and a relieving officer were besieged in a church after confronting protestors and were only saved from the mob by the arrival of troops

A few weeks later at Ampthill in Bedfordshire riots took place when the guardians attempted to replace relief in the form of cash by allowances of bread. *The Times* reported that a mob of up to 500 people had 'commenced a most desperate attack upon the windows with stones, brick-bats, cabbage-stalks, and every missile that could be found.' The reading of the Riot Act failed to quell the protestors, and a posse of twenty-two metropolitan police arrived the next day to restore order.

One of the most dramatic incidents during this period happened after dark on the evening of Saturday 21 November, 1835, at Abingdon. Only a few weeks after the union had opened its new workhouse, shots were fired at the master and his family as they sat in their quarters at the centre of the building. An officer from Bow Street was called in to take charge of the case and a reward of £200 offered. Three men were later apprehended.

In July 1836, new unions were created at Leicester and Nottingham, and in both cases the new Boards of Guardians proceeded with enthusiasm to implement the new principle of denying out-relief to able-bodied applicants. The first signs of trouble came at the end of the year. A severe depression hit East Midlands hosiery towns such as Nottingham where the workhouse could not cope with the numbers seeking relief. The Nottingham Board of Guardians were forced to demand that the PLC suspend their prohibition on out-relief. Similar problems at Leicester in 1841-2 led to violent riots which were only quelled with military assistance.

The most serious resistance to the New Poor Law came in textile manufacturing areas of North-East Lancashire and West Yorkshire, such as Oldham, Rochdale, and Huddersfield.

A bread token issued by the Bedford Union, probably in the late nineteenth century.

This came not only from the labouring classes, but also from the local landowners and ratepayers whose cooperation was required to operate the new system. During periods of manufacturing slump, the traditional method of poor relief in many industrial towns was to give short-term handouts to unemployed workers suffering hardship. A new workhouse was seen as a wasteful expense that would involve large capital expenditure, spend most of its time empty, and be unable to cope with the large numbers of relief claimants during periodic downturns. Giving short-term payments to a worker were viewed as much preferable to having to maintain a whole family in the workhouse.

One of the first major protests took place in Huddersfield in December 1836. News of the imminent introduction of the New Poor Law in the town provoked a demonstration by 8,000 people in the market place at the end of which an effigy of a Poor Law Commissioner was burned. In protests elsewhere, violence regularly erupted with police and even armed cavalry having to be called in to restore order. Opposition also included the boycotting of guardians' elections, the withholding of poor rates, and the refusal of Boards of Guardians to elect officers or conduct union business.

Faced with such sustained resistance, the PLC was forced to make concessions. From 1837 onwards, individual unions could be issued with a Labour Test Order which permitted out-relief to able-bodied men in return for manual labour such as stone-breaking. Many northern unions also exploited the various 'permitted exceptions' in the PLC's regulations and issued out-relief under the guise of it being medical relief or 'sudden and urgent necessity'. Despite the PLC's best efforts, the complete abolition of out-relief to the able bodied was a vision that was never to materialise.

In 1842 a widespread manufactuing slump led to demonstrations and riots in many northern areas. Stockport's workhouse was attacked by a mob of unemployed workers who stole 672 7lb loaves and about £7 in copper.

five

The 1835 Workhouse Dietary

In December 1835, the PLC published a set of six model 'dietaries' from which Boards of Guardians were required to select the one 'best adapted' for their particular union. The Commissioners' declared benchmark in formulating the workhouse diet was that on no account should it be 'superior or equal to the ordinary mode of subsistence of the labouring classes of the neighbourhood'. Although by 1842 this principle was no longer mentioned in the PLC's 'Workhouse Rules', it had already created a mindset in which the quantity and quality of the food provided for inmates was to be kept at a minimum.

The model dietaries were primarily constructed for able-bodied inmates and varied only a little in their range and amount of food they provided. The simplest diet was No. 3, which offered an unvarying menu of bread and gruel for breakfast, and bread and cheese for supper. Midday dinner was also bread and cheese five days a week (with extra soup on Thursdays), and meat and vegetables on the other two days. The remaining dietaries broadly differed by the inclusion of one or two other foods: for example, Dietary No. 1 added soup and broth, while No. 5 featured potatoes.

Men received, on average, around 25 per cent more food (by weight) than women. Children under nine were given a locally decided proportion of the adult amount, while the diets for the sick were left to the workhouse medical officer's discretion. The elderly usually had a ration of butter, sugar and tea although is some cases, this had to be traded for gruel.

The PLC's 1836 annual report contained a report by assistant Poor Law Commissioner Charles Mott which indicated the thinking behind the formulation of the new dietaries:

> Uniformity of diet as to quality can hardly be attained, nor indeed is it absolutely necessary. Provincial habits are difficult to conquer. The labourers of Norfolk and Suffolk would hardly be prevailed upon to forego their dumplings, or the Cornish men their pies. In one of the seasons of scarcity in Ireland, when the potato crops had failed and great distress existed amongst the poor, the Marquess of Lansdowne sent over to his tenantry supplies of rice oatmeal and potatoes. When his Lordship next visited his estates in Ireland, he enquired if the supplies were timely and acceptable; his kindness was acknowledged with gratitude for the oatmeal and potatoes, but the rice was new to them; no one knew its use; consultations were held; it was condemned as being intended to cause sterility, and by common consent was thrown into the sea.

The uptake of the dietaries by unions in different parts of the country bore out this theory, with dietaries in Kent and Sussex mainly consisting of bread and cheese, while those adopted in the Northern counties were chiefly composed of potatoes and oatmeal porridge.

Mott calculated that the average weight of food provided to able-bodied inmates by the six standard dietaries was as follows:

Dietary	Ounces per day (grams per day)	Total ounces per week
1	19 (539)	122
2	25.5 (723)	178
3	24 (680)	168
4	26 (737)	182
5	20 (567)	140
6	23.5 (666)	164

Although Mott admitted that Dietary No. 1 was 'somewhat below the quantity used by labourers generally', he claimed that the overall average of 23oz daily or 161oz weekly was 'not only sufficient, but… exceeds the quantity consumed by agricultural labourers and mechanics, who support themselves by their own exertions.'

Mott also drew upon the estimates of daily food requirements calculated by Arctic explorer Sir Edmund Parry whose crew had dragged boats across polar ice. As a result of his deliberations, Mott concluded that 'a fair estimate of the proportions of food, requisite to support human life in a sound and healthy state' was as follows:

1st: For persons of moderate health or constitution, but using little exercise or exertion: Daily allowance of food, 12 to 18 ounces: In nutritive matter equal to an average daily of 10 ounces.

2nd: For persons of good health, accustomed to moderate labour, as sailors and soldiers, on ordinary peace duty, or agricultural labourers or mechanics at their usual work: Daily allowance of food, 18 to 24 ounces: In nutritive matter equal to an average daily of 10 ounces.

3rd: For persons subject to hard labour or other violent exertion, in good bodily health: 24 to 30 ounces of food: Equal to 22 ounces of nutritive matter.

Mott provided further examples of what he saw as the excessive generosity of some parish workhouses – what his colleague Sir Francis Head described as 'pot-bellied philanthropy'. Here is Mott's account of his visit to the parish workhouse at Farnham in Surrey:

On visiting the workhouse in company with the parish officers, I observed a quantity of trenchers, containing the dinner allowances, placed ready for the paupers on their return from work. I requested the governor of the workhouse to state the full quantity of food given daily to the paupers in Farnham workhouse; I doubted the correctness of it when produced; but the governor's representation being confirmed by the officers, that it was a fair average daily supply, I had the food placed in the scales in their presence; when it was found to weigh 66 ounces, equal to 51 ounces of nutritive matter; and the governor added that even with this allowance the paupers often grumbled because they had not enough.

The PLC's standard dietaries were not entirely rigid and unions could – subject to the Commissioners' approval – vary the content and the amount, both downwards as well as upwards. This could lead to large discrepancies in the food given to inmates at different workhouses.

No. 1.—DIETARY for ABLE-BODIED MEN and WOMEN.

		BREAKFAST.		DINNER.				SUPPER.		
		Bread.	Gruel.	Cooked Meat.	Potatoes.	Soup.	Suet, or Rice Pudding.	Bread.	Cheese.	Broth.
		oz.	pints	oz.	lbs.	pints.	oz.	oz.	oz.	pints.
Sunday . .	Men .	6	1½	5	½	..	..	6	..	1½
	Women	5	1½	5	½	..	..	5	..	1½
Monday . .	Men .	6	1½	..	..	1½	..	6	2	—
	Women	5	1½	..	..	1½	..	5	2	—
Tuesday . .	Men .	6	1½	5	½	..	..	6	..	1½
	Women	5	1½	5	½	..	..	5	..	1½
Wednesday .	Men .	6	1½	..	..	1½	..	6	2	—
	Women	5	1½	..	..	1½	..	5	2	—
Thursday . .	Men .	6	1½	5	½	..	..	6	..	1½
	Women	5	1½	5	½	..	..	5	..	1½
Friday . .	Men .	6	1½	..	..	..	14	6	2	—
	Women	5	1½	..	..	..	12	5	2	—
Saturday . .	Men .	6	1½	..	..	1½	..	6	2	—
	Women	5	1½	..	..	1½	..	5	2	—

Old people of sixty years of age and upwards may be allowed one ounce of tea, five ounces of butter, and seven ounces of sugar per week, in lieu of gruel for breakfast, if deemed expedient to make this change.

Children under nine years of age to be dieted at discretion; above nine, to be allowed the same quantities as women.

Sick to be dieted as directed by the medical officer.

The 'Model Dietaries' published by the Poor Law Commissioners in 1835.

		BREAKFAST.			DINNER.				SUPPER.		
		Bread.	Cheese.	Butter.	Meat Pudding, with Vegetables*.	Suet Pudding with Vegetables*.	Bread.	Cheese.	Bread.	Cheese.	Butter.
		oz.	oz.	oz.	oz.	oz.	oz.	oz.	oz.	oz.	oz.
Sunday . .	Men .	6	1	..	16	..	..	..	6	1	..
	Women	5	..	½	10	..	..	..	5	..	½
Monday . .	Men .	6	1	..	..	..	7	1	6	1	..
	Women	5	..	½	..	..	7	1	5	..	½
Tuesday . .	Men .	6	1	..	..	16	..	..	6	1	..
	Women	5	..	½	..	10	..	..	5	..	½
Wednesday .	Men .	6	1	..	..	..	7	1	6	1	..
	Women	5	..	½	..	..	7	1	5	..	½
Thursday . .	Men .	6	1	..	..	..	7	1	6	1	..
	Women	5	..	½	..	..	7	1	5	..	½
Friday . .	Men .	6	1	..	..	16	..	..	6	1	..
	Women	5	..	½	..	10	..	..	5	..	½
Saturday . .	Men .	6	1	..	..	..	7	1	6	1	..
	Women	5	..	½	..	..	7	1	5	..	½

Old people, being all sixty years of age and upwards: the weekly addition of one ounce of tea, and milk or sugar; also an additional meat pudding dinner on Thursday in each week, in lieu of bread and cheese, to those for whose age and infirmities it may be deemed requisite.

Children under nine years of age: bread and milk for their breakfast and supper, or gruel when milk cannot be obtained; also such proportions of the dinner diet as may be requisite for their respective ages.

Sick: whatever is ordered for them by the medical officer.

* The vegetables are extra, and not included in the weight specified.

No. 2 dietary.

		BREAKFAST.		DINNER.					SUPPER.	
		Bread.	Gruel.	Cooked Meat.	Potatoes or other Vegetables.	Soup.	Bread.	Cheese.	Bread.	Cheese.
		oz.	pints.	oz.	lb.	pints.	oz.	oz.	oz.	oz.
Sunday . .	Men .	8	1½	. .	. .	. .	7	2	6	1½
	Women	6	1½	. .	. .	. .	6	1½	5	1½
Monday . .	Men .	8	1½	. .	. .	. .	7	2	6	1½
	Women	6	1½	. .	. .	. .	6	1½	5	1½
Tuesday . .	Men .	8	1½	8	¾	. .	. .	.	6	1½
	Women	6	1½	6	¾	. .	. .	.	5	1½
Wednesday .	Men .	8	1½	. .	. .	. .	7	2	6	1½
	Women	6	1½	. .	. .	. .	6	1½	5	1½
Thursday . .	Men .	8	1½	. .	. .	1½	6	.	6	1½
	Women	6	1½	. .	. .	1½	5	.	5	1½
Friday . . .	Men .	8	1½	. .	. .	. .	7	2	6	1½
	Women	6	1½	. .	. .	. .	6	1½	5	1½
				Bacon.						
Saturday . .	Men .	8	1½	5	¾	. .	. .	. .	6	1½
	Women	6	1½	4	¾	.	. .	. .	5	1½

Old people, of sixty years of age and upwards, may be allowed one ounce of tea, five ounces of butter, and seven ounces of sugar per week, in lieu of gruel for breakfast, if deemed expedient to make this change.

Children under nine years of age, to be dieted at discretion; above nine, to be allowed the same quantities as women.

Sick to be dieted as directed by the medical officer.

No. 3 dietary.

		BREAKFAST.		DINNER.					SUPPER.	
		Bread.	Gruel.	Pickled Pork, or Bacon, with Vegetables.	Soup.	Bread.	Meat Pudding, with Vegetables.	Rice or Suet Pudding with Vegetables.	Bread.	Cheese.
		oz.	pints.	oz.	pints.	oz.	oz.	oz.	oz.	oz.
Sunday .	Men .	8	1 ½	..	2	6	..	..	6	2
	Women	6	1 ½	..	1 ½	5	..	..	5	1 ½
Monday .	Men .	8	1 ½	..	..	..	..	12	6	2
	Women	6	1 ½	..	..	..	..	10	5	1 ½
Tuesday .	Men .	8	1 ½	..	2	6	..	..	6	2
	Women	6	1 ½	..	1 ½	5	..	..	5	1 ½
Wednesday .	Men .	8	1 ½	6	..	..	..	..	6	2
	Women	6	1 ½	5	..	..	..	..	5	1 ½
Thursday .	Men .	8	1 ½	..	..	..	..	12	6	2
	Women	6	1 ½	..	..	..	..	10	5	1 ½
Friday .	Men .	8	1 ½	..	2	6	..	..	6	2
	Women	6	1 ½	..	1 ½	5	..	..	5	1 ½
Saturday .	Men .	8	1 ½	..	..	..	12	..	6	2
	Women	6	1 ½	..	..	..	10	..	5	1 ½

The vegetables are not included in the weight specified, which is for the meat when cooked.

If it be thought desirable, half an ounce of butter may be given to the women in lieu of cheese, for supper.

Old people of sixty years of age and upwards may be allowed one ounce of tea, five ounces of butter, and seven ounces of sugar per week, in lieu of gruel for breakfast, if deemed expedient to make this change.

Children under nine years of age to be dieted at discretion; above nine, to be allowed the same quantities as women.

Sick to be dieted as directed by the medical officer.

No. 4 dietary.

	BREAK-FAST.		DINNER.						SUPPER.		
	Bread.	Gruel or Porridge	Cooked Meat.	Vegetables.	Soup.	Boiled Rice or Suet Pudding	Bread.	Cheese.	Bread.	Potatoes.	Cheese.
	oz.	pints.	oz.	lb.	oz.	oz.	oz.	oz.	oz	lb.	oz.
Sunday . Men .	7	1½	5	¾	•	•	•	•	7	•	1½
Women	6	1½	5	¾					6	•	1½
Monday . Men .	7	1½	•	•	1½	•	7	•	•	¾	•
Women	6	1½			1½	•	6			¾	
Tuesday . Men ,	7	1½	•	•	•	14	•	•	7	•	1½
Women	6	1½				12			6	•	1½
Wednesday Men .	7	1½	•	•	•	•	7	2	•	¾	•
Women	6	1½					6	2		¾	
Thursday . Men .	7	1½	5	¾	•	•	•	•	7	•	1½
Women	6	1½	5	¾					6	•	1½
Friday . Men .	7	1½	•	•	1½	•	7	•	•	¾	•
Women	6	1½			1½		6			¾	
Saturday . Men .	7	1½	•	•	•	•	7	2	•	¾	•
Women	6	1½					6	2		¾	

Old people, of sixty years of age and upwards, may be allowed one ounce of tea, five ounces of butter, and seven ounces of sugar per week, in lieu of gruel for breakfast, if deemed expedient to make this change.

Children under nine years of age, to be dieted at discretion ; above nine, to be allowed the same quantities as women.

Sick to be dieted as directed by the medical officer.

No. 5 dietary.

No. 6.—DIETARY for ABLE-BODIED PAUPERS.

	BREAKFAST.			DINNER.						SUPPER.			
	Bread.	Cheese.	Butter.	Boiled Meat.	Potatoes.	Yeast Dumplg.	Suet Pudding	Bread.	Cheese.	Bread.	Cheese.	Butter.	Broth.
	oz.	oz.	oz.	oz.	oz.	oz.	oz.	oz.	oz.	oz.	oz.	oz.	pints.
Sunday . Men .	6	1	•	•	•	•	16	•	•	6	1	•	•
Women	5	•	½	•	•	•	12	•	•	5	•	½	•
Monday . Men .	6	1	•	•	•	•	••	6	1	6	1	•	•
Women	5	•	½	•	•	•	••	6	1	5	•	½	•
Tuesday . Men .	6	1	•	4	12	5½	••	•	•	6	•	•	1
Women	5	•	½	4	12	5¼	••	•	•	5	•	•	1
Wednesday Men .	6	1	•	•	•	•	••	6	1	6	1	•	•
Women	5	•	½	•	•	•	••	6	1	5	•	½	•
Thursday Men .	6	1	•	4	12	5½	••	•	•	6	1	•	1
Women	5	•	½	4	12	5½	••	•	•	5	•	•	1
Friday . Men .	6	1	•	•	•	11	••	•	•	6	1	•	•
Women	5	•	½	•	•	11	••	•	•	5	•	½	•
Saturday . Men .	6	1	•	•	•	•	••	6	1	6	1	•	•
Women	5	•	½	•	•	•	••	6	1	5	•	½	•

Old people, being all sixty years of age and upwards ; the weekly addition of one ounce of tea, and milk or sugar to those for whose age and infirmities it may be deemed requisite.

Children under nine years of age ; bread and milk for their breakfast and supper, or gruel when milk cannot be obtained ; also such proportions of the dinner diet as may be requisite for their respective ages.

Sick, whatever is ordered for them by the medical officer.

No. 6 dietary.

What dinner actually looked like for adult male inmates receiving the PLC's No. 3 dietary: 7oz of bread (around a quarter of a modern 800gm loaf) and 2oz of cheese.

Towards the end of 1836, a dietary for the Cirencester Union was approved by the PLC for introduction on 26 December. It included a daily breakfast of 7oz of bread (6oz for women) and a pint of gruel; for supper there was the same bread ration with 1oz of cheese; on one day a week, dinner comprised 2 pints of soup (without vegetables), while on other days 1lb of potatoes was served. The only variation was the addition of 5oz of bacon to the Sunday dinner. The total weekly food ration provided to male able-bodied inmates at Cirencester was therefore 105oz of solid food and 9 pints of liquid food without vegetables added. An outcry ensued when it was subsequently discovered that inmates of the City of London Union workhouse were given 163oz of solid food and 26 pints of liquid with vegetables.

NUTRITIONAL VALUE OF THE 1835 DIETS

The science of nutrition barely existed in the 1830s – it was not until 1838 that the term 'protein' was introduced by Dutch physician Gerrit Mulder to describe a common building block of animal substances. Diets at this date were almost wholly judged in terms of the weight of the food they provided. However, a modern analysis of an average of the six 1835 diets allows us to assess the PLC's claims for the adequacy of their dietaries. The table below shows the breakdown of the 1835 able-bodied men's dietary, together with the corresponding 1991 UK daily recommended Dietary Reference Values (DRVs) for males aged nineteen to fifty-nine years.[31]

	Carbohydrate (gm)	Fat (gm)	Protein (gm)	Energy (kcal)
1835 male able-bodied dietary	317	46	67	1900
1991 DRV males aged nineteen to fifty-nine	345	99	55.5	2550

The table shows that with regard to carbohydrate and fat, the diet fell short of modern daily intake recommendations. Although the protein level was more than adequate, there was an overall deficit in energy intake of around 25 per cent.

Overall, the 1835 dietaries were very low in fat. Small amounts were provided in the occasional meat meal, suet pudding, or cheese and milk. However, workhouse milk was often watered down. Cheese was often made from skimmed milk and of variable quality. Aged and infirm paupers received a little extra fat in the form of butter, but again that could be bulked out with water.

The general lack of fruit and vegetables in all the 1835 diets also indicates a deficiency in minerals and vitamins in the diet.

WHAT DID THE FOOD TASTE LIKE?

Regardless of the quantity and nutritional quality of workhouse food, those who consumed it had a rather more important question in mind: what did it taste like?

In the 1830s, Harold Price was a resident of both the old Warminster parish workhouse and its successor the new Warminster Union workhouse. In the latter establishment, one piece of bacon served to the inmates was so tough as to be inedible and was kicked around their exercise yard like a dirty tennis ball. In September 1837, the male inmates of the workhouse refused to attend chapel as a protest against the food they were receiving.

Another view on the matter was expressed by seventy-year-old Charles Shaw in his book *When I was a Child*, published in 1903. In 1842, at the age of ten, Shaw and his family had been forced into the Wolstanton and Burslem Union workhouse at Chell in Staffordshire. On the subject of gruel, or 'skilly' as it was colloquially known, Shaw wrote:

I had heard of workhouse skilly but had never before seen it. I had had poor food before this, but never any so offensively poor as this. By what rare culinary-making nausea and bottomless fatuousness it could be made so sickening I never could make out. Simple meal and water, however small the amount of meal, honestly boiled, would be palatable. But this decoction of meal and water and mustiness and fustiness was most revolting to any healthy taste. It might have been boiled in old clothes, which had been worn upon sweating bodies for three-score years and ten. That workhouse skilly was the vilest compound I ever tasted, unutterably insipid, and it might never have been made in a country where either sugar or salt was known.

Will Crooks, a workhouse inmate during his childhood, later rose to become chairman of the Poplar Board of Guardians. In 1906, he recounted his first visit as a guardian to the Poplar workhouse:

One day I went into the dining-room and found women sitting on the long forms, some sullen, some crying. In front of each was a basin of what was alleged to be broth... The staple diet when I joined the Board was skilly. I have seen the old people, when this stuff was put before them, picking out black specks from the oatmeal. These were caused by rats, which had the undisturbed run of the oatmeal bin. No attempt was made to cleanse the oatmeal before it was prepared for the old people.[32]

A former workhouse inmate, identified only by his initials W.H.R., later recounted his experiences of the food served to children in the 1860s at the Greenwich workhouse:

> If I remember rightly, nearly all our meat dinners consisted of salt beef. It was very salty, there was no water, and the wash-house was generally locked, except when we were washing. How I have suffered with thirst. Not one drop of water to be got, except during washing time.[33]

It was not only the inmates who criticised the food. A local surgeon visiting the kitchens of the Sheffield Union workhouse in 1896 was bold enough to sample the day's menu:

> I was invited to taste the dinner of the day, which happened to be soup. I was rash enough to take a breakfast cupful, with a piece of their excellent bread, and I paid the penalty of a severe attack of indigestion. A professional cook and five bakers are employed here, and have half-a-dozen inmates to assist them. Black beetles, as at Ecclesall, are a great nuisance, and occasionally get into the food, but vigorous steps are being taken to decimate them.

Even those responsible for the dietary could occasionally criticise the food. In December 1880, the subject of the workhouse porridge was discussed at a meeting of the Camberwell Board of Guardians. One member thought it would make a 'very good paste', while another professed that he would be ashamed to give it to one of his servants. The Board eventually agreed that serving a half pint of milk with the porridge would be sufficient to improve its palatability.

Following his election to the Poplar Board of Guardians in 1893, George Lansbury inspected conditions at the union's workhouse:

> On this occasion the food was served up with pieces of black stuff floating around. On examination, we discovered it to be rat and mice manure. I called for the chief officer, who immediately argued against me, saying the porridge was good and wholesome. "Very good, madam," said I, taking up a basinful and a spoon, "here you are, eat one mouthful and I will acknowledge that I am wrong." "Oh dear, no," said the fine lady, "the food is not for me, and is good and wholesome enough for those who want it." I stamped and shouted around till both doctor and master arrived, both of whom pleaded it was all a mistake, and promptly served cocoa and bread and margarine.[34]

The quality of workhouse food was not universally condemned however. In 1841, a report of a visit to the Windsor Union workhouse published in the *Penny Magazine* noted:

> The inmates have recently dined. We taste the food which has constituted their meal; and we acknowledge that the suet pudding, the bread, and the cheese are, in quality, equal to what may be found in the larders of the wealthiest.

six

Workhouse Scandals

For those who opposed the New Poor Law, stories of local opposition, scenes of violent confrontation, and – most of all – headline-grabbing scandals, provided valuable ammunition for their cause. One of the law's most consistent critics was the London newspaper *The Times*, which through its news, editorial and letter columns publicised virtually any story which discredited the new system, no matter how flimsy the evidence for its veracity. According to one analysis, between 1837 and 1842 the paper reported 290 instances of individual suffering that it attributed to 'this odious law'. These included thirty-two accounts of cruel punishments, fourteen stories of overcrowding, fifteen reports of brutal separation of parents and children or husband and wife, and seven of workhouse 'murders'.[35] One notorious story first appeared in the paper on 11 July, 1837, in a letter from anti-Poor Law campaigner Richard Oastler:

> A clergyman, a neighbour of mine, told me the other day, that two friends of his from Cambridge had told him the following anecdote:– At a union workhouse in that neighbourhood a labourer, his wife, and children, had been confined. They were, as a matter of course, separated. The poor fellow was at last tired out; he was 'tested,' as the Duke of Richmond would term it. At length, he thought he would better be half starved at liberty than half starved in prison. He gave notice to the governor 'that he, his wife, and children would leave, and that he would try to obtain work.' The governor said, 'You cannot take your wife out. You and your children may go.' 'Not take my wife!' exclaimed the poor man. 'Why not?' 'We buried her three weeks ago!' replied the gaoler.

A month later, the PLC replied – also in the letter columns of *The Times* – that after 'minute and careful inquiries', they could find no evidence for such an event having taken place. Although many such reports were largely false, the PLC's reputation was undoubtedly harmed by the bad publicity they generated.

Provincial newspapers, too, sometimes published stories that were later shown to be untrue, but which could generate far-reaching adverse publicity. In 1844, the *Nottingham Review* printed allegations of incompetence and corruption at the Basford workhouse. Although proved to be fallacious, and probably the work of Chartist opponents of the New Poor Law, a much exaggerated version was included by Engels in his 1845 work *Conditions of the Working Class in England*:

> The sheets had not been changed in thirteen weeks, shirts in four weeks, stockings in two to ten months, so that of forty-five boys but three had stockings, and all their shirts were in tatters. The beds swarmed with vermin, and the tableware was washed in the slop-pails.

The most comprehensive and lurid collection of anti-Poor Law propaganda appeared in 1841 in *The Book of the Bastiles* edited by radical Tory George Wythen Baxter. 'Bastile' (usually spelt with a single 'l') was then a popular derogatory name for the union workhouse. The book assembled extracts from virtually every newspaper and magazine article, book, letter, pamphlet, and speech thus far promulgated against the new poor law. Prominent amongst the press cuttings were, unsurprisingly, many from *The Times*. There were also clippings from many local papers such as the *Sheffield Iris*, the *Leeds Intelligencer*, and the *Northern Star*. This typical entry is extracted from a letter to Wythen Baxter from the Revd C. Fowell Watts, former chaplain of the Bath workhouse, written in October 1840:

> The nearest relative is not allowed to carry the least thing, not even a bit of fruit, or a bun, into the House, to a dying person. I have had it said to me – 'Oh, Sir! If I had but an orange to suck to moisten my dry mouth!' and oranges I have stealthily carried to the sick and dying. A friend of mine carried a short time ago a little snuff to a man blind and dumb, whom he had long known, and who had taken it for 25 years. He was not allowed to give it. He wrote to the Board, and received for answer, that it was against the rules of the House to allow it, nor could it be allowed unless the medical officer stated it to be necessary for the man's health.

However, such incidents paled into insignificance compared to two major scandals which achieved national prominence. The first of these took place at Bridgwater in Somerset.

THE BRIDGWATER WORKHOUSE SCANDAL

In 1836, the new Bridgwater Union workhouse was still under construction and two former parish workhouses were being used by the union in the interim. Conditions in these old buildings were far from satisfactory, with children sleeping up to six to a bed.

The Bridgwater Union had, however, already carried the new dietary orders into effect and had chosen the PLC's Dietary No. 3 which provided a breakfast of bread and 1½ pints of gruel. Oatmeal was not a normal part of the labourers' diet in the area, and it was widely held locally that gruel was unhealthy. This view was backed up by a report from the union medical officer that, after gruel replaced milk in their diet, many of children in the workhouse had become affected with 'white mouth' said to be caused by irritation of the stomach and bowels and accompanied by severe diarrhoea and dysentery. In this debilitated state, sufferers then became susceptible to other conditions such as measles. It later emerged that over a six-month period during the winter of 1836-37, twenty-seven workhouse inmates had died.

In March 1837, after the annual guardian's elections, the Bridgwater Board was joined by John Bowen – an engineer, journalist, wine-merchant, and opponent of much of the New Poor Law. Bowen launched a crusade exposing conditions in the workhouse which he described as 'murderous pesthouses'. According to Bowen, the stench of diarrhoea pervaded the workhouse 'infecting others who were obliged to breathe an atmosphere saturated with foetid exhalations'. Even the workhouse governor was afflicted – he was said by Bowen to have given the following stomach-turning description of the effect of the gruel:

> It did not affect the poor people so much at first, but after the use of it for a few days, they became terribly bad; it ran from them while they were standing upright as they took it. It affected them upwards and downwards. All the way down the stairs, across the hall, and down the garden path, was all covered every morning, and the stench was horrible all through the house; making the people ill and sick who had not got the diarrhoea.[36]

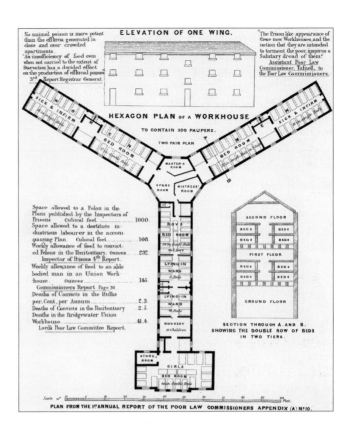

The PLC's model Y-shaped workhouse design with annotations by John Bowen, to illustrate his claim that prisoners were better off than workhouse inmates

Much of Bowen's campaign was conducted through the letters column of *The Times* newspaper which itself opposed the 1834 Act. As well as complaining about the conditions and diet in the old workhouses, Bowen also accused the Bridgwater guardians of deliberating placing a vagrant with fever in the workhouse with the aim of infecting and killing inmates.

Even when the new Bridgwater workhouse was opened in December 1837, Bowen continued to criticise the diet and space provided for each inmate. In the new workhouse dormitory inmates had 108 cubic feet each, he claimed, while convicted criminals in prison were each provided with 1000 cubic feet. He also quoted official figures to demonstrate that workhouse inmates typically received 145oz of food a week – just less than half the 292oz given to prison inmates. The new building was also afflicted with medical problems – within a few months of its opening, scabies (otherwise known as 'the itch') and other conditions were rife amongst the inmates.

Although official inquiries were held to investigate the operation of the workhouse and the conduct of the guardians and officers, none of Bowen's specific allegations was upheld.

THE ANDOVER WORKHOUSE SCANDAL

The biggest workhouse scandal of all surfaced in 1845 at Andover in Hampshire. Andover had a reputation as an extremely strict workhouse, largely due its fearsome master, Colin McDougal, a former sergeant-major and veteran of Waterloo, and his wife, Mary Ann, who was once described by the chairman of the guardians as 'a violent lady'. The McDougals ran the workhouse like a penal colony, keeping expenditure and food rations to a minimum, much to the approval of the majority of the guardians. Inmates in the workhouse had to eat their food with their fingers, and were denied the extra food and drink provided elsewhere at Christmas or for Queen Victoria's coronation. Any man who tried to exchange a word with his wife at mealtimes was given a spell in the 'refractory cell' – up to forty-eight hours of solitary confinement on a diet of bread and water.

Andover had adopted the PLC's No.3 dietary but, owing to some administrative error, had been given incorrect figures for the breakfast bread ration (6oz for men and 5oz women, rather than the correct amounts of 8oz and 6oz respectively). Figures for the twice-weekly portions of dinner vegetables had also been wrongly set at ½oz rather than the correct amount of ¾oz.

The workhouse's favoured occupation for able-bodied men was the strenuous task of crushing old animal bones to turn them into fertilizer. In 1845, rumours began to spread in the neighbourhood that men in the workhouse bone-yard were so hungry that they resorted to eating the tiny scraps of marrow and gristle left on the old bones they were supposed to be crushing. Fighting had almost broken out when a particularly succulent bone came their way.

One of the guardians, Hugh Mundy, raised concerns about the issue but found little support from his fellow guardians. He then took the matter to his local MP, Thomas Wakeley, who on 1 August, 1845, asked a question in Parliament concerning the paupers of Andover who 'were in the habit of quarrelling with each other about the bones, of extracting the marrow... and of gnawing the meat.' The Home Secretary expressed disbelief that such things were happening but promised to instigate an inquiry. The next day, Henry Parker, the Assistant Commissioner responsible for the Andover Union, was sent to investigate.

Parker soon established that the allegations were largely true. By now, however, the affair was receiving attention from the press, and Parker was under pressure from the PLC to resolve matters quickly. Then, on 29 September, McDougal resigned as master. Trying to be helpful, Parker recommended as a replacement an acquaintance of his own, the unemployed former master of the Oxford workhouse. Unfortunately, it transpired that the man had been dismissed for misconduct. In October, the beleaguered Parker was asked to resign by the PLC who, under attack from all sides, needed a scapegoat for the affair.

On 8 November, 1845, the Commissioners implicitly acknowledged the validity of the outcry against bone-crushing by forbidding its further use. The disquiet rumbled on until, on 5 March, 1846, a Parliamentary Select Committee was set up to inquire into the affair and began work a fortnight later. The shortfall in the inmates' diets was confirmed. A succession of witnesses then revealed the grim and gory details of bone-crushing – it was heavy work with a 28lb solid iron 'rammer' being used to pummel the bones in a bone-tub. Apart from the appalling smell, it was back-breaking and

Andover workhouse, now converted to residential use, where in 1845 the hungry inmates sucked the marrow from rotting bones that they were supposed to be pounding into dust.

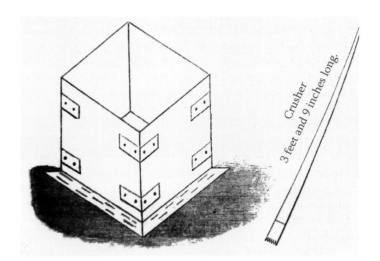

A sketch of the bone-crushing equipment used at the infamous Andover workhouse.

Crusher 3 feet and 9 inches long.

hand-blistering work, yet even boys of eight or ten were set to it, working in pairs to lift the rammer. Men also suffered scarred faces from the flying shards of bone. Bone crushing could, however, make a good profit for the workhouse with old bones being bought at 20s a ton and the ground bone dust fetching up to 24s a ton. It was embarrassingly revealed that the some of Andover guardians had themselves bought ground bones at a bargain price of 17s to 19s a ton.

The workhouse master, Colin McDougal, was revealed to have been regularly drunk and having had violent and bloody fights with his wife who had threatened suicide. McDougal had also attempted to seduce some of the young women inmates (as, too, had his seventeen-year-old son who had been taken on as a workhouse schoolmaster).

The Committee heard evidence from a large number of witnesses, including the workhouse inmates themselves. Here is part of the testimony of one of them, sixty-one-year Samuel Green:

I was employed in the workhouse at bone-breaking the best part of my time…We looked out for the fresh bones; we used to tell the fresh bones by the look of them, and then we used to be like a parcel of dogs after them; some were not so particular about the bones being fresh as others; I like the fresh bones; I never touched one that was a little high; the marrow was as good as the meat, it was all covered over by bone, and no filth could get to it… I have picked a sheep's head, a mutton bone, and a beef bone; that was when they were fresh and good; sometimes I have had one that was stale and stunk, and I eat it even then; I eat it when it was stale and stinking because I was hungered, I suppose. You see we only had bread and gruel for breakfast, and as there was no bread allowed on meat days for dinner, we saved our bread from breakfast, and then, having had only gruel for breakfast, we were hungry before dinner-time. To satisfy our hunger a little, because a pint and a half of gruel is not much for a man's breakfast, we eat the stale and stinking meat. If we could get a fresh bone we did not take the stale and stinking meat. The allowance of potatoes at dinner on meat days is half a pound, but we used to get nearly a pound, seven or eight middling sized potatoes. The food we got in the workhouse was very good; I could not wish better, all I wanted was a little more… I have seen a man named Reeves eat horse-flesh off the bones.

The Select Committee's report, published in August 1846, criticized virtually everyone involved in the scandal. The McDougals were found to be totally unfit to hold such posts; the guardians had failed to visit the workhouse and had allowed the inmates to be underfed;

Assistant Commissioner Parker, although competent in his everyday duties, had placed too much confidence in the Andover guardians; the Poor Law Commissioners had dismissed Parker and Day in an underhand manner and had mishandled the whole affair. No direct action was taken against the PLC as a result of the report but the findings undoubtedly contributed to its abolition the following year. In its place, a new body – the Poor Law Board – was set up, which was far more accountable to Parliament. The Poor Law Board was itself replaced in 1871 by the Local Government Board (LGB).

The Andover guardians appear to have come out of the affair little the wiser. The master appointed as successor to McDougal was a former prison officer from Parkhurst gaol. After only three years in the post, he was dismissed for taking liberties with female paupers.

THE CITY OF LONDON GUARDIANS AND THEIR LUNCHES

Although nothing ever equalled the Andover affair, scandals and controversies large and small continued to erupt periodically over the years. As at Andover and Bridgwater, they usually involved workhouse conditions, or the behaviour or misdemeanours of the staff and guardians. When it came to food, it wasn't always the fare served up to inmates that evoked public outcry.

At a meeting of the City of London guardians in March 1897, one of the Board members, Mr John Lobb, proposed an innocuous sounding motion 'that the dining by the guardians at the workhouse at Homerton and the infirmary at Bow after the business... be discontinued.' Press reports subsequently revealed that the Board's meetings were conducted in a manner worthy of the pages of *Oliver Twist*. Proceedings began with a light luncheon of bread and cheese, beer, spirits etc. After the main business of the meeting, typically an hour to an hour and a half later, the guardians were served a repast of fish (salmon for preference), fowl, roast mutton and beef, and sundry other dishes followed by a selection of puddings and sweets. The food was accompanied by champagne and other wines as well as spirits. Then came the important matter of a long series of well-lubricated toasts to the Queen and Royal family, the chairman of the Board, the vice-chairman of the Board, the chairman for the day, the vice-chairman for the day, and so on, concluding with a toast for the oldest guardian and one for the youngest guardian. Finally, the members rounded off their meal with tea, coffee, biscuits, cakes, and other dainties and delicacies. As well as the unseemliness of such consumption and cork-popping taking place in earshot of the workhouse inmates, concerns were raised over the financing of such feasts and whether they were being subsidized by the ratepayers. Mr Lobb's motion, needless to say, was defeated.

An artist's impression of the 'banquet' that accompanied the City of London guardians' meetings as viewed by the diners and the workhouse inmates.

seven

A Chorus of Disapproval

Although much of the criticism of the New Poor Law was aired through the news and letters columns of publications such as *The Times*, the workhouse – and in particular its food – was sometimes the target of more literary or satirical attacks. One of the most erudite of these was a new version of one of the witches' scenes from Shakespeare's *Macbeth*, originally published the *Weekly Dispatch* and reprinted in the *Book of the Bastiles*:

Macbeth.–Act IV, scene I *(Workhouse laboratory – a cauldron boiling – groans – three guardians discovered.)*

First Guardian: Thrice hath the dying pauper groan'd,

Second Guardian: And once his starveling child hath moaned;

Third Guardian: Rot-gut cries, ''tis time, 'tis time':

First Guardian: Round about the cauldron go;

                               In the loathsome victuals throw:
                               Bone that in the shambles' drain
                               Thirty days and nights hath lain,
                               Ta'en from sheep that had the rot,
                               Boiled there in the charmed pot.

All: Double, double, toil and trouble,
                               Fire burn and cauldron bubble.

Second Guardian: Fillet of a new-slunk calf.
                               In the cauldron put but half;
                               Horn of goat and hoof of hog,
                               Head of cat and lights of dog,
                               Asses' tongue and weavled wheat,
                               Sundry scraps of putrid meat
                               For a charm of powerful trouble,
                               Like a hell-broth, boil and bubble.

| All: | Double, double, toil and trouble |
| | Fire burn and culdron bubble. |

Third Guardian:	Shell of oyster, chicken's claw,
	Duckling's entrails, turkey's maw;
	Measled pork and moudy meal,
	Clods and Sticking, greasy heel;
	Swealtered cabbage, eye of ox,
	Scaly tail of mangy fox,
	Add thereto the back of ferret;
	Round about the cauldron stir it.

| All: | Bubble, bubble, toil and trouble, |
| | Fire burn and cauldron bubble. |

| First Guardian: | Cool it with a pauper's blood, |
| | Then the charm is firm and good. |

(Enter Assistant Pinch-pauper.)

Pinch-pauper:	Well-done, I commend your pains,
	And every one shall share the gains.
	Round about the cauldron sing,
	Like good guardians in a ring,
	Praising all that you put in.

(Enter relieving officers and the churns of guardians – groans and lamentations.)

Pinch-pauper:	Black gruel and white,
	Green gruel and grey,
	Mingle, mingle, mingle,
	That they can eat it may.

| First Guardian: | Now for water; make it thin. |

| Second Guardian: | Put of that a plenty in. |

| Third Guardian: | That will make the paupers grin. |

| All: | Around, around, around, about, about, |
| | All bad come running in – all good keep out. |

PUNCH

The Poor Law was often a subject of attention for the satirical magazine *Punch*, which was launched in 1841. Typical of its attacks was the cartoon captioned 'The "Milk" of Poor Law "Kindness"' published in 1843 following a report that in Bethnal Green workhouse 'an infant, only five weeks old, had been separated from the mother, being occasionally brought to her for the breast.'

THE "MILK" OF POOR-LAW "KINDNESS."

Inquisitive Guardian. "BY THE WAY, HAVE YOU ANY CHILDREN?"
Applicant for Relief. "No."
Guardian. "BUT—ER—SURELY I KNOW A SON OF YOURS?"
Applicant. "WELL, I DON'T SUPPOSE YOU'D CALL A CHILD CHILDREN!"

Above left: The 'Milk' of Poor Law 'Kindness' – a 1843 cartoon from the satirical magazine *Punch*.

Above right: This jocular 1899 *Punch* cartoon portrays a much-changed attitude towards the once terrifying ordeal of the guardian's interview – the applicant is now shown trying to get the better of the Board.

Over the years, the pages of *Punch* chart the changing attitudes towards the workhouse system. An 1899 cartoon depicting a Board of Guardians' interrogation of an applicant for poor relief has a remarkably light-hearted tone, indicating how ordinary a part of everyday life the system had become. The image makes a striking contrast with the 1844 illustration of a similar scene from the novel *Jessie Phillips* included earlier.

BROADSIDE BALLADS

From the sixteenth to the early twentieth century, broadside ballads were the popular songs of their day, performed in taverns, homes, or fairs. Printed sheets containing the words were sold in the street for a penny or halfpenny.

Not surprisingly, the workhouse was the subject of a number of broadside ballads. One of the most popular was *The Workhouse Boy* – a macabre story of a young workhouse inmate 'going to pot'. The song has an interesting pedigree – it was a parody of *The Mistletoe Bough* by Thomas Haynes Bayly who took his inspiration from an earlier poem by Samuel Rogers (whose verses were based on an old Italian tale from the eighteenth century). *The Workhouse Boy* appeared in around 1836 and is referred to in Dickens' *Bleak House* when shrill youthful voices taunt the Beadle with having boiled a boy and then chorus fragments of a popular song 'importing that the boy was made into soup for the workhouse.'

The Workhouse Boy

The towels were spread in the workhouse hall,
Our caps were hung up on the whitey brown wall;
W'ed hoshuns of soup, and nothing to pay,
For keeping our Christmas holiday.
We'd a baron of beef, and pudden beside,
A beautiful one – it was Missus's pride
We feasted our eyes with the pudden and beef,
But as for our bellies, t'was all make belief,
For the poor workhouse boy! Oh, the poor workhouse boy.

'I'm tired,' cried one, 'of the soup I'm sick,
But stop here a minute – I'll play 'em a trick.
Bill Lovell,' says he, 'will you come and go,
Where the pudden is hid, I thinks I know.'
Away he ran and his pal began
The wash-house to search and the larder to scan.
And Bill Lovell cried, 'Now where do you hide?
I can't find the pudden nor you beside.'
Oh the poor workhouse boy! Oh, the poor workhouse boy.

He sought him next night, and he sought him next day,
He sought him in vain when a week passed way.
On the pantiles, the cellars, the coal-hole ('Why Not?')
Bill Lovell sought wildly but found him not.
A month flew by and his grief at last
Was just like a story of woe long past.
But Bill he still wept o'er his lonesome lot,
For his pal he felt certain had gone to pot.
Oh the poor workhouse boy! Oh, the poor workhouse boy.

The soup copper was cleaned out once a year,
The mops and the birch brooms were all brought near.
They put out the fire, they looked all around,
And what do you think in the copper was found?
A little boy's coat and a small-tooth comb
Showed very well that was a poor boy's tomb.
He'd lost his way and like poor Lovell too,
Had been for a month in a terrible stew.
Oh the poor workhouse boy! Oh, the poor workhouse boy.

eight

Workhouse Kitchens

Most early Victorian workhouse kitchens would have had fairly basic facilities, sometimes comprising little more than one or two large pots or 'coppers' in which to make gruel, or boil potatoes or meat. Cooking was generally done on a kitchen range. Former parish workhouses might still have the old-style open range with an open fire over which pots were hung. By the 1830s, however, new buildings would normally be fitted with a closed range or 'kitchener' which had an enclosed fire heated a hotplate above and one or more ovens each side.

An idea of the operation of a modest-sized workhouse kitchen can be gained from the auctioneer's catalogue for the disposal of the contents of the old Oxford workhouse in 1859. The workhouse was listed as having two kitchens equipped as follows:

| Kitchen No. 1 | Dough bin, two steamers, six tin porringers, two colanders, two spouts, eight buckets, two stands, two pails, bowl, and five coalboxes. |
| Kitchen No. 2 | Scales and weights, four tables, saw, cleaver, knife-box, skewers, three trenchers, two skimmers, ladle, fork, funnel, saucepan, two porridge measures, two buckets, tub, sieve, shovel, range of four coppers as fixed, meat screen, and two buckets. |

As well as the obligatory porridge or gruel, this particular kitchen appears to have cooked meat, vegetables, sauces, and produced its own bread. Some workhouses were rather more limited in their facilities. A visitor to one workhouse kitchen discovered:

> They had two coppers so set that their tops were separated only by a space of three inches. When I was there, they were boiling clothes in one and soup in the other; and there were no lids on them. When the soup boiled over into the clothes, I raised no objection, but when the clothes boiled over into the soup, I said I would not stay to dinner.[37]

In a similar vein, an official inspection of the old Kirkheaton township workhouse at Huddersfield in 1866 revealed that the copper in which the establishment's 'foul linen' was boiled, was used also for cooking the food of the inmates.

For workhouses with large numbers of inmates, fairly elaborate kitchen facilities were required. A visitor to Manchester's Chorlton Union workhouse in 1881 recorded:

> We were formally introduced to the family teapot which holds the modest quantity of 175 gallons, while the soup tureen is capable of containing 120 gallons. Everything here is on a gigantic scale. The room is lofty and well ventilated, the rack for steaming the potatoes looks as if it would hold the produce of half an acre, and the enormous milk-cans are suggestive of many cows.[38]

The technology used in workhouse kitchens also evolved. The coal and wood used to fire the traditional kitchen range were joined by gas and steam which both offered clean and efficient sources of heat. Steam was particularly versatile – not only did it provide heat for cooking and for warming the building, but could also power mechanical devices such as pumps, laundry equipment, and dynamos.

By the 1860s, the Victorian talent for mechanical and engineering inventiveness was beginning to make its mark on institutional kitchens such as those found in larger workhouses. All manner of novel machines for preparing and cooking industrial quantities of food were devised, and heavily advertised in the trade press of the day in journals such as the *Local Government Chronicle* and the *Poor Law Officers' Journal*.

An 1870 advertisement for the London firm of Clements, Jeakes & Co. included gas roasting ovens and potato steamers, as well as more conventional ranges. By 1901, the company of Benham & Sons listed its specialities as: roasting ranges, pastry and roasting ovens, potato and vegetable steam ovens, grills, refrigerators, hot closets and carving tables, steam-jacketed cooking pans, milk sterilizers, tea and coffee-making apparatus, and beef-tea infusers.

In 1902, the new kitchen at the St Marylebone workhouse was described by one observer as:

A large lofty room, lined with whie glazed bricks, and with a score of steam-jacketed coppers, tea coppers, roasting ovens, and the like… here they make sixty-gallon milk pudding, have three teapots of eighty gallons capacity each, cook a quater of a ton of bacon and a ton of cabbage at an operation, and steam potatoes by the ton.

WORKHOUSE COOKS

In the first few decades of the union workhouse era, it was common for the workhouse's cooking to be supervised by the matron, with the kitchen work carried out by women inmates. Larger

A 1901 advertisement for Benham and Sons, purveyors of institutional kitchen equipment. They succeeded in persuading the Holborn Guardians to allow the workhouse kitchen (and cook) to be featured.

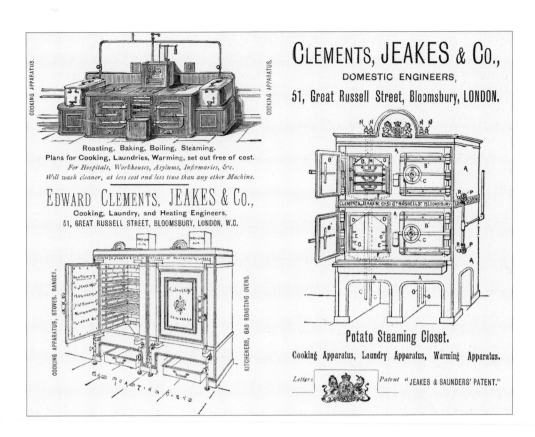

Above: An 1870 advertisement for institutional cooking equipment.

Right: Another kitchen equipment advertisement listing the company's numerous existing clients.

In 1858 the kitchens of the St Marylebone workhouse hosted the trial of a new invention – Stevens's bread-making machine – which claimed to make dough more efficiently and hygienically than by using manual labour.

St Marylebone workhouse kitchens in around 1902. At the left, a cook stirs a large pot, while supplies of bread are stacked on the scales to the right.

workhouses sometimes had a separate bakehouse – in this case, the baking would generally have been carried out by male inmates.

In the second half of the nineteenth century, the employment of paid and even trained cooks became more usual. Recruitment was often done via the local press – on 31 May 1856 the *Manchester Times* carried an advertisement for 'a respectable unmarried female, not exceeding 42 years of age' to act as cook in the Manchester workhouse. The salary offered was £16 a year with board, washing and lodging included.

Obtaining the services of a suitable person was not always easy, however. In April 1864, the Halifax Union advertised for a cook in the *Leeds Mercury* specifying an 'active, unmarried woman… with testimonials as to character and for honesty, sobriety, morality, and general competency'. The post came with a salary of £15 a year plus board and lodging. Apparently, this met with little success as a similar advertisement was placed in November of the same year, although the salary on offer was now £25, with free washing thrown in. Applicants were now also required to be between 25 and 45 years in age.

Analysis of a sample of 100 workhouse returns from the 1881 census reveals that roughly half of the institutions had a resident cook listed on the staff. Their average age was around thirty-eight, with the youngest aged twenty-one and the eldest, at Battle workhouse, still going strong at eighty-eight! The large majority were unmarried or widowed. Although being single was frequently a requirement of the post, there was the occasional exception: at Swaffham workhouse, for example, the cook was married to the workhouse porter. Seven out of eight cooks were women, with male cooks most likely to be found in London workhouses.

Despite the potential difficulties in obtaining a good cook, the employment was not necessarily secure. On 17 October 1881, the *Western Mail* reported that the Cardiff workhouse cook had been ill and unable to attend to her duties. After the housemaid had stepped in and performed the work very satisfactorily, the cook was given notice that her services were no longer required and the housemaid was appointed in her place.

WORKHOUSE DINING HALLS

Although a few workhouses had separate dining rooms for different categories of inmate, the most common arrangement was a single communal dining hall. This had some practical advantages in terms of the easy distribution and serving of food from the workhouse kitchens. A single room also required less staff to supervise than was the case with multiple dining areas. The obligatory

Biggleswade Union, Beds.
FEMALE COOK.

WANTED, a Female Cook. Salary £25 per annum, with rations, apartments, and washing, and £3 5s. per annum in lieu of beer.

For the purposes of superannuation the value of the rations, &c., is assessed at £35 a year.

The applicant must have had experience in Cooking for Inmates and Officers in a Public Institution ; she will also be required to superintend Female Vagrants, and act under the direction of the Matron.

Applications, upon forms to be obtained from the undersigned, together with copies of three recent testimonials, to be sent to me not later than first post on Tuesday, the 25th July, 1905.

Selected candidates will have notice to attend the Board.

GEO. WAGG,
Clerk to the Guardians.
Biggleswade, July 12, 1905.

Above left: A London workhouse cook in the 1890s, location unknown.

Above right: A 1905 advertisement by the Biggleswade workhouse seeking a cook. Although kitchen and laundry workers were traditionally provided with beer while at work, this practice had fallen foul of temperance campaigners. Thus the post came with £3 5s 'in lieu of beer'.

saying of grace before and after each meal was also simplified. Where a workhouse had a single dining hall, it was common for it to be used as a chapel on Sundays or for other communal events such as the occasional entertainments which were provided in later years.

The separation of the sexes that was required by the workhouse regulations was achieved in various ways. Some workhouses had physical partitions down the middle of the dining hall with separate entrances for men and women. By the end of the century it appears that merely having segregated seating and serving areas was sufficient. In the 1830s, workhouse regulations demanded that during meals 'silence, order and decorum shall be maintained', though from 1842 the word 'silence' was dropped.

Every workhouse dining hall was required to have a set of scales available. Any inmate who suspected that his allotted portion of food fell short of the regulation weight could demand to have it weighed in front of witnesses. It is not clear how often inmates took advantage of this privilege which, presumably, would not be looked upon too kindly by the workhouse staff.

In the 1830s and 1840s, the provision of cutlery and crockery was not at all commonplace. For consuming liquid food such as gruel, a wooden or metal spoon would probably be provided – otherwise, fingers would be used. Food was often eaten from a trencher – a plate or shallow dish made from a solid piece of wood, often sycamore which did not taint the food. Tin plates or pannikins were used by some workhouses up until the 1860s when they were gradually replaced by pottery dishes. The provision of a knife, fork and spoon for each workhouse inmate was a recommendation in a Poor Law Board report in 1866.[39]

WORKHOUSE LAUNDRIES

One of the principle sources of work for women in the workhouse was the laundry where large amounts of bedding and clothing were washed and ironed every week. In the 1890s, the laundry at the large Sheffield Union workhouse washed 20,000 articles every week and employed about thirty able-bodied inmates, together with a dozen women from outside who received 1s 6d a day plus three meals.

Most workhouse laundries had distinct areas for different stages in the washing process: the wash-house, where dirty items were washed, a drying room where items were dried on large wheeled racks, and the laundry itself where articles were ironed, folded, and so on.

As with the kitchen, the workhouse laundry became the target of labour-saving technical innovations such as steam-powered washing machines and driers.

SANITATION

The toilet or latrine facilities in workhouses, like most others of their day, would be considered primitive by modern standards. The simplest form of provision was the 'privy', a room without plumbing, often placed away the main workhouse building and well ventilated, perhaps even lacking a door. The user would sit on a hole cut into a wooden plank which dropped through either to a large cesspit, or to a pan or pail whose contents could periodically be removed. (In domestic urban premises, this material would often be deposited at the side of the road for overnight removal by 'night-carts' – thus 'night soil' became a term for human excrement.) As well as privies for single occupancy, communal privies could accommodate up to six users at a time sitting side by side.

From the 1840s, various forms of water closet, where a reservoir of water was used to flush away the matter deposited by the user, gradually became more common. If a workhouse did provide such a luxurious facility, a single closet would probably serve a very large number of inmates. For night-time use in workhouse dormitories, chamber pots could be provided or, failing that, a communal bucket or tub which was carried away and emptied each morning.

A dining hall at a smaller workhouse. The religious mottoes were intended to instil piety and gratitude into the inmates.

The ornate dining hall of the new Holborn Union workhouse erected in 1885. The room was also used as a chapel.

The old folks' mealtime at the Mitcham workhouse in 1896 – the men are seated at the rear of the hall.

A view from around 1902 of the dining hall at St Marylebone workhouse – women are seated at the rear part of the hall. The plates appear to have a 'meat-and-two-veg' dinner with a dessert spoons to hand for a second course.

In 1857, St Pancras workhouse installed the latest in laundry technology: the steam-powered Macalpine's washing machines, coupled with Manlove's dashwheel rinsing machine and hydro-extractor. These could do the weekly wash of 8,000 articles in four days.

Even where water closets were fitted, they were often poorly maintained and the supply of water to them might be far from guaranteed. In 1865, the medical journal *The Lancet* surveyed the conditions in a number of London workhouses. At St George the Martyr in Southwark, conditions in the workhouse sick wards were particularly unpleasant:

> Thirty men had used one closet, in which there had been no water for more than a week, and which was in close proximity to their ward; and in an adjoining ward so strong was the ammoniacal smell that we had no doubt respecting the position of the cabinet, which we found dry. In No. 4 ward (female), with 17 beds, the drain-smell from a lavatory in a recess of the room was so offensive that we suspected a sewer-communication, and soon discovered that there was no trap; indeed it had been lost for some considerable time. Apart from this source of contamination of the ward, there were several cases with offensive discharges: one particularly, a case of cancer, which, no disinfectant being used, rendered the room almost unbearable to the other inmates.[40]

In around 1860, a rival to the water closet appeared in the form of the earth closet, invented by the Revd Henry Moules. Moules had discovered that a small amount of dry sifted earth scattered by each user into the closet's under-seat receptacle would quickly deodorize the deposited material. After re-drying, the mixture could be re-used a number of times before being employed as fertiliser. Although some use was made of earth closets, particularly in rural workhouses or in situations where no ready water supply existed, the water closet became the standard.

WATER SUPPLIES

Until the second half of the nineteenth century, most people obtained their water from sources such as a well, spring, or river, perhaps supplemented by the collection of rain water. The piped domestic water supplies that did exist were mostly provided by private water companies. They were thus expensive and generally only available in towns and cities. Union workhouses were often sited on the edge of a town and aimed to be run as economically as possible. Even if piped water was available in their locality, the cost would probably be more than the guardians would be prepared to pay. The principle of 'less eligibility', that a workhouse inmate should be no better off than the lowliest of independent labourer outside the workhouse, also weighed against the use of commercially supplied water.

The remains of a communal privy (toilet) at an Irish workhouse at Bawnboy in County Cavan.

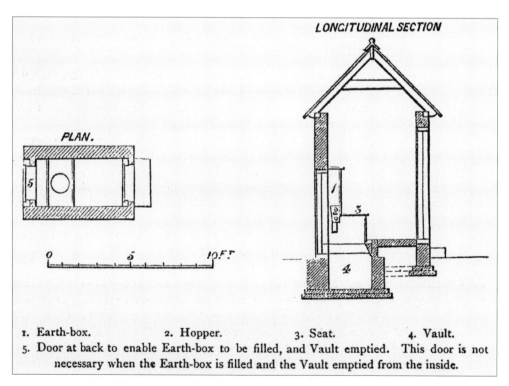

LONGITUDINAL SECTION

PLAN.

1. Earth-box.   2. Hopper.   3. Seat.   4. Vault.
5. Door at back to enable Earth-box to be filled, and Vault emptied. This door is not
   necessary when the Earth-box is filled and the Vault emptied from the inside.

A diagram of Moules' earth closet fitted with a small hopper so that each user could easily sprinkle a fixed amount of earth into the 'vault' below.

Above left: A typical workhouse water pump in one of the inmates' yards at the Holywell workhouse in North Wales.

Above right: The impressive clock tower at the Rochdale Union workhouse conceals a large water tank.

Workhouses thus often relied on natural sources of water for their supply. Water for the Shrewsbury workhouse was hand-pumped from the river by the paupers using a 'small machine'. At Longtown in Cumberland, water for the workhouse was supplied by a pump in the kitchen supplemented by water from a stream adjoining the premises.

Larger workhouses might have four or five wells, with a bucket or hand-pump being used to raise the water. Water could also be pumped to an elevated storage tank for distribution around the rest of the workhouse. The Malton workhouse in North Yorkshire had a treadmill, which was used both to pump water for the workhouse, and to provide a punishment task for the inmates. When a new workhouse was opened in Tamworth in 1859, the main cold water tank was in a central tower, to which the water was supplied by a crank pump from the well in the able-bodied men's yard. Hand pumping was gradually replaced by the use of powered pumps – at the new Medway Union workhouse, which opened in 1859, the initial plan was that water for the new building would be manually pumped from a well but a steam pump was later included in the scheme.

Large elevated water storage tanks were erected at many workhouses (and other institutions such as hospitals or asylums) and took various forms. The simplest method was to place the tank above a simple metal framework. In other cases, it could be placed on top of a brick-built block. Later workhouse designers often cunningly concealed tanks inside the central tower of the main building. In 1872, at Huddersfield's new Crosland Moor workhouse, the upper part of the central tower contained a large tank which held 10,000 gallons of water and supplied all the water closets, lavatories, baths etc. Provision was also made to attach a plug and hose on each landing in case of fire.

Building engineers often had to go to great lengths, or rather depths, in order to locate suitable sources of water. In 1881, the St Marylebone guardians opened a new infirmary at Rackham

The St Olave Union's Ladywell workhouse turned its water storage facilities into a feature in the shape of this imposing water tower.

Some workhouses obtained their water from artesian wells, where natural pressure was sufficient to bring water to the surface. This 1920s picture shows new artesian wells being drilled at the Aylsham workhouse in Norfolk.

Street in Ladbroke Grove. To provide water for the establishment, they had to sink a well 500ft deep from which powerful pumps raised 6,000 gallons per hour. Even more severe difficulties were encountered at Brighton in the 1850s when it was decided to erect a new workhouse on an elevated site at Race Hill, together with a nearby workhouse school at Warren Farm. The guardians were reluctant to pay for piped water to supply the new buildings so workhouse labour was used to dig a new well at the Warren Farm site. Progress was slow and the lack of water led to a long postponement of the building work on the new workhouse. On Sunday 16 March, 1862, after four years of digging by workhouse inmates, down to a world-record depth of 1,285ft, they finally reached water. Church bells were rung and there were great celebrations locally, but it was the engineers that were honoured with a parade, medals, and a banquet, not the pauper labour force. The wife of a man who died during the digging work was given £6 in compensation.

nine

Supplying the Workhouse

A typical union workhouse, a household with a population of 200-300 inmates, had a large weekly shopping list. The provisions it required covered all manner of items from basic foodstuffs such as bread, milk, potatoes, and oatmeal, through to coal for heating, candles for lighting, soap for washing, clothing for the inmates, linen for their beds, or even the beds themselves. For those who ended their days in the workhouse, a supply of coffins and shrouds was also needed.

Many of these items were bought in, usually from local suppliers, and the workhouse could make a considerable contribution to the local economy. Advertisements for sealed bids to supply goods regularly appeared in local newspapers and contracts were usually awarded to the lowest tender. The quality of the goods was often very much a secondary consideration, however.

The alternative to buying in supplies was for the workhouse to produce them itself. Not only was this a way of saving money, but also provided useful work for the workhouse inmates. Some workhouses had their own bakery – this not only fed and employed the inmates, but could also be used for producing loaves given to paupers on out-relief. Agriculture, too, provided both food and employment. At Abingdon workhouse, around ten acres of land at the rear of the workhouse was turned over to growing vegetables: swedes, mangold wurzels, parsnips, carrots, potatoes, peas and barley. In addition, a dozen pigs were kept. The piggery, supplemented by the contents of the workhouse privies, provided a steady source of manure for the crops. In May 1849, workhouse master Richard Ellis reported to the PLC on the matter of 'Profitable Employment of Paupers on Workhouse Land':

> By keeping, upon an average, twelve large pigs, which we purchase in a very poor condition, (spayed sows being preferred), we can use all our spare offal from the garden, and this description of pigs will eat it, and get half fat upon it. We obtain a large quantity of manure from them, and, with a small purchase of stable dung, are enabled to manure the ground sufficiently. The liquid obtained from the washhouses, privies, &c., is all conveyed into close cesspools in the garden, from which it is pumped, and conveyed between the rows of the crops, particularly mangold wurzel, by which means this plant attains a weight of from 20 to 25lbs each, and sells at 20s. per ton. In winter the liquid manure is pumped up and distributed over such parts of the ground as are dug in, and the ground is trenched and prepared for spring crops. A gravel pit is kept always open for the employment of those who are not otherwise employed; the gravel sold to surveyors and others produces more than sufficient to purchase manure and straw for the piggery. The seeds we grow ourselves, so that no extra charge is made upon that account in this return.

Many workhouses followed Abingdon's example and either cultivated crops on part of their grounds, or acquired additional land for the purpose. In 1856, the Tonbridge Union purchased

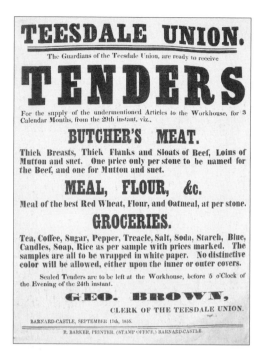

Above: A handbill requesting tenders for the supply of foodstuffs to the Teesdale workhouse in 1855.

Right: A typical advertisement for the supply of workhouse provisions placed by the Dartford union in 1905.

12 acres of land adjoining the workhouse and the bacon and produce were used in the workhouse with any surplus being sold locally. Some establishments, such as the Mitford and Launditch workhouse at Gressenhall, and the Holborn Union workhouse at Mitcham, operated their own separate farms where workhouse inmates provided labour. The Mitcham farm was unusual in having a gasworks which supplied the nearby workhouse.

The largest of these agricultural enterprises was probably the Doe Royd dairy farm set up in around 1898 by the Sheffield Board of Guardians. The 156 acre farm produced around 200 gallons of milk a day, some of which was used to make butter. Produce from the farm was used to supply the Sheffield workhouse and union infirmary. However, a veto by the land's owner, the Duke of Norfolk, meant that pauper labour was not used on the farm.

SHADY DEALINGS

Traders who supplied a workhouse often saw it as an easy target for swindling. The most common deception was to provide a good quality sample item when tendering for a contract, but to supply inferior goods afterwards. This could be done by simple measures such as watering down milk, or providing bread that was adulterated or made from an inferior grade of flour. Some frauds were more sophisticated. In 1896, Messrs Berringer & Co., had contracted to supply the South London District Poor Law School at Sutton with best quality margarine from the well-known manufacturers Otto Monstead. It was later discovered that they had, in fact, been providing a much inferior foreign product packed in boxes stencilled and labelled to resemble those which Otto Monstead used.

Like many other workhouses, Wincanton workhouse in Somerset turned its grounds over to the growing of vegetables, even though these were often conspicuously lacking from the inmates' own diet.

The extensively cultivated grounds of the Tonbridge Union workhouse in Kent. The better quality produce would probably sold off rather than being used in the workhouse.

The bakery of the Bath Union workhouse.

Members of the Board of Guardians and workhouse officers were forbidden by the 1834 Act from being involved in the supply of goods or provisions to the workhouse in case it led to financial impropriety. Despite such regulations, workhouse officials sometimes succumbed to temptations that were placed before them. At the Loddon and Clavering Union in 1842, the workhouse master was dismissed after being discovered replacing cheese in the inmates' diet by cheap broth, and selling off for his own gain honey and plants produced at the workhouse.

A much more serious case came to light in 1906 during an official inquiry at the Poplar workhouse following a catalogue of complaints from local ratepayers. It was revealed that the level of comfort for inmates in the workhouse was rather superior to that of a typical working labourer, with rations of beer issued to inmates amounting to over 200 pints a day on occasion. Members of the Board of Guardians, and also tradesmen supplying the union, were reported as often taking meals and drinking with the master at the workhouse and, contrary to normal practice, contracts were regularly being awarded to suppliers who had not tendered the lowest price. In the case of one milk contract, over £200 would have been saved if the lowest tender had been taken. In some cases, bribes had been paid by suppliers to secure such contracts. The workhouse master, who had resigned by the start of the inquiry (supposedly due to ill-health), was shown to have been neglecting his duties because of a relationship he had been conducting with a former nurse at the workhouse. Because of this, inmates performed virtually no work and discipline in the workhouse was said to be non-existent.

The anonymous author of *Indoor Paupers* in 1885 claimed that 'plundering' of food stocks by officials was rife. He described a typical method by which this was done:

> Different days are selected for the raids on the different sorts of food – one day for the meat, another
> for the flour, a third for the vegetables, a fourth for the meal, and so on. Tuesday, let us suppose, is

Holborn Union's workhouse farm at Mitcham in 1896. As well as the piggery, the site also had its own gasworks which supplied the workhouse.

one of the porridge or gruel days. The paupers will receive precisely the same quantity morning and evening – say a pint and a half on each occasion. But the quality? The best answer to that question is a fair statement of what ought to happen, contrasted with what has happened. A pound of meal to a gallon of water is the regulation amount; but on the raiding-day the proportion is known to have been 70lb of meal to 120 gallons of water, or fifty pounds of meal – nearly one-half – short. The paupers complain; but of what use is that? The master admits that there is some justice in the complaint. He calls for the cook, and receives a plausible excuse which he does not care to search too closely, orders that the thing shall not occur again, and then forgets all about it. Next day the gruel is all correct, and the next, and the next, until the raiding-day returns, when what has just been described is repeated. It is the same with the meat, which is stolen on one of the days when there is soup for dinner; and the same with everything eatable.

The same author also alleged that the workhouse 'scullery-men' – themselves paupers – regularly sold basins of sweetened tea to their other inmates, thereby 'fleecing' their fellows, to say nothing of workhouse stores.

As often happens in large institutions, an undercover economy existed in many workhouses. At the 1845 inquiry into the Andover scandal, an inmate named Samuel Green described how workhouse bread could be used as a currency to buy tobacco:

I did not eat my bread any one morning in the week. I did not eat it, but not because I had too much. I used to sell it to buy a bit of 'bacco. I used to sell it in the workhouse. Most all the people who take 'bacco, sell their bread. 'Bacco is a very wholesome thing, especially in such a place as the workhouse. The master once found that I had saved five allowances of bread, and he took them away from me, but afterwards gave them me again. He told me he should not allow us to save bread in that way. The saving of bread used to cause a good deal of quarrelling, because some of them would steal it. I used to save a bit of bread for Sunday, because on Sundays, when you are standing about the yard doing nothing, you want more to eat than when you are working; the time seems so long when you are standing about.

THE ADULTERATION OF FOOD

Prior to the 1880s, the adulteration of commercially produced or distributed food was rife, the most common targets being bread and flour, oatmeal, milk, tea, cocoa, and beer. The extent of the problem was first highlighted by the work of Frederick Accum whose *Treatise on Adulterations of Food and Culinary Poisons* was published in 1820 and described some of most common adulteration techniques then in use.

Because of the premium placed on white bread, all sorts of methods were used to adulterate it, both to whiten inferior flour, and to increase the amount of bread that could be produced from a given amount of white flour. Common additives used for this purpose included alum, lime, chalk, and powdered bones.

Oatmeal could be replaced by cheaper but less nutritious barleymeal. Milk was frequently watered down and had chalk and flour added to restore its body. Tea could be completely fabricated from dust and gum and then coloured with Prussian blue, verdigris (copper acetate) or turmeric. Used tea leaves could be boiled with sheep's dung and copperas (iron sulphate) then dried and resold. Tea could also have iron filings added. Cocoa might be adulterated with brick-dust, tallow, iron peroxide, and ground biscuit. Beer, like milk, could be watered down then have sugar and salt added to restore its flavour, plus the addition of copperas to give it a good head. Many foods were brightly coloured using toxic dyes containing lead, copper or mercury. The situation could be made even worse by 'double-adulteration' – for example, if a baker was supplied with already adulterated flour which he then further contaminated himself. Likewise, a workhouse could buy in milk that was already watered down and then further dilute it so that the nutritional content was then minimal.

The system of tendering for supplies made workhouses particularly susceptible to food adulteration since the lowest tender was usually given the contract. Workhouse inmates, who had a restricted diet to begin with, were also especially vulnerable to any diminution of what limited food they had.

From 1851 to 1854, *The Lancet* published a long and detailed series of reports on the adulteration of every major item of food and drink. The investigation, conducted by Dr Arthur Hassall, revealed, for example, that every single one of the forty-nine random samples of bread he analysed was found to contain alum.

A gradual increase in food quality was brought about by several factors. In the case of bread, the adulteration of bread and flour remained widespread until the 1870s, a decade which saw a drop in the cost of imported flour and the introduction of new technology in the form of roller mills. However, legal force eventually brought about a general improvement in food quality through the Adulteration of Food, Drink and Drugs Act of 1872 and the Sale of Food and Drugs Act of 1875. The inclusion of ingredients to add bulk or weight to a food product now had to be declared to the customer, and any adulteration injurious to health became punishable by a heavy fine.

ten

Medical Care in the Workhouse

Every union workhouse had some kind of facilities for the care of sick inmates, usually in the form, of a small infirmary. Although a union was obliged to employ a fully qualified doctor, early nursing care in the workhouse was invariably in the hands of female inmates. Such nurses would often not be able to read – a serious problem when dealing with labels on medicine bottles. Before 1863, not a single trained nurse existed in any workhouse infirmary outside London.

In the 1860s, pressure began for improvements in workhouse medical care. Some of the most notable campaigners were Louisa Twining, a prominent figure in the Workhouse Visiting Society, Florence Nightingale, and the medical journal *The Lancet,* which in 1865 published a series of detailed reports about conditions in London's workhouse infirmaries. Its description of a women's ward for the insane at Clerkenwell workhouse is typical:

> Twenty-one patients live entirely in this ward, which affords them an allowance of only 459 cubic feet each; and the mixture of heterogeneous cases which ought never to be mingled is really frightful. There is no seclusion ward for acute maniacs, and accordingly we saw a poor wretch who for five days had been confined to her bed by means of a strait-waistcoat, during the whole of which time she had been raving and talking nonsense, having only had two hours' sleep: and there was the prospect of her remaining several days longer in the same condition. There were several epileptics in the ward, and one of them had a fit while we were present, and there were imbeciles and demented watching all this with curious, half-frightened looks, which said very plainly how injurious the whole scene must be to them.[41]

As a result of such reports, the government was forced into action and in 1867 the Metropolitan Poor Act was passed, requiring London workhouses to locate their hospital facilities on sites separate from the workhouse. The Act also led to the creation of the Metropolitan Asylums Board which took over the provision of care for the sick poor across the whole of the capital and set up its own institutions for the treatment of smallpox, fever, tuberculosis, and venereal diseases. Florence Nightingale's campaigning led to improvements in the standard of nursing care, with the founding in 1860 of the Nightingale Fund School at St Thomas's Hospital.

It was a similar story outside London. An 1866 Poor Law Board inspection of the Oldham workhouse infirmary found that:

> The sick are not always supplied with separate beds; in one ward two old men were in the same bed together. In another ward I found together a girl 13 years old afflicted by a "urinary complaint", a woman with "itch", a child four years old with "whooping cough", a middle-aged woman with "venereal disease" and an aged woman who, from infirmity, was unavoidably of extremely offensive

habits. Into these wards was lately sent a case of cholera, which shortly afterwards terminated fatally. The convalescent patients from the fever wards are sent to the infirmary, and they mix with the other patients there.[42]

In 1865, Liverpool workhouse pioneered the use of trained nurses through an experiment funded by local philanthropist William Rathbone. He financed the placement in the workhouse infirmary of twelve nurses trained at the Nightingale School. These were assisted by eighteen probationers and fifty-four able-bodied female inmates who received a small salary. Although the experiment had mixed results – the pauper assistants needed constant supervision and obtained intoxicants at the slightest opportunity – it was generally perceived overall to have been a success, largely due to the efforts of the infirmary superintendent, Agnes Jones. Eventually, a skilled nursing system spread to all union infirmaries in the country.

One particular burden that workhouse infirmaries had to bear was that of patients with venereal diseases. Such cases were often refused admission to charitable and subscription hospitals, or would be offered only one course of treatment. Many workhouse infirmaries had special sections – the so-called 'foul wards' – set aside for this type of patient.

From the 1880s onwards, workhouse infirmaries increasingly provided care not just for workhouse inmates, but also for those outside who although not destitute were too poor to afford private medical treatment. Such patients could enter the infirmary directly without going through the normal workhouse admission process. Those with some money might also be required to contribute towards the cost of their board while receiving treatment. The difference between these two routes into the workhouse infirmary was significant because, prior to 1918, the receipt of poor relief normally disqualified the recipient from voting. In 1885, this issue was addressed by the Medical Relief Disqualification Removal Act which stipulated that anyone who was in receipt only of poor-rate-funded medical care no longer lost their vote.

To accommodate this widening clientele, many workhouse infirmaries were enlarged or replaced by new and much bigger buildings: in some cases, the workhouse's medical facilities became larger than its pauper accommodation. In this way, the workhouse infirmary gradually became the primary source of medical care for the nation's poor. It effectively laid the foundations for the National Health Service which began in 1948, incorporating many former workhouse sites amongst its facilities.

A women's ward in the Whitechapel Union infirmary in about 1902. Although the floor is largely bare, there are pictures on the walls and plants on the table.

DIETS FOR THE SICK

The PLC's 1835 dietaries had contained no specific provision for the sick other than that they should be 'dieted as directed by the medical officer'. However, by 1842 the Commissioners had realised that such open-endedness could lead to problems. Their annual report noted that there was 'not only much confusion and error in the master's accounts, but the auditor has considerable difficulty in ascertaining the quantities of food actually consumed in the workhouse.' The PLC now proposed that each union frame a sick dietary similar to that used in hospitals, containing up to four kinds of diet labelled as High Diet, Middle (or Half) Diet, Low Diet, and Fever Diet. An early example of a sick dietary comes from the Stoke Damerell workhouse in 1844:

	Bread	Beef or mutton	Potatoes	Pearl barley	Broth	Salt	Sago or embden groats	Tea	Sugar	Milk
Half Diet	12oz	8oz	8oz	1oz	1 pint	6 drms		1½ oz	1oz	¼ pint
Low Diet	8oz	4oz		1oz	1 pint	6 drms	1oz	1½ oz	1oz	½ pint
Fever Diet	½lb bread or ¼lb sago or rice or sago pudding or fish as the medical officer may prescribe.									½ pint

Rice pudding to contain 2oz of best rice, 16 drachms of sugar, half pint milk, one egg, and one blade of cinnamon.
To 1oz of sago or 1oz of embden groats crushed oats, half ounce of sugar, or 2oz of oatmeal, and one ounce of sugar daily, for gruel.

By 1847, the classifications had changed slightly to include the House Diet (for healthy inmates), Full Diet, Low Diet, and Fever Diet. However, examples of the 'Half' or 'Middle' dietary still appear – in the 1860s, the Wycombe Union's sick dietary for women comprised:

	Breakfast	Dinner	Supper
Full Diet	6oz bread ½oz butter 1 pint tea milk sugar	8oz mutton 1lb potatoes	Same as breakfast
Middle Diet	Same as Full Diet	6oz mutton 1lb potatoes On Monday, Wednesday, and Friday, 1 pint of beef tea or mutton broth with 6oz bread	Same as breakfast
Low Diet	1 pint oatmeal gruel	½ pint mutton broth or beef tea	Same as breakfast
Lying-in Diet	To consist of Low Diet for first week, Middle Diet for second week, Full Diet for third week. Beer, wine, spirits, or any other extras, to be ordered in writing by the medical officer.		

The 'extras' which the medical officer could order for sick inmates could be virtually anything he felt could be justified on medical grounds. They included not only items such as tea, butter, and sugar but also beer or spirits which were now otherwise forbidden in the workhouse.

BEEF TEA

One of the most popular drinks provided for sick or convalescing workhouse inmates was beef tea. The beverage could be produced by the prolonged boiling of raw meat, either a shin of beef or minced beef that had been soaked in water. Alternatively, it could be made by adding hot water to a commercially manufactured beef extract. The first such product was developed in 1840 by the German-born chemist Baron Justus von Liebig. Liebig subsequently co-founded the Liebig Extract of Meat Co. ('Lemco') which later became known as Oxo. The company's factory opened in 1864 at Fray Bentos in Uruguay where the cost of meat was around a third of that in Europe. In the 1870s, John Lawson Johnston developed a rival product, 'Johnston's Fluid Beef', later renamed Bovril, which was produced in Argentina.

The remarkable claims made by Liebig for his meat extract – that 1lb of extract had the nutritional value of 32lb of beef – were disputed by Dr Edward Smith, the Poor Law Board's medical officer. Smith's view, presented in a letter to *The Times* on 16 October 1872, was that Liebig's extract was 'meat flavour… and has good qualities, but it is not food.' He also noted Liebig's own words that, like tea, meat extract was not 'nutriment in the ordinary sense.' Liebig did not reply.

Institutions such as workhouses were natural targets for beef-extract suppliers. In 1900, a Bovril salesman made a successful bid to get his product into the Thanet workhouse. At their meeting on July 19, the workhouse medical officer Dr J.S. Harris reported to the guardians:

A short time ago the Bovril Company's agent called upon me, proposing that he should send to the workhouse a sample of Bovril to make beef-tea, which he did, and the master had it tried last week, and it gave entire satisfaction to those who tried it. I now propose that the Board should order some for further trial, as the cost of a pint is only 3½d., which is much less than it costs by the present system, not counting the cost of the firing, and I think it is quite as nutritious.

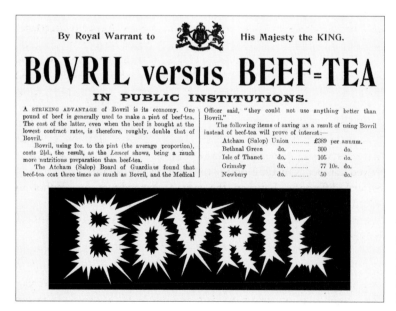

This advertisement for Bovril from around 1900 was keen to promote its money-saving benefits.

The chairman said such a recommendation, coming from the doctor, was worthy of their consideration. Personally, he thought Bovril would be more palatable to the sick, in water. Another guardian, Dr A. Flint quite agreed with the recommendation. Bovril, he said, was one of the few preparations that retained the fibrine. The recommendation was agreed to.

In 1907, the guardians of the Droitwich Union received a letter proposing that 'beef tea' be removed from the inmates' diet and replaced by meat extract. The letter claimed that beef tea was derived from worn-out English horses sent abroad for slaughter and then re-imported in the form of a supposedly nourishing drink. The guardians declined to follow the letter's proposals.

ALCOHOL ON PRESCRIPTION

The consumption of alcohol was generally banned in union workhouses, other than at special occasions such as Christmas Day and royal celebrations. However, there were two purposes for which its use was permitted: sacramental purposes, such as the taking of Holy Communion, or medicinal use when ordered by the workhouse medical officer.

In addition to these general exceptions, some workhouses appear also to have occasionally provided beer to able-bodied inmates engaged in certain types of work. In some cases, this was with the support of the central authorities. For example, in 1886 the Wirral Union was allowed to provide extra food and 'fermented liquor' to paupers employed in harvest work on land belonging to the guardians. In 1903, when an auditor surcharged a workhouse master for allowing beer to able-bodied inmates without such approval, the strange response came that if such an allowance were not made, 'some of the paupers would leave the workhouse.'

The consumption of alcohol, like virtually every other activity that took place in the workhouse, was carefully recorded and periodic returns made to the central authority. The parliamentary returns of alcohol consumption in workhouses make interesting reading. In 1893, the average workhouse population of England and Wales was almost 191,000. Over the year, they consumed around 113,000 pints of spirits, 51,000 pints of wine, and 430,000 gallons of 'malt liquors' (beer and so on) at a total cost to the ratepayers of £32,911 – these figures include alcohol distributed on special occasions.[43] For each inmate this would roughly equate to an annual ration of half a pint of spirits, a quarter of a pint of wine, and 18 pints of beer, although such a calculation ignores the turnover of inmates through the year.

There were surprisingly large variations in the use of alcohol by different Boards of Guardians, most of whom operated several institutions. Just looking at the Metropolitan area in 1893, the Strand Union spent a total for the year of £695 on its average inmate population of 1,394 – roughly 10s per head. Wandsworth and Clapham, on the other hand, spent only £4 14s 9d on alcohol on its average of 1,196 inmates – around 1d per head and less than 1 per cent of the Strand's expenditure. Some workhouses, such as Greenwich, used wine only for sacramental purposes; others, such as Woolwich, issued wine and spirits for infirmary use. The Strand workhouse at Edmonton got through almost ten thousand gallons of beer in the year, while Lambeth's two workhouses consumed only two pints between them – it would be interesting to know what condition swayed Lambeth's medical officer to relent on this occasion!

There were large regional differences between the average expenditure on alcohol in workhouses. In the 1891 returns, the county of Rutland had the largest average annual expenditure at 12s 10d per inmate, while the most abstemious county was Northumberland whose unions spent only 4d per head.

THE TIDE TURNS

The 1880s and 1890s saw a large drop in alcohol consumption in workhouses. In part, this was due to the growth of the temperance movement in Britain. Pressure for a reduction in the use of alcohol or even its complete abolition came both from teetotal guardians and also from organisations such as the Workhouse Drink Reform League. The League publicised the large amounts of alcohol being consumed in workhouses at the ratepayers' expense, such as the £2 per inmate spent in 1881 by the East Preston Union in Sussex. Even worse, in the League's view, was the imbibing of alcohol by workhouse staff and union officers – such as the barrel of beer consumed each week by the guardians at their weekly Board meetings at the Wolverhampton workhouse. In 1884, the Local Government Board decreed that workhouse masters would be liable for the cost of any alcohol that was not supplied under medical instruction – a master at Islington subsequently faced a bill for over 200 gallons of port consumed by his nursing staff.

Attitudes were also gradually changing amongst doctors as to the medical efficacy of alcoholic beverages although this topic remained controversial until the beginning of the twentieth century. The London Temperance Hospital, which opened in 1873, prescribed almost no alcohol to its patients but achieved a very low mortality rate among its patients. The changing tide of medical opinion was also demonstrated by the British Medical Association: from 1880, tickets for its annual dinner did not include wine in the price.

The following table, based on parliamentary returns, shows that alcohol consumption in workhouses in England and Wales almost halved between 1881 and 1893. During the same period, the average daily number of inmates rose from around 170,000 to 190,000.

	1881	1885	1891	1893
Spirits (pints)	183,233	141,664	120,123	112,906
Wine (pints)	114,407	75,153	54,456	51,126
Malt Liquors (gallons)	817,641	610,990	456,221	429,608
Total Cost (£)	60,303	44,721	34,832	32,011

Despite this downward trend, some doctors clearly remained convinced of the therapeutic effects of alcohol. The 1906 Royal Commission on the Poor Laws was told that all seventeen inmates of the tiny Welwyn Union workhouse each recieved a daily pint of beer by order of the workhouse medical officer.

eleven

Children in the Workhouse

In 1838, Assistant Commissioner Dr James Phillips Kay noted that children who ended up in the workhouse included 'orphans, or deserted children, or bastards, or children of idiots, or of cripples, or of felons'. Such children were not in the minority: according to the 1905 Royal Commission on poor relief, around half the children under the care of Boards of Guardians in the nineteenth century were without parents or close relatives.

Although families were separated on entering a workhouse, a child under seven could, if deemed 'expedient' by the union's Board of Guardians, be accommodated with its mother in the female section of the workhouse and even share her bed. She was supposed to have access to the child 'at all reasonable times'. Parents were allowed a daily 'interview' with a child living in the same workhouse, or an 'occasional' interview if the child was in a different workhouse or school. Much of this depended on the discretion of the guardians – for example, a minimum length of the 'interview' was not laid down.

The physical conditions in which workhouse children ended up were often appalling. The PLC's Annual Report in 1838 recorded a visit by a physician to the Whitechapel workhouse who witnessed:

> The pale and unhealthy appearance of a number of children in the workhouse, in a room called the Infant Nursery. These children appear to be from two to three years of age; they are 23 in number; they all sleep in one room, and they seldom or never go out of this room, either for air or for exercise.
>
> In another part of the same workhouse, 104 girls slept four or more to a bed in a room 88 feet long, 16½ feet wide and 7 feet high. 89 of the 104 had, perhaps unsurprisingly, recently been attacked with fever.

EDUCATION

The PLC's orders relating to the operation of workhouses contained a single regulation relating to children's education:

> The boys and girls who are inmates of the Workhouse shall, for three of the working hours, at least, every day, be instructed in reading, writing, arithmetic, and the principles of the Christian religion, and such other instruction shall be imparted to them as may fit them for service, and train them to habits of usefulness, industry, and virtue.

Boards of Guardians were, however, sometimes reluctant to spend money on even the most basic equipment such as writing slates. Occasionally, it was questioned whether pauper children even needed to be taught basic literacy. This was partly justified by the 1834 Act's principle of 'less eligibility' which, it was argued, demanded a lower quality of education than would be enjoyed by the children of those of modest means outside the workhouse. In 1836, the guardians of the Bedford Union suggested a compromise by teaching workhouse children to read but not to write. Likewise, in 1839 the guardians of the Pershore Union decided that 'it is quite unnecessary to teach the children in the union workhouse the accomplishment of writing'. However, they were forced to change their minds in 1844 when the Parish Apprentices Act demanded that 'pauper apprentices be able to read and write their own names unaided'. Teaching pauper children to read and write would, in the long run, it was argued, make them less likely to need poor relief.

DISCIPLINE

Unlike their education, the use of corporal punishment on children received rather more official attention. The PLC's regulations specified that corporal punishment could only be inflicted on boys and then only after two hours had elapsed since the related offence had been committed. Nonetheless, discipline of children in the workhouse could, by modern standards, appear remarkably cruel. Charles Shaw's recollections of the Chell workhouse include a chilling example of the punishment given to a boy who had run away:

> The boys who had been longest in the workhouse said he would be flogged in the presence of the other boys with a pickled birch rod – that is a rod which has been kept soaking in salt water. After the usual skilly supper that night we were all told to remain in the room. The long table was cleared, and a smaller square table was brought in and placed in the middle of the room... The boy was lifted upon the table, and four of the biggest boys were called out to hold each a leg or an arm. The boy was laid flat on the table, his breeches well pushed down, so as to give as much play as possible for the birch rod. The lad struggled and screamed. Swish went the pickled birch on his back, administered by the schoolmaster, who was too flinty to show any emotion. Thin red stripes were seen across the poor lad's back after the first stroke. They then increased in number and thickness as blow after blow fell on his back. Then there were seen tiny red tricklings following the course of the stripes, and ultimately his back was a red inflamed surface, contrasting strongly with the skin on his sides. How long the flogging went on I cannot say, but screaming became less and less piercing, and at last the boy was taken out, giving vent only to heavy sobs at intervals. If he was conscious, I should think only partially so. The common rumour was that he would have his back washed with salt water.[44]

RECREATION

Life for workhouse children was not entirely bleak, however. From 1891, unions could buy toys for the workhouse. Some workhouses had a band for the boys. From 1868 until his death in 1872, Thomas Beale held the post of schoolmaster at the Beaminster workhouse. During this time he taught the boys to play the fife, and established the Union Fife and Drum Band which became popular with the local townspeople. Occasionally, the workhouse children would process – in their workhouse uniforms – into Beaminster led by the band. The band provided the music at the Church Sunday-school summer treat at Parnham in 1869. Children from the same union also enjoyed the occasional trip to the seaside, as reported by this item from the *Bridport News* in August 1899:

> On Monday, the children of Beaminster Union were given a real treat. About 10 o'clock they were conveyed in a brake from Beaminster to West Bay. They were accompanied by Mrs JB Dunn, Miss Hine, Mrs Andrews the Matron, and Miss Bevan the industrial trainer, who did all they could to see the little folks had a happy day. Between meals they enjoyed themselves on the beach as only children can. Mrs Dunn, who with her husband takes a keen interest in the welfare of the Union, provided a capital tea.

CHILDREN'S DIETS

From April 1856, unions were required to produce official dietaries for children aged from two to five, and from five to nine. In order to assist them in this task, the Poor Law Board published a sample dietary for each age group:

DIETARY FOR CHILDREN FROM 2 TO 5									
	Breakfast		Dinner				Supper		
	Bread	Milk	Meat	Potatoes	Suet Pudding	Rice Pudding	Bread	Butter	Milk and Water
	oz	pints	oz	oz	oz	oz	oz	oz	pints
Sunday	4	½	3	8	-	-	4	¼	½
Monday	4	½	-	-	8	-	4	¼	½
Tuesday	4	½	3	8	-	-	4	¼	½
Wednesday	4	½	-	-	-	8	4	¼	½
Thursday	4	½	3	8	-	-	4	¼	½
Friday	4	½	-	-	8	-	4	¼	½
Saturday	4	½	3	8	-	-	4	¼	½

DIETARY FOR CHILDREN FROM 5 TO 9									
	Breakfast		Dinner				Supper		
	Bread	Milk	Meat	Potatoes	Suet Pudding	Rice Pudding	Bread	Butter	Milk and Water
	oz	Pints	oz	oz	oz	oz	oz	oz	pints
Sunday	5	½	3½	8	-	-	5	½	½
Monday	5	½	-	-	10	-	5	½	½
Tuesday	5	½	3½	8	-	-	5	½	½
Wednesday	5	½	-	-	-	10	5	½	½
Thursday	5	½	3½	8	-	-	5	½	½
Friday	5	½	-	-	10	-	5	½	½
Saturday	5	½	3½	8	-	-	5	½	½

Until the 1870s, the nine to thirteen age group was usually given the same diet as able-bodied women. They, too, were then provided with a separate dietary.

OTHER TYPES OF CHILDREN'S ACCOMMODATION

By the end of the nineteenth century, a number of schemes had been devised to take children away from what was widely seen as the malign influence of the workhouse.

District schools – also known as 'barrack' schools – were, to some degree, miniature workhouses for children. They were set up from the 1840s onwards by large urban unions such as Manchester and Liverpool, and by a few groupings of smaller unions such as Walsall and West Bromwich. London set up half a dozen district schools, such as the Central London at Hanwell. The children were taught trades to equip them for later life: for boys, these included tailoring, shoemaking, and carpentry; girls were taught knitting, needlework, washing, ironing, and cooking, to qualify them for domestic service.

Cottage homes were used by some unions from the 1870s and housed children in 'family' groups of fifteen to twenty children plus a house-mother or father. Ideally, cottage homes were constructed as a self-contained 'village' in a rural location, typically with a dozen cottages plus a school, infirmary, administration and reception block, and even a swimming pool. Large cottage home sites such as Birmingham's Marston Green housed over 400 children. However, many unions set up much smaller cottage homes with just two or three houses.

Scattered homes originated in the 1890s at Sheffield where cottage homes were seen as isolating children from the real world. The alternative system of 'scattered' homes placed groups of children in ordinary suburban domestic houses. Unlike cottage homes, children in scattered homes attended ordinary local schools. Otherwise, scattered homes were run much like cottage homes with a group of children under the care of one or two house-parents. Unions with many scattered homes usually erected a headquarters home to act as an administrative centre and probationary home for new arrivals.

Boarding out was a system for placing workhouse children in the long-term care of foster parents who received a weekly allowance for each child staying with them. The system, which is usually said to have originated in Scotland, was seen as the nearest approximation to a 'normal' home life that could be provided by a union, and was also financially economical. Boarding out was generally restricted to orphans or children who had been abandoned by their parents.

A dining room at Marlesford Lodge in Hammersmith – the Kensington and Chelsea District's intermediate school for pauper children.

The Central London
District School at
Hanwell, where Charlie
Chaplin was once an
inmate.

Youngsters on the
'village street' at the
Shoreditch Union's
cottage homes site at
Shoreditch.

Compass instruction for
the lads aboard training
ship *Arethusa, c.* 1910.

Training ships were operated by a number of organisations to provide a naval training for boys aged from about twelve to sixteen. A few of these vessels took boys from Poor Law institutions and included the *Exmouth* on the Thames, the *Indefatigable* on the Mersey, and the *Mercury* at Hamble near Southampton. Many of the new boys needed to be taught to swim – unfortunately, some drowned before they mastered the skill! Discipline was strict and the birch often used to enforce it. Food was limited in quantity and variety – biscuits, potatoes, and meat were the staples, with occasional green vegetables.

After 1915, it was prohibited for any child to reside in a workhouse other than a brief temporary period.

INDUSTRIAL TRAINING

Regardless of the type of accommodation in which pauper children were placed, there was a growing emphasis on equipping them with practical skills that would make them employable in later life and so not be a burden on the poor rates. This so-called 'industrial training' could take a variety of forms. For boys it could include instruction in crafts such as carpenty, plumbing, blacksmithing, cobbling and tailoring. In rural areas, agricultural training could be provided, especially if the workhouse had its own farmland. Some children's establishments had their own military bands which could equip boys for a future career as military bandsmen. For girls, domestic service was the most common destination and the workhouse might provide training in needlework, laundry, cookery, and domestic economy.

Leaving the care of the Poor Law system, where they might have spent much or all of their lives, could be quite a traumatic experience for workhouse youngsters. To help them make the transition into the outside world, particularly in the larger cities, a number of voluntary organisations were set up. These included the 'Homes for Working Boys in London' which ran a number of hostels, each housing up to sixty boys and young men, and MABYS – the Metropolitan Association for Befriending Young Servants.

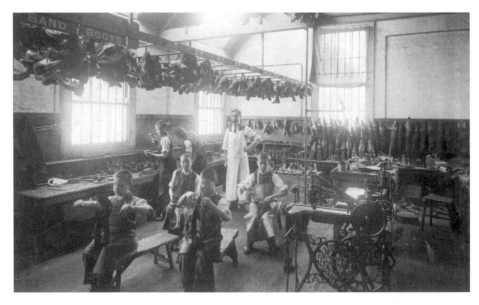

Boys learning a trade in the shoe-making workshop at eh Kensington and Chelsea District School in 1902. Boots made for the use of the school's band can be seen hanging above.

twelve

Births, Marriages and Deaths

UNMARRIED MOTHERS

Throughout its history, the workhouse was a place of refuge for poor unmarried pregnant women. The workhouse could provide the medical help needed during and after the delivery of a child; it also offered the basic necessities of survival for women whose situation made it virtually impossible to otherwise support themselves and their child.

Prior to 1834, an unmarried mother could try and obtain financial support from the child's putative father by applying for an affiliation order through local Petty Sessions (i.e. magistrates) courts. The 1834 Poor Law Amendment Act made the obtaining of such orders much more difficult and expensive. Applications now had to be heard at county quarter sessions and could only be initiated by overseers or Boards of Guardians. Evidence of paternity claims now also had to be 'corroborated in some material particular', something that was often impossible to achieve. The Act effectively made illegitimate children the sole responsibility of their mothers until they were sixteen years old. If mothers of such children were unable to support themselves and their offspring, the only poor relief on offer would be the workhouse. It was expected that the Act would make the consequences sufficiently unattractive to deter women from risking extra-marital pregnancy. Perhaps unsurprisingly, it was a highly unpopular and contentious measure and was diluted in 1839 by a measure which allowed affiliation claims again to be heard by local magistrates at Petty Sessions. The U-turn was completed by a further Act in 1844 which enabled an unmarried mother to apply for an affiliation order against the father for maintenance of the mother and child, regardless of whether she was in receipt of poor relief.

One other important change in the 1834 Act was that an illegitimate child now took its mother's settlement at birth. This replaced the previous situation, where such a child gained settlement from its place of birth. There was thus no longer an incentive for parishes to try and eject unmarried pregnant women to avoid the burden of being responsible for the child.

Unmarried mothers in the workhouse could be stigmatised, for example by being made to wear uniforms of a particular style or colour, usually yellow. In 1839, the Poor Law Commissioners issued a minute entitled *Ignominious Dress for Unchaste Women in Workhouses* in which they deprecated these practices. However, more subtle forms of identification sometimes continued. At Gressenhall workhouse in Norfolk, unmarried mothers were made to wear a 'jacket' of the same material used for other workhouse clothing. This practice, which led to them being referred to as 'jacket women', continued until 1866.[45] Unmarried mothers (or other categories of inmate of which the guardians disapproved) might also receive an especially unappetising diet. For example, at the Strand Union workhouse, single women in the lying-in ward were kept on a diet of gruel for nine days.[46]

Being born in a workhouse also carried a stigma, although an attempt to change this was made in 1904 when the Registrar General instructed local registrars that birth certificates of such children should now disguise this fact. As a result, workhouse births were then registered with a (sometimes fictitious) street address. For example, births in the Liverpool Workhouse were recorded as having taken place at 144a Brownlow Hill although no such address actually existed. The practice was later extended to death certificates.

HUSBANDS AND WIVES

Males and females in the workhouse were strictly segregated – this included husbands and wives. An exception to this rule was introduced in 1847 when elderly married couples who were both aged over sixty could request a shared bedroom. In practice, little such accommodation was provided – in 1895 only 200 couples in the whole of England and Wales were enjoying this luxury.[47] In some cases, Boards of Guardians argued that many long-married couples were glad of an excuse to be away from each other.

In 1896, the Hampstead Board of Guardians debated the case of two of their inmates, Mr and Mrs 'Pigeon' Hill, who had left the workhouse for an hour or so, went to church, and got married. They had then returned and demanded a place in the workhouse's special married couples' quarters. The couple were both over sixty and each had been married twice before. The guardians, who clearly felt they were being manipulated, called for an alteration in the law so that the privilege of special quarters should be extended only to those who had been married for six months previously.

For some married couples though, separation was undoubtedly a hardship. Vera Underwood, whose parents ran the Ongar Union workhouse in Essex in the early 1900s, recalled:

> We only had one married couple there. All the rest were either widows, widowers or spinsters, and all 'without visible means of support'. The couple used to sit next to each other at the service on Sunday afternoon and hold hands all the time, as they were separated on admission – living in male and female accommodation respectively. As a child, this upset me very much. My father and mother, unofficially, used to arrange for them to be together as much as possible – easy in summer in the garden, but difficult in winter.

Despite the strict segregation of the sexes, the workhouse could still be a place to meet one's soulmate. In March 1911, the *Nuneaton Chronicle* carried the following heart-warming story concerning the Rugby workhouse:

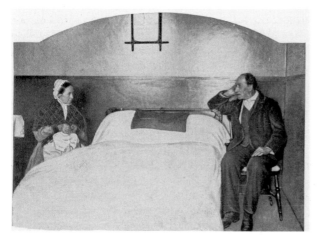

An aged couple's bedroom at the St Marylebone workhouse, *c.* 1902.

At the meeting of the Rugby Board of Guardians, on Monday, the workhouse master reported that a young woman and her two children left the house on Saturday. It appears that last Christmas a young widower, hailing from a Northern town, was admitted to the casual wards. He was a painter, and stayed on at the workhouse for the three weeks and did some painting. He saw the girl, and, taking a fancy to her, asked her to be his wife. She declined at first, but before he left about the middle of January he had so far been successful in his suit that he told the workhouse master he would return and marry her on March 26th. He returned to his home, where he secured regular employment, and kept up a constant correspondence with the girl. Most of those who had a knowledge of the affair were sceptical as to the man's sincerity, but, travelling all night last Friday he presented himself at the Workhouse soon after nine o'clock with an outfit for his intended bride. This she put on, was married by the Registrar at the Union Offices, and before midday was travelling northward with her husband and children.

Workhouse brides were the subject of another unusual incident in 1895 at Bishop Auckland in Durham. The *Poor Law Officers' Journal* newspaper reported on the matter:

At last week's meeting of the Auckland Board of Guardians, the following letter was read from a miner:– 'Having noticed that you have some orphan children and other class of people you want rid of from your Workhouse, I thought it a likely place to get a wife. I am a respectable working man under 40 years of age, a widower with no encumbrance, a good set-up house, a coal-hewer by trade, and wants a wife, as I am completely sickened of housekeepers, having had no less than 18 in as many months. If you can fit me up with a respectable lassy between 30 and 50 I would be glad, and would be glad to take an orphan girl into the bargain free of charge. I prefer a single woman before a widow, as widows won't do for me. I have no particular fancy for beauty; a plain girl will do for me, only she must be clean and industrious. If you have one please let me know and I will come with a trap and take her away free of charge to the Guardians. Let me know soon, please.'

The letter was handed over to the workhouse master.

THE ELDERLY

Despite the Spartan conditions that prevailed in many workhouses, inmates could live to a ripe old age. Workhouse census records, for example, often include a sizeable number of inmates in their seventies, eighties or nineties. Across the country, the number of workhouse inmates aged over sixty-five rose from around 25,000 in 1851 to just over 76,000 in 1901. As a proportion of the workhouse population, this equated to a rise from 3.0 per cent to 5.0 per cent over the same period.

One celebrated inmate of the Wandsworth Union infirmary in 1896 was a Mrs Blower who, at the age (it was said) of 107, was reckoned to be the oldest workhouse inmate in the country. She was still active and cheerful and regularly ran the length of the workhouse ward. Her son (or her 'boy' as she referred to him), a mere youth in his eighties, was also an inmate of the Wandsworth workhouse.

In 1834, the Royal Commission, whose report had been the basis of the Poor Law Amendment Act, had recommended that 'the old might enjoy their indulgences'. The diets published by the PLC in 1836 had offered a modest concession to the over-sixties in the form of additions of tea, sugar, milk or extra meat pudding – so long, of course, as the guardians deemed that it was 'expedient'.

For the next half century, things improved relatively little for the elderly, who formed a substantial and increasing part of the workhouse population. In the 1891 census, the over-sixty-fives comprised just under one third of the total inmates. Changes began to come about in the early 1890s with a

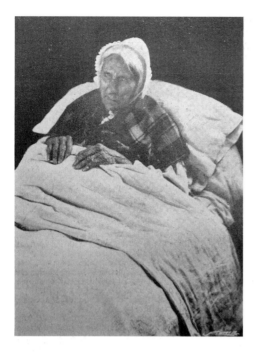

107-year-old Mrs Blower, the oldest inmate of the Wandsworth Union infirmary in 1896.

relaxation on the use of tobacco by elderly inmates of good character. In 1894, old women were allowed extra 'dry tea' with milk and sugar, in addition to what was already included in their dietary. This allowance was subsequently extended to include dry coffee or cocoa, and also made available to old male inmates. By 1896, the LGB were recommending that well-behaved aged and infirm inmates should, within reasonable limits, be allowed to go out of the workhouse for walks, to visit friends, or attend church. It was also proposed that they could receive visits from friends, not be required to wear a uniform, and choose their own times for breakfast and supper, and for rising or for going to bed. Other improvements during this period for the aged and infirm included a more varied diet which could include sago, semolina, rice pudding, stewed fruit, lettuce, onions, and seed cake.

By the 1860s, many workhouses had acquired some kind of library for the use of their inmates. In 1864, the guardians of the Haslingden Union asked the Lancashire and Yorkshire Railway for permission to place collecting boxes at local railway stations, so that travellers could donate discarded books and periodicals for use by the workhouse. By the early 1900s, entertainments provided for elderly inmates of the Stoke-upon-Trent workhouse included nine concerts during the winter months, a phonograph and gramophone, games such as dominoes and draughts, and a good supply of reading matter, some of which was donated by residents of the union. Workhouses could also by now subscribe to a lending library or buy newspapers. From around 1903, unions could spend money on a piano or harmonium. By the 1920s, some workhouse dayrooms had a communal wireless, while in Abingdon in the late 1920s, some inmates were even allowed a weekly trip out to the local cinema.

Aged inmates could also have occasional outings away from the workhouse, although these were not always the sedate affairs that might be expected. From 1891, inmates from Camberwell's Gordon Road and Constance Road workhouses had an annual summer excursion to the seaside. For their 1896 day out to Bognor Regis, a special 650-seat train was chartered and at around 9 a.m. the party set off. The group consisted mostly of elderly inmates aged sixty to ninety,

'Sunday music for the indigent poor: a concert given by the National Sunday League at the City Road workhouse.' An illustration from *The Graphic* magazine in 1901 – some of the audience (and band) appear less than attentive.

Elderly men enjoy a pipe and a newspaper in the 'airing yard' of St Marylebone workhouse, *c.* 1902.

together with a number of young children from the workhouse. They were also accompanied by a boys' band from the South Metropolitan District School. Dinner and tea were provided at the Bognor Town Hall after which the men were given tobacco, and the women and children sweets. However, many of the group had apparently obtained money from their friends and after being liberated from the workhouse had headed straight for the nearest public house before boarding the train. On arrival at Bognor, they had continued drinking and had then gone for their dinner at which beer was also served. After dinner, there were more visits to the local public houses. It was later reported that a number of cases had occurred of disorderly conduct and indecent behaviour on secluded parts of the beach.

DEATH IN THE WORKHOUSE

As we have already seen, the quality of workhouse medical facilities significantly improved from 1870 onwards. However, in many people's minds, the workhouse was inextricably associated with death. In the early years of the New Poor Law, wild rumours circulated that children in workhouses were killed to make pies, while the old when dead were used to fertilise the workhouse fields. Even in more enlightened times, the workhouse infirmary acquired a grim reputation as 'the place where old people go to die'. This was in a sense true – although not because it was necessarily an awful place but, for many aged poor, it was the only form of medical care available at the end of their life when they were beyond the help that their family could provide.

Elderly inmates from Camberwell workhouse enjoying their annual outing to Bognor Regis in 1896. The bottles of beer that line their dinner table contributed to high jinks on the beach later in the day.

Some workhouses had a special coffin for transporting bodies to the cemetery. This one at Londonderry had a hole on top where a warning flag would be placed when the coffin contained a body.

If an inmate died in the workhouse, the death would be notified to their family who could, if they wished, organize a funeral themselves. If this did not happen, which was often the case because of the expense, the guardians arranged a burial in a local cemetery or burial ground – this was originally in the parish where the workhouse stood, but later rules allowed it to be the deceased's own parish if they or their relatives had expressed such a wish. In a few instances, workhouses had their own burial ground on or adjacent to the workhouse site.

The burial would be in the cheapest possible coffin and in an unmarked grave, into which several coffins might be placed on the same occasion – large workhouses often did a 'cemetery run' once or twice a week. There would probably be no mourners – at Bourne in 1901, the workhouse master reported that despite repeated invitations, workhouse inmates always declined to attend funerals. This was perhaps a testimony to the old saying: 'rattle his bones, over the stones, he's only a pauper whom nobody owns.'

Under the terms of the 1832 Anatomy Act, bodies unclaimed for forty-eight hours could also be disposed of by donating them for use in medical research and training – this was not specific to workhouses, but applied to any institution whose inmates died while in its care.

thirteen

Tramps and Vagrants

The Poor Law Act of 1834 made no mention of vagrants, with the result that new union workhouses made no provision for them; Boards of Guardians regarded vagrancy as a matter for the police rather than the Poor Law. The settlement laws, too, still operated so that a union was obliged to offer relief only to those holding legal settlement within its boundaries. However, tramps continued to demand relief at union workhouses which, it turned out, were usually located within a day's walk of one another. Several instances of tramps dying from exposure or starvation after being turned away from the workhouse door resulted in the PLC having to compromise. In 1837, a new regulation was introduced which required food and a night's shelter to be given to any destitute person in case of 'sudden or urgent necessity', in return for them performing a task of work.

Accommodation for vagrants then became a standard feature of workhouses. At first, this was often provided in existing infectious wards which were often separated from the main workhouse and recognised that tramps often carried contagious diseases such as measles. Gradually, purpose-built tramps' blocks were added, usually of a single storey and located near the workhouse entrance. They were designed to provide the most basic level of accommodation, inferior to that in the main workhouse. One observer in 1840 reported that:

> In general they have brick floors and guardroom beds, with loose straw and rugs for the males and iron bedsteads with straw ties for the females. They are generally badly ventilated and unprovided with any means of producing warmth. All holes for ventilation in reach of the occupants are sure to be stuffed with rags or straw; so that the effluvium of these places is at best most disgustingly offensive.[48]

These quarters were known by various names – tramp wards, vagrant wards, or casual wards – with their occupants officially referred to as the 'casual poor', or just as 'casuals'. Another term that became popular for the tramp ward was 'the spike' – a name whose origins are much debated, with the most popular contenders being: the 'spiky' nature of the beds, a small metal tool sometimes used in the task of oakum picking, and the spikes that often topped the perimeter wall of the vagrants' section of the workhouse.

THE CASUAL WARD

The routine for those entering a casual ward began in late afternoon by joining the queue for admission. A spike had only a certain number of beds and latecomers might find themselves turned away. The spike was sometimes supervised by the workhouse porter, with his wife looking after the female casuals. Some spikes were in the charge of a 'tramp major', probably a former tramp himself, and now employed by the workhouse in return for his keep.

Casuals queuing for admission to the Whitechapel workhouse casual ward on Thomas Street in 1902.

When the spike opened at 5 or 6 o'clock in the evening, the new arrivals would be searched and any money, tobacco or alcohol confiscated. It was common practice for vagrants to hide such possessions in a nearby hedge before entering the spike. George Orwell's essay *The Spike* revealed an unspoken rule that searches never went below the knee so that illicit goods could be hidden in the boots or stuffed into the bottoms of trouser legs. Entrants then had to strip and bathe in water that may already been used by a number of others. They were then issued with a blanket and a workhouse nightshirt to wear while their own clothes being fumigated or 'stoved', dried, and stored. Each was given a supper, typically 8oz of bread and a pint of gruel (or 'skilly' as it was colloquially known), before being locked up for the night from 7 p.m. until 6 or 7 a.m. the next morning.

Until the 1860s, the norm was for casual wards to have communal dormitories where the inmates either slept in rows of low-slung hammocks or on the bare floor.

CASUAL WARD FOOD

The food provided to the casual poor was the worst and least regulated of all the workhouse diets and often consisted of no more than a piece of stale bread and water. The treatment of casuals was one area where the central authorities allowed unions considerable discretion – at Driffield in Yorkshire, for example, casuals were provided with neither food nor baths, apparently because it was felt that such luxuries would encourage vagrancy.

In 1866, the Poor Law Board issued a dietary to be used in London casual wards. For breakfast and supper, all persons aged nine or over were to receive 6oz of bread and a pint of gruel; children under nine were to be given 4oz of bread and half a pint of gruel. The same dietary was recommended but not compulsory outside London. From 1882, casuals could be detained two nights and thus require a midday dinner. An amended dietary recommended that breakfast and supper for adults should now comprise 8oz of bread and a pint of gruel, while dinner should consist of either 8oz of bread and 1½oz of cheese, or 6oz bread and one pint of soup. However, this was largely wishful thinking – by 1904, in over half of the country's casual wards, vagrants received only a piece of bread for breakfast and supper.

Nonetheless, a small number of workhouses did treat casuals well. At Oxford, for example, in the 1920s, new arrivals sat down to a helping of bread, margarine and cocoa.

NEW CASUAL WARD DESIGNS

In 1864, the Metropolitan Houseless Poor Act introduced new guidelines for the facilities to be provided in casual wards in the capital. Separate wards were to be provided for men and for

St Marylebone's new-style casual ward with its coffin-like beds opened in 1875. Scriptural texts printed in large red letters adorned the blue walls.

women and children, each having a yard with a bathroom and water-closet, and a work shed. It was also recommended that wards have raised sleeping platforms, divided down the middle by a gangway, and each side divided up by boards to give a sleeping space of at least 2ft 3in. A narrow shelf along each side of the room provided an area at the head of each compartment where clothes could be placed. Bedding was to consist of coarse 'straw or cocoa fibre in a loose tick', and a rug 'sufficient for warmth'. A casual ward based on these recommendations was erected at St Marylebone workhouse in 1867. Its walls were heavily decorated with religious texts no doubt intended to 'improve' the building's occupants.

From around 1870, a new form of vagrants' accommodation began to be adopted known as the cellular system. It consisted of individual cells, very much like those in a prison, usually arranged along both sides of a corridor. Sleeping cells contained a simple bed, perhaps hinged so that it could be folded up against the wall when not in use. Work cells were usually fitted out for stone-breaking, with a hinged metal grille which could be opened from the outside to allow unbroken lumps of stone to be deposited in the cell. The inmate then had to break up the stone into lumps small enough to pass back through the holes in the grille, or in a separate horizontal grid fitted beneath it. The broken stone was collected on the outside.

WORK IN THE SPIKE

In 1843, workhouses had been given the power to detain male tramps for up to four hours while they performed the required task of work. One common task was oakum picking where a certain weight (usually one or two pounds) of old rope had to be unpicked into its constituent fibres – the resulting product could then be sold off (perhaps the origin of the expression 'money for old rope'!). Another task favoured by Boards of Guardians was stone-breaking. Not only was it hard work, but the amount broken (typically two hundredweight) was easily measured, and the resulting small stones could be sold off for road-making. For female casuals, the work given could also include oakum-picking but was often washing, scrubbing or cleaning.

Once vagrants had done their stint of work, they were given a lump of bread and released to go on their way. However, even with an early start to the work, this meant that only half the day remained to tramp to another workhouse. The Casual Poor Act of 1882 made it a requirement for casuals to be detained for two nights, with the full day in between spent performing work.

The casuals could then be released at 9 a.m. in the morning after the second night. Return to the same spike was not allowed within thirty days with the penalty being four nights detention (with three days work being performed in between).

To avoid this restriction, tramping circuits evolved which linked a long progression of spikes before eventually returning to the first. Nights at a spike might also be interspersed with sleeping rough or in farm outhouses, especially in the summer months. Those entering the casual ward on a Saturday evening were detained an extra day since no work was performed on Sunday.

In 1890 William Booth, founder of the Salvation Army, published his book *In Darkest England and the Way Out,* which included some experiences of London casual wards:

> J.C. knows Casual Wards pretty well. Has been in St. Giles, Whitechapel, St. George's, Paddington, Marylebone, Mile End. They vary a little in detail, but as a rule the doors open at 6; you walk in; they tell you what the work is, and that if you fail to do it, you will be liable to imprisonment. Then you bathe. Some places the water is dirty. Three persons as a rule wash in one water. At Whitechapel it has always been dirty; also at St. George's. I had no bath at Mile End; they were short of water. If you complain they take no notice. You then tie your clothes in a bundle, and they give you a nightshirt. At most places they serve supper to the men, who have to go to bed and eat it there. Some beds are in cells; some in large rooms. You get up at 6 a.m. and do the task. The amount of stone-breaking is too much; and the oakum-picking is also heavy. The food differs. At St. Giles, the gruel left over-night is boiled up for breakfast, and is consequently sour; the bread is puffy, full of holes, and don't weigh the regulation amount. Dinner is only 8 ounces of bread and 1½ ounces of cheese, and if that's short, how can anybody do their work?

Many casual wards issued vagrants with meal-tickets or bread-tickets which could be redeemed for food at a specific location en route to their next stated destination. These were intended to try and ensure that casuals kept to their supposed destination, and also aimed to reduce begging.

SOCIAL EXPLORERS

Life in the 'underworld' presented a particular fascination for the Victorian middle classes and 'inside' descriptions of institutions such as the workhouse and spike proved highly popular. These were often compiled by so-called social explorers disguising themselves as down-and-outs to obtain admission to a casual ward. Such investigations were carried out by people as diverse as a clergyman, an American novelist, a politician, and a 'Lady'.

One of the earliest and best-known undercover reports was *A Night in a Workhouse*, published by James Greenwood in 1866 in the *Pall Mall Gazette* (of which he was the founder and first editor). Greenwood's titillating prose described not only the repugnant conditions in the Lambeth spike, but the characters who entered it, such as an old-timer known as 'Daddy':

> The porter went his way, and I followed Daddy into another apartment where were ranged three great baths, each one containing a liquid so disgustingly like weak mutton broth that my worst apprehensions crowded back.
>
> 'Come on, there's a dry place to stand on up at this end,' said Daddy, kindly. 'Take off your clothes, tie 'em up in your hank'sher, and I'll lock 'em up till the morning.'
>
> Accordingly, I took off my coat and waistcoat, and was about to tie them together when Daddy cried, 'That ain't enough, I mean everything.'
>
> 'Not my shirt, Sir, I suppose?'
>
> 'Yes, shirt and all; but there, I'll lend you a shirt,' said Daddy. Whatever you take in of your own will be nailed, you know. You might take in your boots, though – they'd be handy if you happened to want to leave the shed for anything; but don't blame me if you lose 'em.'

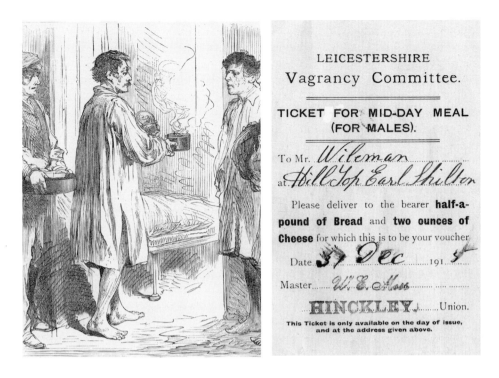

Above: An 1887 illustration of the sleeping cells in a London casual ward, and a bread ticket issued by the Hinckley Union to provide vagrants with bread en route to their next destination.

An outside view of the stone-breaking cells at Stratford-upon-Avon workhouse. The grilles could be rapidly opened from the outside to provide an escape route for the inmates in case of fire.

The other inmates in the spike were a very rough crowd:

> Towzled, dirty, villainous, they squatted up in their beds, and smoked foul pipes, and sang snatches of horrible songs, and bandied jokes so obscene as to be absolutely appalling. Eight or ten were so enjoying themselves, the majority with the check shirt on and the frowsy rug pulled about their legs; but two or three wore no shirts at all, squatting naked to the waist, their bodies fully exposed in the light of the single flaring jet of gas fixed high upon the wall.

In the summer of 1902, the American writer Jack London spent some time incognito in London's East End, staying in doss-houses and casual wards and recording his experiences. Here is part of his account of a night at the Whitechapel workhouse:

> At six o'clock the line moved up, and we were admitted in groups of three. Name, age, occupation, place of birth, condition of destitution, and the previous night's 'doss,' were taken with lightning-like rapidity by the superintendent; and as I turned I was startled by a man's thrusting into my hand something that felt like a brick, and shouting into my ear, 'Any knives, matches, or tobacco?' 'No, sir,' I lied, as lied every man who entered. As I passed downstairs to the cellar, I looked at the brick in my hand, and saw that by doing violence to the language it might be called 'bread.' By its weight and hardness it certainly must have been unleavened.
>
> The light was very dim down in the cellar, and before I knew it some other man had thrust a pannikin into my other hand… The pannikin contained skilly, three-quarters of a pint, a mixture of Indian corn and hot water… It was coarse of texture, unseasoned, gross, and bitter. This bitterness which lingered persistently in the mouth after the skilly had passed on, I found especially repulsive. I struggled manfully, but was mastered by my qualms, and half a dozen mouthfuls of skilly and bread was the measure of my success.
>
> By seven o'clock we were called away to bathe and go to bed. We stripped our clothes, wrapping them up in our coats and buckling our belts about them, and deposited them in a heaped rack and on the floor – a beautiful scheme for the spread of vermin. Then, two by two, we entered the bathroom. There were two ordinary tubs, and this I know: the two men preceding had washed in that water, we washed in the same water, and it was not changed for the two men that followed us. This I know; but I am quite certain that the twenty-two of us washed in the same water.

The next morning, London was allocated what was considered a plum job – 'scavenging' the rubbish from the infirmary sick wards. He was then given breakfast:

> At eight o'clock we went down into a cellar under the Infirmary, where tea was brought to us, and the hospital scraps. These were heaped high on a huge platter in an indescribable mess – pieces of bread, chunks of grease and fat pork, the burnt skin from the outside of roasted joints, bones, in short, all the leavings from the fingers and mouths of the sick ones suffering from all manner of diseases. Into this mess the men plunged their hands, digging, pawing, turning over, examining, rejecting, and scrambling for. It wasn't pretty. Pigs couldn't have done worse. But the poor devils were hungry, and they ate ravenously of the swill, and when they could eat no more they bundled what was left into their handkerchiefs and thrust it inside their shirts.

In 1904, 'A Lady' (later revealed to be Mary Higgs, a Cambridge University-educated minister's wife) published an anonymous account of undercover stays in several lodging houses and casual wards. At the Dewsbury workhouse, she was propositioned by one of the paupers who was acting as gate keeper:

He talked to me in what I suppose he thought a very agreeable manner, telling me he wished I had come alone earlier, and he would have given me a cup of tea. I thanked him, wondering if this was usual, and then he took my age, and finding I was a married woman (I must use his exact words), he said, 'Just the right age for a bit of funning: come down to me later in the evening.' I was too horror-struck to reply: besides I was in his power, with no one within call but my friend, and all the conditions unknown and strange. Probably silence was best; he took it for consent, and, as other tramps were coming, let me pass on. I made a mental vow to expose him before I left the place...

Put to bed, like babies, at about half-past six, the kind woman in charge brought us our food... We were given a small lading-can three parts full of hot gruel and a thick crust of bread. The latter we were quite hungry enough to eat, but when we tasted the gruel it was *perfectly saltless*. A salt-box on the table, into which many fingers had been dipped, was brought us; the old woman said we were 'lucky to get that.' But we had no spoons; it was impossible to mix the salt properly into the ocean of nauseous food. I am fond of gruel, and in my hunger and thirst could easily have taken it, if fairly palatable. But I could only cast in a few grains of salt and drink a little to moisten the dry bread: my companion could not stomach it at all, and the old woman, being accustomed to workhouse ways, had a little tea in her pocket, and got the kind attendant to pour the gruel down the w.c. and infuse her tea with hot water from the bath tap.

In the 1920s, former Oxford MP Frank Gray made undercover visits to a number of Oxfordshire casual wards as part of his efforts to save teenage vagrants from a life on the road. His stay at Thame was typical:

We reach the gates. It is not six o'clock yet. With some eighteen others we loaf, huddle, and cringe before the gate. There is one woman among us. Women tramps are scarce; but all tramp women look like tramps. All men tramps don't. This is curious, for in every other walk of life women are the better dissemblers.

The gates open; we walk up the garden. A clerk takes particulars under a lamp at the front door, and we pass to the back, isolated from the higher grade of the workhouse, the permanent inmates. We shamble into this workhouse from the outer world, and then past the quarters of the permanent inmates to our den at the back midst the refuse heaps, well-nigh like lepers – the unclean. I made a slip as I gave my answers, for I noticed the clerk momentarily start as he detected a pitch of voice unusual in a casual ward. I must be more careful thereafter.

In the Thame workhouse there is no strict search; there is no suggestion of a bath or a wash. We retain our clothes and sleep in some of them. To-night I have a pillow – my boots with my trousers wrapped over them. We sleep on boards on a gradient raised from the floor, and the slope helps sleep. As we arrived at this workhouse and answered the stereotyped questions – as listlessly as they were asked – we received our hunk of bread, and with it we said good-bye to all officialdom and supervision and entered the casual ward. As the tramps have lost heart so have the officials.

fourteen

The Workhouse in Ireland

Although workhouses existed in Ireland prior to the 1834 Poor Law Amendment Act, their use was on a much smaller scale than was the case in England and Wales.

In the early 1700s, a House of Industry was erected in Dublin. Its inmates were mostly 'sturdy beggars', 'disorderly women', the old and infirm, and orphan children. Up to a hundred men and sixty women slept in bunk-beds crammed into the workhouse cellars which were 240ft long by 17ft wide. The diet included bread, milk, porridge, gruel, and 'burgoo' – oatmeal in cold water seasoned with salt and pepper. For those who disobeyed workouse regulations, punishments could include flogging, imprisonment or deportation. The workhouse also housed abandoned and foundling children. At one of its gates, a basket was fixed to a revolving door. Someone wishing to leave a child anonymously could place it there, ring the porter's bell, and then depart.

Other early workhouses or Houses of Industry were set up at Belfast, Cork, Clonmel, Ennis, Limerick, Waterford, and Wexford.

THE 1838 IRISH POOR LAW ACT

After the Act of Union in 1800, when Ireland came under British administration, the British government made numerous but ineffectual attempts to address the desperate and widespread poverty in the country. What finally stirred them to action was increasing concern over the growing influx of Irish immigrants to Britain and in 1833 a Royal Commission was appointed to investigate 'the conditions of the poorer classes in Ireland'. While the Commission was deliberating, the landmark 1834 Poor Law Amendment Act was passed whereby the only form of poor relief for the able-bodied was to be via the workhouse. The 1833 Commission, reporting in 1836, felt that such a scheme would not be suitable for Ireland. Despite this, in September 1836, one of the English Poor Law Commissioners, George Nicholls, was sent to Ireland to assess whether the English poor-relief system could be established there. Following his visit, Nicholls suggested – perhaps unsurprisingly – that Ireland adopt the English system, with poor relief being locally financed through a poor rate, and offered only through the workhouse – out-relief formed no part of the scheme. Despite considerable opposition, the Act 'for the more effectual Relief of the Destitute Poor in Ireland' passed into law on 31 July 1838. Ireland was then dvided into 130 Poor Law Unions, each of which was required to raise a poor rate and set up a workhouse.

For those entering an Irish workhouse, conditions were even more miserable than those in the English institutions. For economy, walls and ceilings were left unplastered. Ground-level floors were covered in earth or clay, rather than more expensive wood or stone, because, it was argued, the former would be 'better adapted to the habits of the people, most of whom will be without shoes and stockings, and have been accustomed to floors of common earth in their cabins'.[49]

Dormitories were cramped and lacking ventilation. Beds frequently consisted of a platform of planks and a straw mattress covered with rough rags. There was often a lack of water and the only toilet facilities were large urine tubs in each ward – which often overflowed.

THE IRISH WORKHOUSE DIET

The diet provided to the inmates of Irish workhouses was based on the principle that 'the food of a pauper maintained at the public cost, should not be more abundant or better than that of a poor man maintaining himself in independence by his industry'. This had proved hard enough to achieve in some parts of England and Wales, but in Ireland, where much of population lived almost entirely on potatoes, this was to be even more of a challenge.

The task of framing new workhouse diets was given to Assistant Poor Law Commissioners in Ireland who looked at two main sources of information: typical labourers' diets in their area, and the diets already employed at other institutions such as prisons and asylums.

As a result of their observations, the Assistant Commissioners decided that workhouse inmates should receive only two meals a day – breakfast and dinner – with no supper being served, as was often the case both in prisons and in labourers' own homes. They proposed the following general diet for able-bodied inmates between the ages of fourteen and sixty:

	Males	Females
Breakfast	8 oz oatmeal stirabout ½ pint new milk	6oz oatmeal stirabout ½ pint new milk
Dinner	3½lbs (raw weight) of potatoes 1 pint of skimmed milk	3½lbs (raw weight) of potatoes 1 pint of skimmed milk

'Stirabout' was another variation of gruel or porridge – typically 3oz of oatmeal stirred into a quart of boiling water, milk or buttermilk, and seasoned with salt.

Unlike their elders, children in Irish workhouses were allowed three meals a day. From 1842, the official dietary for those aged nine to fourteen comprised:

Breakfast	3½oz oatmeal and ½ pint of new milk
Dinner	2lbs potatoes and ½ pint of new milk
Supper	6oz of bread

Children aged five to eight received smaller portions of the same diet, while the under-fives could be given rice or bread.

Meat was notably absent from new dietary. However, the Boards of Guardians of the North Dublin and South Dublin Unions took exception to this and decided that 'on two days of the week, the dinner should consist of ox-heads and shins, and other coarse pieces of beef, together with potatoes, to be mashed up therein'. From 1 January 1842, all unions were given the option on two days each week of providing soup instead of milk at dinner time.

The main accommodation block of the Larne Union workhouse in county Antrim.

EQUIPPING AN IRISH WORKHOUSE

The architect of the new Irish workhouses, George Wilkinson, published a detailed 'shopping-list' of the furniture and utensils that needed to be purchased for a new workhouse. His recommended list of items for the kitchen and provision stores included:

Platters for potatoes, either of wood or tin.
Large flesh knife and fork. Potato shovel. Ladle for skimming.
Ladles for stirabout. Scrapers for stirabout and soup.
Fire raker and poker.
Baskets, size of coppers for boiling potatoes.
Baskets or trays for carrying potatoes to dining-hall. Salt-box.
Tins for stirabout and gruel, of quart and pint measures.
Ditto for milk, of about 6 to 10 gallons each.
Boxes for cleaning potatoes, or tubs 3–4ft in diameter, with holes at bottom for letting water out.
Baskets for carrying away offal.
Potato-nets of 4lbs, 3lbs, or 2lbs each (for boiling and distributing potatoes).
Large bread-knife on cut board of mahogany.
Bread-baskets or deal trays for carrying bread.
Milk-tubs with iron handles for poles to carry the milk.
Deal trays to carry tins to dining-hall. Flat hand-barrows for carrying ditto.
Small scales and weights.
Knives, forks, plates, dishes, etc. for use of master and matron etc.
Iron pots, saucepans, and kettles. Iron spoons.
Branding-irons for wood, and brass stamps for the bedding and clothes.

The list gives some interesting indications of how the workhouse kitchen and dining room operated. A weighed amount of potatoes was put into a net for each inmate before being boiled in a large copper. The still-netted cooked portions were then carried to the dining hall and distributed to the tables. The absence of inmates' plates etc. indicates that potatoes at least may have been eaten directly off the table without cutlery.

THE POTATO

As the Assistant Commissioners' investigations confirmed, for a great many of Ireland's eight million inhabitants, the potato was the staple – if not the sole – item of their diet.

The potato (*Solanum tuberosum*) is a member of the *Solanaceae* or 'nightshade' family which also includes the tomato, aubergine, sweet pepper, and deadly nightshade. It originated in Chile and the Andes region, and was introduced to Europe via Spain in around 1570. Sir Francis Drake is often credited with its introduction to England in 1586 after acquiring some when he seized the port of Cartegena in Columbia. Drake later called at Virginia to pick up some English settlers – this led to his samples mistakenly being attributed as having originated in Virginia rather than in South America.

The potato's introduction to Ireland is often credited to Sir Walter Raleigh who was part of the forces sent to quell the anti-English Desmond Rebellion. Raleigh was given an estate of 42,000 acres by Elizabeth I and in around 1587 the first potatoes to be grown in Ireland were planted in the gardens of his residence, Myrtle Grove, at Youghal. The story goes that in September, when the plant had flowered and produced a small hard green fruit, Raleigh's unimpressed gardener took him a specimen and asked 'is this the fine fruit from America you prized so highly?' Raleigh was, or pretended to be, ignorant of the matter and told him to dig up the weed and throw it away. The gardener soon returned with a good parcel of potatoes.

The Irish quickly appreciated the advantages of the new crop – it was easier to grow than cereals such as oats or barley and did not need milling. Furthermore, in times of military conflict, a field of potatoes was much more resilient against wanton destruction by an enemy.

In the seventeenth century, four main types of potatoes were distinguished in England: 'Spanish' or sweet potatoes, 'Canadian' potatoes (what we now refer to as Jerusalem artichokes), 'Virginian', and 'Irish' potatoes. The latter two were actually just two varieties of the common potato which differed only in the colour of their flowers.

The popularity of the potato gradually spread through England and they were taken up most enthusiastically by oat-growing areas such as Lancashire, where lobscouse was created. In 1750, *The Country Housewife's Family Companion* by William Ellis enthused about the multitude of uses to which potatoes could be put. It included the following entry:

> At Manchester, a great market in Lancashire, potatoes stand in many sacks as well as oatmeal for publick Sale, for here they are in common Use by both poor and rich; and as I have had potatoes brought me from that part, I think I may say they are the best sort in England, for whiteness, shortness, and sweetness. And therefore they are much eaten by the poor people, first boiled, then mashed, and the pulp boiled again in milk in which they stir some flower and eat it like hasty-pudding.

THE GREAT FAMINE

In the summer of 1845, reports of potato blight began to appear, first in continental Europe and then in southern England. By August it had reached Ireland, and a substantial part of that year's crop rapidly became black and inedible. Initially, the full significance of the blight was underestimated. A similar problem had occurred in 1832, and it was widely assumed that only that year's crop would be affected. Through the end of 1845 and into 1846, the most obvious effect was on the price and availability not only of the remaining potato stocks, but also of other foods such as wheat and oatmeal.

Official action to relieve the growing food shortages was primarily through the Relief Commission for Ireland, set up by the Prime Minister, Sir Robert Peel, in November 1845. The Commission set up local fund-raising committees, and encouraged landlords to create employment schemes, up to half of whose costs would be borne by the Government. The

Board of Works was authorized to instigate new road-building projects from which extra employment would result. The Commission also set up food depots around the country for the storage of 'Indian meal' (maize corn imported from America and often used as pig-feed) which local relief committees would be able to resell at cost price should food prices continue to rise. As it turned out, Indian meal was to become a major part of many Irish people's diet for several years.

The summer of 1846 saw the return of the blight and an escalation in the desperation and misery. Bad harvests across Europe led to a general shortage of food and escalation of prices. Government attempts to buy Indian meal at the end of August were unsuccessful. That which did come onto the market was rapidly snapped up at high prices. Much of it ended up in the hands of small Irish traders who then sold it at exorbitant prices. On 28 September 1846, the scarcity and price of food, and the shortage of work, resulted in the Dungarvan riots where grain stores on Dungarvan Quay were looted.

Inside the workhouses, conditions were steadily getting worse. Stables and washrooms were being pressed into service as overflow accommodation, and auxiliary workhouse accommodation was being rented to cope with the rising numbers. However, the finances of many unions, which had already been parlous, were now exhausted, and they closed their doors to further admissions. The costs of providing extra accommodation, as well as the increased costs of feeding the inmates, were already pushing some unions into insolvency. On top of this, diseases such as typhus fever and dysentery were now widespread. The situation in November 1846 at Swineford workhouse was described by Quaker relief worker James Tuke:

> On the dreadful 10th November 120 were admitted beyond the regulated number. Hundreds were refused admission for want of room, some unhappy being pushed on the high roads and in the fields. Influenced by terror and dismay – leaving entire districts almost deserted – the better class of farmers, in numbers, sold their property, at any sacrifice, and took flight to America. And the humbler classes left the country in masses, hoping to find a happier doom in any other region. In this Union 367 persons died in the workhouse; the Master of the workhouse also died. In the adjoining Union, Ballina, 200 were admitted to the workhouse beyond the number it was built for (1200). Hundreds were refused admission for want of room and 1,138 died in the workhouse; medical officer of the workhouse was also carried off. In another adjoining Union, Ballinasloe, all the officers of the workhouse were swept away, and 254 inmates of the workhouse perished.[50]

The Relief Commission's attempts to generate employment through increased public works schemes proved hopelessly inadequate. There was insufficient work to satisfy demand, the wages were insufficient to keep up with escalating food prices, and food was often impossible to obtain because of the poor distribution network.

Potatoes were not, of course, the only food crop grown in Ireland. Oats and other grains were grown by Irish peasants; however, cereals were primarily used as cash crops by tenants to pay their rent rather than to be eaten. Some landlords did agree to reduce or forgo their rents during the crisis, but many insisted on their rent. As a result, many Irish poor were given the stark choice between starvation and homelessness. The fear of eviction led many to sell their grain and pay their rents, even though this meant their families would go hungry.

Throughout the famine years, Ireland continued to export large amounts of high quality foods such as grain and meat. Not surprisingly, the sight of food leaving their country's shores led to great resentment and, in some cases, riots. On 25 September 1846, troops were summoned to the port of Youghal near Cork when a large angry crowd attempted to hold up a boat carrying oats for export: 2,000 troops were subsequently deployed as a number of rapid response units to protect against such disturbances or to guard food depots. Naval escorts were provided to escort some grain-carrying vessels.

SOUP KITCHENS

By the start of 1847, several voluntary famine relief schemes had been set up by groups such as the Quakers and the British Relief Association, the latter receiving a £2,000 donation from Queen Victoria. In February, the passing of an Act for the Temporary Relief of Destitute Persons in Ireland, sometimes known as the 'Soup Kitchen' Act, led to the setting up of soup kitchens offering some minimal relief for those outside the workhouse. To spearhead the scheme, the government approached the Reform Club's flamboyant *chef de cuisine* Alexis Soyer, who became one of this country's first 'celebrity chefs'. Soyer was despatched to Ireland with a brief to provide a meal a day in the form of bread and soup – the latter to cost no more than one pound per hundred gallons.

Soyer's model soup kitchen opened on 5 April, 1847, in front of the royal barracks near the entrance to Dublin's Phoenix Park. The marquee, measuring 48ft by 40ft, had its entrance at one end and exit at the other. The central kitchen area was fitted with a large oven producing a hundredweight of bread per batch, and a 300-gallon steam boiler. Eight *bains marie* held a further thousand gallons. The outer area was taken up by rows of wooden tables which seated a total of 100. At each place, a hole was cut to hold a two-pint white enamel basin with a spoon attached by a metal chain. The bowls were filled with soup and a bell was rung, at which point the next 100 people waiting in a queue outside would be admitted to take up their places at the tables. After grace was said, the diners had five minutes in which to consume their soup before another bell signalled that their time was up. As they left at the rear of the tent, they each received a quarter of a pound of bread. The bowls and spoons were then rapidly wiped, and the whole process repeated. With each batch of 100 taking six minutes to process, the kitchen could feed up to 1,000 persons an hour. As a result of his efforts, Soyer quickly acquired the local soubriquet of 'head cook to the people of Ireland' and was also referred to as 'a broth of a boy'.

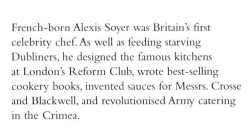

French-born Alexis Soyer was Britain's first celebrity chef. As well as feeding starving Dubliners, he designed the famous kitchens at London's Reform Club, wrote best-selling cookery books, invented sauces for Messrs. Crosse and Blackwell, and revolutionised Army catering in the Crimea.

The soup prepared by Soyer, which he called 'the poor man's regenerator, used the following recipe:

> ## The Poor Man's Regenerator
>
> *(For 2 gallons of soup)*
> 2oz of dripping.
> ¼lb of a pound of solid meat (cut into dice one inch square).
> ¼lb of onions, sliced thin.
> ¼lb of turnips; the peel will do, or one whole one cut into small dice.
> 2oz of leeks; the green tops will do, sliced thin.
> ¾lb of common flour.
> ½lb of pearl barley, or one pound of Scotch.
> 3oz of salt.
> ¼oz of brown sugar.
> 2 gallons of water.
>
> I first put 2oz of dripping into a saucepan (capable of holding two gallons of water), with a quarter of a pound of leg of beef without bones, cut into squares of about an inch; and two middling-sized onions, peeled and sliced; I then set the saucepan over a coal fire, and stirred the contents round for a few minutes with a wooden (or iron) spoon until fried lightly brown. I had then ready washed the peeling of two turnips, fifteen green leaves or tops of celery, and the green part of two leeks (the whole of which, I must observe, are always thrown away). Having cut the above vegetables into small pieces, I threw them into the saucepan with the other ingredients, stirring them occasionally over the fire for another ten minutes; then added one quart of cold water and three quarters of a pound of common flour, and half a pound of pearl barley, mixing all well together. I then added 7 quarts of hot water, seasoned with 3oz of salt, and a quarter of an ounce of brown sugar, stirred occasionally until boiling, and allowed it to simmer very gently for three hours; at the end of which time I found the barley perfectly tender. The above soup has been tasted by numerous noblemen, members of Parliament, and several ladies who have lately visited my kitchen department, and who have considered it very good and nourishing.

Soyer claimed of his recipe that 'a bellyful once a day, with a biscuit, will be more than sufficient to maintain the strength of a strong healthy man.' However, *The Lancet* was highly critical of the soup's content, and also of its 'talented, but eccentric, self-deceived originator'.[51] The solid content of the soup, they calculated, amounted to less than 3oz per two-pint serving, which was only one third of that required by a healthy adult.

Like *The Book of the Bastiles* five years earlier, the Irish nationalist newspaper *The Nation* drew upon the witches' scenes in Macbeth to give vent to its opinion of Soyer's soup:

> Round about the boiler go,
> In twice fifty gallons throw
> Water in the noisome tank.
> In the boiler then you'll throw
> Onion slice and turnip top,
> Crust of bread and cabbage chop,
> Tomtits' gizzards, head and lungs
> Of a famished French-fed frog,
> Root of pratee digged in bog.[52]

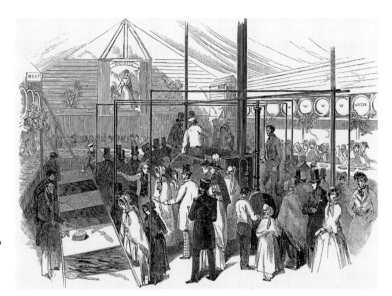

Soyer's model kitchen in Dublin where a soup production line fed up to 1,000 people an hour.

A commemorative display of famine cooking pots at the Carrick-on-Shannon workhouse.

The 'boiler' used by many soup kitchens and workhouses for making their brew was often a large cast-iron pot or cauldron. It was usually about 4ft in diameter, weighed around a third of a ton, and had lugs attached to the rim so that it could be suspended over a fire. It could hold from eighty to a hundredgallons.

The 'Soup Kitchen' Act lasted for only six months, during which soup kitchens were set up across the country. It was replaced by the Poor Law Extension Act of 1847 which introduced a system of discretionary out-relief, again funded by the local poor rate. Although the PLC indicated that out-relief was to be distributed as cooked food, many unions provided only supplies of uncooked Indian meal and rice as it was a cheaper and less troublesome procedure. The Commissioners subsequently issued a circular explaining the advantages of providing food in cooked form, namely that it required no expenditure on fuel by the recipient, and was unlikely to be sold by the recipient – this was of particular benefit to women and children as it prevented a selfish husband selling their rations.

The Great Famine is commemorated in this striking sculpture which now stands in front of the former Roscommon union workhouse.

THE END OF THE FAMINE

During 1847, often known as 'Black '47', workhouses struggled to provide extra accommodation to cope with the ravages of typhus fever and dysentery. A number of workhouse fever hospitals were rapidly erected, although in some cases these consisted of little more than wooden sheds. Financial crises continued – Ballina workhouse had debts of £2,000 and Castlebar of £3,000, while the debts of Ennis Union reached £20,000 by 1849. Throughout all this, the Government Exchequer continued to demand repayments on the loans taken out by most unions to finance the building of the workhouse.

As it turned out, the direct effects of potato blight diminished relatively quickly – even as early as the 1847 season, what potatoes were planted seemed to have cropped reasonably well. What contributed to the continuing food shortages was the difficulty in obtaining seed potatoes for planting, and also an understandable general reluctance to risk wasting money in planting such seed.

At the beginning 1849, when it was starting to seem that the worst was over, a final misery descended on the weakened population in the form of an epidemic of Asiatic cholera. It was not until October that the epidemic abated.

At the end of the famine years, it was estimated that at least a million people had died, either directly from starvation, or from the diseases it brought in its wake, such as typhus fever and dysentery. A further contributory factor was the nutritionally poor Indian meal which became a major part of the diet of many poor, particularly in the workhouses.

That the building of the Irish workhouse system so closely coincided with the Great Famine was purely an accident of history. Whether the existence of the workhouses during this period was a help or a hindrance to the starving Irish poor is a matter for debate. Either way, the British Government's behaviour at this time of national disaster earned it lasting dishonour and discredit.

fifteen

The Scottish Poorhouse

Scotland, too, has its place in the story of the British workhouse. Although Scotland's poor-relief system always remained separate from that operating in England, Wales and Ireland, it too had its workhouses – or rather poorhouses, as the Scottish institutions were most often known. The 1845 Scottish Poor Law Act created a new central advisory body, the Board of Supervision, but kept parishes responsible for poor relief. Poorhouses could be set up by large parishes, or by 'combinations' or parishes. By the 1890s, there was accommodation for over 15,000 poorhouse inmates in Scotland, though the average number was usually between 8,000 and 9,000. In addition to 'official' poorhouses, smaller parishes often operated local parish lodging houses or parish-funded almshouses.

Although poorhouses largely catered for the sick, the elderly and children, they could also be used as 'test' workhouses for those whose relief claim was considered 'doubtful' – those who were suspected of being capable of maintaining themselves, or those who would squander out-relief in drunkenness and debauchery.

POORHOUSE OPERATION

The day-to-day operation of poorhouses in Scotland was in many respects similar to that adopted for workhouses in England and Wales, with overall control of each poorhouse under an annually elected 'house committee' rather than a Board of Guardians.

Inmates were classified as follows: males above the age of fifteen years; boys above the age of two years, and under fifteen years; females above the age of fifteen years; girls above the age of two years, and under fifteen years; children under two years of age.

For paupers entering the poorhouse, life was strictly regulated. The different classes of inmate, particularly males and females, were segregated. Inmates were required to wear the poorhouse uniform. On admission, an inmate's own clothing was 'purified' by steaming it for three hours and then placing it in store until they left the poorhouse. Inmates were bathed once a week, under supervision, in water between 88 and 98 degrees Fahrenheit. Children under fifteen had their hair regularly cut to keep the length at two inches for boys and three inches for girls. There was a prescribed daily routine and work was expected to be performed by inmates according to their capabilities. Tasks suggested by the Board of Supervision included oakum picking, firewood chopping, and the making of mats and fire-lighters. No 'spirituous or fermented liquor' was allowed, except under medical direction.

THE 1850 POORHOUSE DIETARY

In their second annual report in 1847, the Scottish Board of Supervision examined some of the existing poorhouse diets that were in operation. They recommended that the one used at

The main block of the former Aberdeen poorhouse which served as a military hospital during both world wars. The cone-roofed structures flanking the entrance are the inmates' outdoor privies.

Edinburgh's Charity Poorhouse should form the basis of the poorhouse diet to be adopted nationally. A slightly revised version of this dietary was issued by the Board in 1850 as part of their 'Rules and Regulations for the Management of Poorhouses'.[53] A notable feature of the revised version was the removal of an option enjoyed by Edinburgh inmates to have beer instead of milk at six meals per week.

The 1850 dietary distinguished seven classes or 'rates' of diet for healthy inmates: 'A', aged persons who are not working; 'B', adults who are not working; 'C', adults who are working; 'D', infirm persons; 'E', children aged five to eight; 'F', children aged two to four; 'G', infants under the age of two.

Unlike workhouses in the rest of Britain, Scottish poorhouses gave male and female inmates exactly the same rations. It was also specified that all food served to inmates was to be 'of good quality, and in a wholesome state'. The 1850 dietary is shown below.

Class A	*Breakfast:*	3oz meal; ½ pint milk
	Dinner:	6oz bread; 1½ pints broth
	Supper:	3oz meal; ½ pint milk
Class B	*Breakfast:*	4oz meal; ¾ pint milk
	Dinner:	8oz bread; 1½ pints broth
	Supper:	4oz meal; ¾ pint milk
Class C	*Breakfast:*	4oz meal; ¾ pint milk
	Dinner:	8oz bread; 1½ pints broth; 4oz boiled meat
	Supper:	4oz meal; ¾ pint milk
Class D	*Breakfast:*	4oz meal; ¾ pint skimmed milk
	Dinner:	6oz bread; 1½ pints rice-soup
	Supper:	6oz bread, ½ pint tea

Class E	Breakfast:	4oz meal; ¾ pint milk
	Dinner:	6oz bread; 1 pint broth
	Supper:	3oz meal; ½ pint milk
Class F	Breakfast:	3½oz meal; ½ pint new milk
	Dinner:	5oz bread; ¾ pint broth
	Supper:	3oz meal; ½ pint new milk
Class H	Daily:	8oz white leavened bread or 7oz of meal, and 1 pint of new milk

Notes:

The meal may be either oatmeal or Indian meal, or a mixture of the two.

The milk may be buttermilk, where new or skimmed milk is not specified.

The broth shall be made with 2oz of meat, exclusive of bone, 2oz of barley, ½oz pease, 1½oz carrots, turnips, or other vegetables, and a due quantity of salt, for each ration of 1½ pints.

The rice-soup in Class D shall be so made, that for each ration for an infirm inmate, there shall be 4oz of meat (which shall be left in the soup or not, as the medical officer shall direct, in each case); 1½oz rice; 2oz vegetables; the due quantity of salt and pepper.

The tea for Class D shall be made with ½oz sugar; 1oz new milk; and ⅛oz tea, for each ½ pint.

In Classes A-C, there may be substituted up to three times a week for the broth at dinner, 1½ pints of pea soup, made with 2oz of whole or split pease, 1½oz of pease-flour, 1oz of vegetables, and a due proportion of salt and pepper.

In Classes A-C, there may be substituted, not more than once a week, for the broth at dinner, 3oz of skimmed-milk cheese; and, for the broth and meat together, 4½oz.

In Classes A and B, there may be substituted, not more than twice a week, for the broth at dinner, 8oz of white fish; and, in Class C, 12oz of white fish, for the broth and meat together.

In Class A, there may be substituted, not more than twice a week, for the bread and broth at dinner, 1½lbs boiled potatoes with ¾ pint skimmed milk and, in Classes B and D, 2lbs of boiled potatoes, with ¾ pint skimmed milk and in Class C, for the bread, broth, and meat together, 3lbs boiled potatoes, with 1 pint of skimmed milk.

EDINBURGH

In 1869, Edinburgh's old Charity workhouse was replaced by the Craiglockhart poorhouse which housed over 1,500 inmates. It was intended to provide both a 'comfortable home for the aged and poor' and also a reformatory for the 'dissipated, the improvident, and the vicious'. The male wing had divisions for 'old men of good character', 'dissolute men', 'doubtful old men', and 'boys', with similar divisions in the women's quarters.

Edinburgh's St Cuthbert's parish opened a new poorhouse and hospital in 1868. The poorhouse had separate sections for 'very decent', 'decent', 'bastardy', and 'depraved'. In 1873, St Cuthbert's merged with Canongate, forming St Cuthbert's Combination.

GLASGOW

After 1845, Poor Law provision in Glasgow was split between four parishes: City, Barony, Govan and Gorbals. Gorbals never set up a poorhouse and was absorbed by Govan in 1873. The City poorhouse on Parliamentary Road was originally erected in 1809 as a lunatic asylum. With 1,500 beds, it was one of the largest pauper institutions in Britain. Poor conditions and overcrowding in the city poorhouse were a recurring subject of concern. It closed in 1905 following a merger with Barony parish.

The Barony parish poorhouse at Barnhill opened in 1853 and was described in 1882 as 'a very capacious asylum for the children of poverty and well adapted by its cleanliness, ventilation and

A surviving portion of the east Edinburgh's former Charity Poorhouse. It was once used to house the establishment men's ward in Port Bristo.

position to mitigate the ills of their condition.' After the merger with the City parish, it was enlarged and became Scotland's largest poorhouse.

In 1894, the Board of Supervision was replaced by a more powerful Local Government Board, which was directly responsible to Parliament. An increasing emphasis was then placed on the provision of improved hospital facilities. In Glasgow, following the creation of a single Poor Law authority in 1904, three new establishments were built: Stobhill Hospital (for the infirm and chronic sick poor, and for children), the Eastern General Hospital (an acute hospital with psychiatric assessment wards), and the Western General Hospital (for acute medical and surgical cases).

THE HIGHLANDS AND ISLANDS

The first poorhouse erected in the highlands was in 1850 at Tain, which served a combination of nine parishes in Easter Ross. Tain achieved a certain notoriety because meat featured nowhere on its menu – in its place the inmates recieved herrings twice a week. Under pressure from the Board of Supervision, poorhouses were eventually erected in most parts of the highlands and islands. However, they often were larger than demand warranted and proved costly to build and to run, never approaching anywhere near their capacity. The situation was aggravated in the 1880s by factors such as the failure of potato and grain crops, difficulties in the fishing industry, and disputes over land rights, all of which contributed to some combinations going into debt. By the early twentieth century, proposals were being made for the conversion of poorhouses in the highlands and islands to other uses, such as accommodation of the mentally ill. This first came into effect at the Long Island in 1907 when the poorhouse at Lochmaddy was licensed for the reception of twenty-eight 'harmless lunatics' in addition to the ordinary poor. The parishes of the Long Island Combination were thus saved the expense of sending such cases from the Hebrides to the asylum at Inverness.

The Long Island combination poorhouse at Lochmaddy on North Uist was one of Scotland's remotest poorhouses. It later became Lochmaddy Hospital.

THE 1898 POORHOUSE DIETARY

The 1850 dietary remained the basis of poorhouse food until 1898 when a revised version was issued. The main innovation in the new dietary was the addition of a new 'privileged' category of inmate, Class H, who were deemed deserving of a more varied diet. For other classes, there was very little change except for a reduction in the use of butter-milk, whose consumption in Scotland had significantly fallen since 1850.

	1898 DIETARY FOR PRIVILEGED INMATES (CLASS H)
Breakfast	Meal, 3oz; skimmed milk, ¾ pint; or tea, ½ pint; butter, ½oz; bread, 4oz
Dinner	Bread, 6oz daily, along with – one day in week – rice soup (without the meat with which it is prepared), 1½ pints; suet pudding (sweetened), 2oz (occasionally apples may be used in making this pudding.) Two days in week – broth, 1½ pints; one day in week – lentil or pea soup, 1½ pints. One day in week – white fish, 8oz, with plain butter sauce (¼oz butter to each person). Two days in week – minced meat, 2oz; with 4oz of potatoes one of the days, and 2oz of suet pudding (unsweetened) the other day.
Tea (at 4 o'clock)	Tea, ½ pint; bread, 3oz; butter, ½oz, four days in the week; and marmalade (or other preserve), ½oz, on the remaining three days.
Supper	Skimmed milk ¾ pint; meal, 3oz, four days in the week; and bread, 4oz (instead of porridge), the remaining three days.

POORHOUSE RECIPES

The food provided in at least some poorhouses appears to have been a little more varied than the 1850 and 1898 dietaries suggest. Some 'standard' poorhouse recipes devised by the matron of Glasgow's Eastern District Hospital were published in 1908.[54] Dishes included stewed liver, Irish stew, English stew, and the following:

Sago Soup

6 potatoes, 1 large onion, 1 small turnip, a bit of celery or parsnip, ¼lb sago, 4 pints water, ½ pint milk, salt and pepper, 1 dessert-spoonful dripping. Pare the potatoes and cut them in small pieces, put them in a saucepan with the dripping, onions chopped, turnip and parsnip, and stir all over the fire for five minutes; then put in the water, and allow to boil for one hour; then put the whole through a cullender, and put it back in a saucepan with the sago (which should be soaked in the milk one hour); salt and pepper; stir till it boils – five minutes. Serve.

Scrap bread pudding

½lb bread, 1½ table-spoonfuls chopped suet or dripping, 2oz currants, 1oz sugar, 1/16oz ground ginger, 5oz milk, 1 egg. Take all the scraps that are clean, and neatly cut from them all very dark crust; put the bread into a basin of water to soak for an hour, have very clean hands, and, after squeezing the water entirely out, put the bread into a dry basin, and add to it the sugar, dripping or suet, and the fruit; boil the milk and pour over bread, &c., in the basin; whisk it up well with a fork; beat up the egg and add it, also the ground ginger; butter a basin, into which put the pudding, and allow it to steam for one and a half hours.

THE LATER YEARS OF THE POORHOUSE

As in the rest of Britain, a number of poorhouse buildings were used during the First World War for military accommodation or for the treatment of military casualties.

After the passing of the Local Government Act of 1929, many poorhouses evolved into Public Assistance Institutions, offering care for the elderly, infirm, chronic sick, and unmarried mothers-to-be. In 1946, as part of preparations for the setting up of the National Health Service, many former poorhouse buildings were re-evaluated. Some were refurbished or upgraded to take on a role under the NHS. Others were condemned and sold off or demolished.

sixteen

Christmas Day in the Workhouse

In the era of the parish workhouse prior to 1834, Christmas Day was the traditional occasion of a treat for most workhouse inmates. In 1828, for example, inmates of the St Martin-in-the-Fields workhouse received roast beef, plum pudding, and one pint of porter (dark beer) each. At Bristol in the 1790s, the Christmas Day (and Whit Sunday) dinner included baked veal and plum pudding. At Carlisle on Christmas Day workhouse inmates were allowed roast mutton, plum pudding, best cheese, and ale.

However, in the new union workhouses set up by the 1834 Poor Law Amendment Act, things were rather different, at least to begin with. The Poor Law Commissioners ordered that no extra food was to be allowed on Christmas Day (or any other feast day). The rules also stated that 'no pauper shall be allowed to have or use any wine, beer, or spirituous or fermented liquors, unless by the direction in writing of the medical officer.' Nevertheless, some unions chose to disregard the rules and celebrate Christmas in the traditional way. In Cerne Abbas, for example, the new workhouse's first Christmas dinner in 1837 included plum pudding and strong beer. At Andover, the inmates received bread and cheese on the previous 'meat day' so as to save a ration of beef for Christmas Day. Despite the lack of festive fare, Christmas Day was (along with Good Friday and each Sunday) one of the special days when no work, except the necessary household work and cooking, was performed by the workhouse inmates.

By 1840, the Poor Law Commissioners revised their rules to allow extra treats to be provided, so long as they came from private sources and not from union funds. Following the Queen's marriage to Prince Albert in 1841, the Victorian celebration of Christmas took off in a big way, with the importation of German customs such as Christmas trees and the giving of presents. Dickens' *A Christmas Carol*, published in 1843, also raised the profile of the event. In 1847, the new Poor Law Board who succeeded the Poor Law Commissioners relented further and sanctioned the provision of Christmas extras from the rates.

By the middle of the century, Christmas Day – or more often Boxing Day (26 December) – had become a regular occasion for local dignitaries to visit their union workhouse and dispense food and largesse. The workhouse dining hall would be decorated and entertainments organised. The *Western Gazette*'s 1887 report on the Christmas festivities in Chard is typical:

> The inmates, thanks to the liberality of the Guardians and the kindness of Mr and Mrs Pallin, spent a very enjoyable time on Christmas Day and Boxing Day. The pretty chapel was nicely decorated with holly and over the Communion-table was a cross of Christmas berries. On the walls were the words 'Emmanuel, God with us'. The inmates afterwards had cake and tea, which was much enjoyed. On Monday the usual festivities took place. The dining hall was elaborately decorated with evergreens, mottoes, gilded stars and Prince of Wales' plumes… The mottoes were of the usual festive character

but one, expressive of esteem, "Long Life to Mr and Mrs Pallin" showed the feeling entertained by the inmates towards those put over them. Dinner was served at two p.m. and consisted of prime roast beef, potatoes, baked and boiled, and each adult had a pint of beer. One ounce of tobacco was given to each man, snuff to the old ladies, and oranges and sweets to the children. After tea, which comprised cake and bread and butter, a capital magic lantern display was given and was thoroughly enjoyed by young and old. Then followed some ancient ditties, sung by the old people, and those who liked tripped it merrily. Songs were sung by the Master, Porter and several friends, and a very enjoyable evening came to an end. Cheers were given for those who had strived to make them happy.

Such occasions were, however, seen by some as condescending and patronising. One of the best known pieces of workhouse literature, the melodramatic ballad or monologue 'In the Workhouse: Christmas Day', was written from this standpoint. Its author, George R. Sims, was a campaigning journalist specialising in stories on poverty and poor housing published in the series entitled 'How the Poor Live' and then in a column in the new *Sunday Referee*. His monologue, first published in 1877, tells the story of inmate whose wife had been refused out-relief the previous Christmas and had starved to death rather than enter the workhouse and be separated from him. Here are the ballad's opening stanzas:

It is Christmas Day in the workhouse,
And the cold, bare walls are bright
With garlands of green and holly,
And the place is a pleasant sight;
For with clean-washed hands and faces,
In a long and hungry line
The paupers sit at the table,
For this is the hour they dine.

And the guardians and their ladies,
Although the wind is east,
Have come in their furs and wrappers,
To watch their charges feast;
To smile and be condescending,
Put pudding on pauper plates.
To be hosts at the workhouse banquet
They've paid for — with the rates.

Oh, the paupers are meek and lowly
With their 'Thank'ee kindly, mum's!'
So long as they fill their stomachs,
What matter it whence it comes!
But one of the old men mutters,
And pushes his plate aside:
'Great God!' he cries, 'but it chokes me!
For this is the day she died!'

Despite a number of flaws in its narrative (regulations allowed couples over sixty to share a bedroom, and the union was obliged to take in and feed anyone in case of 'sudden and urgent necessity'), Sims's ballad became immensely popular.

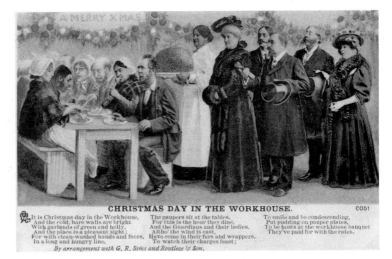

A postcard from the early 1900s illustrating a scene from 'In the Workhouse Christmas Day'.

CHRISTMAS DAY IN THE WORKHOUSE.   C051

It is Christmas day in the Workhouse,
And the cold, bare walls are bright
With garlands of green and holly,
And the place is a pleasant sight;
For with clean-washed hands and faces,
In a long and hungry line,

The paupers sit at the tables,
For this is the hour they dine,
And the Guardians and their ladies,
Altho' the wind is east,
Have come in their furs and wrappers,
To watch their charges feast;

To smile and be condescending,
Put pudding on pauper plates,
To be hosts at the workhouse banquet
They've paid for with the rates.

By arrangement with G. R. Sims and Routlege & Son.

Hubert von Herkomer's sentimental illustration 'Christmas in a Workhouse', from the Christmas 1876 issue of *The Graphic* magazine. A sign on the wall reads 'God Bless Our Master & Matron'.

A Christmas scene in the Whitechapel workhouse from *The Pictorial World* magazine in December 1874. Despite the festive mood, men and women were still strictly segregated.

For good or bad, Christmas continued to be the high point of the years as far as workhouse residents were concerned. In 1897, the 998 inmates of the City of London workhouse and infirmary received treats which included roast beef and vegetables, muscatels and almonds, dessert biscuits, Savoy cakes, French plums, figs, oranges, apples, mixed sweets, tobacco and snuff. At Paddington in the same year, the Christmas extras included nine turkeys, 12lb of sausages, coffee, and one pint of beer each for each patient in the infirmary.

As well as the food and drink, Christmas celebrations in the workhouse were often enlivened by entertainments. For children, this could include treats such as Punch and Judy shows and outings to local attractions such as museums. For the adult inmates, concerts and entertainments were often provided by the workhouse master or officers or various local societies. Apparently, these could be of a quite risqué nature – at the Holborn workhouse in 1897, the boys' school band was barred from the usual custom of attending and taking part in the entertainment at the workhouse because the songs were 'not of a kind that young boys should hear.'

The culinary highlight of most workhouse Christmas Day festivities was the Christmas pudding whose colossal ingredient list often featured in local newspaper reports of the occasion. Islington's St John workhouse pudding in 1897 was typical: 6cwt suet, 480lb flour, 3,000 eggs, 60 gallons milk, 5cwt currants, 6cwt raisins, 4cwt sultanas, 254lb sugar, 6lb spice, 3cwt peel, 3lb salt.

The following recipe for a Christmas pudding for 300 persons was provided by Pat Constable, whose family includes several generations of workhouse master. The recipe was perfected over many years by her parents Lionel and Annie Williams, who ran several Poor Law institutions (including the former Bridport workhouse in the 1940s). By this time, they were fortunate enough to have the benefit of a food mixer to help prepare the mixture.

Christmas Pudding for 300

36lbs of currants
42lbs of sultanas
9lbs of dates
9lbs of mixed peel
26lbs of flour
16lbs of breadcrumbs (prepared)
24lbs of margarine
26lbs of Demerara sugar
102lbs of golden syrup
102lbs of marmalade
144 eggs
2lbs 10oz of mixed spice
13lbs of carrots (prepared)

Cream fat and flour in Hobart mixer (to fairly thin consistency). Mix breadcrumbs with chopped dates and add to fat mixture Put shredded carrots and all dried fruit (washed) into separate bowl and mix thoroughly. Then gradually add the first mixture. Add brown sugar, stirring all the time. Add marmalade. Add spice and stir well. Add eggs, which have already been well beaten. Finally add the hot melted syrup.

N.B.
1 – Eggs are beaten in the Hobart mixer
2 – Wash all dried fruit in hot water before adding shredded carrots

---

In January 1863, the St Marylebone workhouse kitchens were used to prepare a monster plum pudding. However, this was not for the inmates' consumption: it was made by members of the United Cooks Society for despatch to Lancashire cotton-mill operatives put out of work by the cotton famine during the American Civil War.

The dining room of the Caistor Union workhouse decorated for Christmas dinner in 1905.

For cost-conscious keepers of the public purse, even the Christmas pudding could be a source of contention. At a meeting of the Newark Board of Guardians in December 1896, a heated debate ensued when it was revealed that a pudding for twenty-five inmates of the workhouse infirmary was to use 35lb of currants, 21lb of sugar, 30 eggs, and 20lb of raisins. One Board member calculated this would amount to 4lb of pudding per head whereas half that amount would surely suffice. However, a motion to reduce the quantities was declared out of order when it was pointed out the ingredients had been passed without comment at a previous meeting.

seventeen

The Evolution of the Workhouse Diet

Although the food served up at each union workhouse was initially based on one of the PLC's original six model dietaries, changes could be requested by the Board of Guardians. The procedure for doing this was made quicker and simpler in 1847, largely as a result of the Andover scandal. The new Poor Law Board also engaged the scientist Dr Lyon Playfair to analyse the 1835 dietaries and calculate the weight of food in each, and their basic composition in terms of carbon and nitrogen. Playfair produced tables that allowed the PLB to compare any proposed changes against the 1835 dietaries, and also against those used by other unions in the same area to try and set a consistent standard.

A union could request a modification to its dietary for a number of reasons: the ready availability of a certain commodity in a certain area, for example fish in coastal unions such as Penzance, an increased use of vegetables where a workhouse cultivated such crops. In 1856, the Worcester Board of Guardians applied for a temporary change in the dietary 'for the purpose of consuming the crop of cabbage now growing in the workhouse garden'. Other reasons might include the particular nutritional views held by a workhouse medical officer or the saving of money by reducing the variety or quantity of food – which could also deter new applicants.

Circumstances could occasionally force dietary changes onto a union. Although the Great Famine in the 1840s is particularly associated with Ireland, potato crops in England and Wales were also afflicted with the same potato blight resulting in potatoes rapidly becoming rotten. As a result, workhouses were obliged to serve alternatives, such as boiled rice or additional bread; in other cases, turnips, carrots, parsnips, cabbage, peas, or hominy (corn kernels) were used. Cost saving was always uppermost in the mind of the Poor Law Commissioners who issued a circular giving details of how to extract starch or 'farina' from rotting potatoes: pulp and soak the potatoes, strain the liquor, leave to settle, then pour off the excess water leaving a layer of starch which is then spread on cloths to dry.[55]

By the mid-1860s, the accumulation of small changes over the previous thirty years had resulted in a total lack of uniformity of workhouse diets. Even where two unions supposedly had a similar dietary, there was no requirement that they use the same recipes for basic dishes such as gruel. The extent of the variations was highlighted in 1866 in a survey conducted by Dr Edward Smith who had recently taken on the dual roles of inspector and medical officer for the Poor Law Board. Smith's investigations into the diets of the poor and of institutions were conducted at a time when workhouses conditions, particularly those of workhouse infirmaries, were under close scrutiny. Although Smith's work and his subsequent recommendations can be seen, with hindsight, as highly significant, at the time his work was largely unrecognised.

DR EDWARD SMITH

Edward Smith, who was born in around 1818, had a somewhat erratic medical career, then spent the 1850s and early 1860s working at London's Charing Cross and Brompton hospitals.

He became interested in the emerging disciplines of physiology and nutrition, particularly in the metabolism of different foodstuffs. At the time, the content of food was primarily categorised as either 'carbonaceous' (what we would now generally refer to as carbohydrates) and 'nitrogenous' (proteins). A leading figure in this field was the Baron Justus von Liebig, whose beef extract enterprises have already been mentioned. In 1842, Liebig had published his highly influential book *Animal Chemistry* which maintained that protein was the only true nutrient and the primary source of the body's energy. In the late 1850s, Smith's own experiments on himself, and on prisoners doing hard labour on treadmills at Coldbath Fields Prison, showed that increased exercise led to an increased production of carbon dioxide, but not to any change in the excretion of nitrogen-containing urea. Contrary to Liebig's theory, Smith found that urea production was related to the amount of protein in the diet. Thus, it was carbohydrates rather than proteins that that were the body's primary source of energy.

In 1863, at the height of the Lancashire cotton famine, Smith undertook a government sponsored study to examine how unemployed mill workers could best be relieved and avoid 'starvation diseases'. Smith's analysis of a large number of workers' diets showed that the daily intake of an average man required to maintain good health was 4,000 grains (9.1oz or 259gm) of carbon and 200 grains (0.46oz or 13gm) of nitrogen. This was one of the first such estimates to be produced and in more modern terms equates to a daily intake of about 2,600 kilocalories of energy and 80 grams of protein. This is remarkably close to the present-day recommended dietary intake of 2,550 kilocalories per day for an adult male. His report on the 'Nourishment of Distressed Operatives' revealed that the poorest diets mostly comprised bread and treacle, and that providing fresh vegetables and skimmed milk would be the most cost-effective form of supplement.

THE 1866 WORKHOUSE DIETARY SURVEY

Smith's survey into the dietaries of sixty-five workhouses in the North of England made some revealing discoveries. First of all, he found 'an inconceivable want of uniformity' in the dietaries of different workhouses. Dinner was the meal which varied most and the number of permutations proved mind-bogglingly complex, despite Smith's attempt to provide a summary:

> The largest number of workhouses in which the same rotation of foods occurs is 10, and in them meat and vegetables are provided thrice, soup or broth and bread, thrice, and pudding once in each week. Five others give meat and vegetables twice, meat pie twice, soup or broth twice, and pudding once in each week. Four supply meat and vegetables twice, soup or broth and bread twice, and pudding twice weekly. Three give meat and vegetables thrice, soup or broth and bread thrice, and a pudding once weekly. In five other cases of two workhouses each the same rotation of food is provided...[56]

Smith also found 'every possible diversity in the composition and consequent nutritive values of foods having the same designation in different workhouses... this is a most serious evil, since no idea can be formed of the value of the food from the name, and in many a good name is given to very poor food.' His investigation of the various recipes used for making one pint of gruel showed that the amount of oatmeal used was most often 1½oz but ranged from a miserly ¾oz at unions such as Easingwold, to a glutinous 4oz at Scarborough. Some recipes included additions such as 1oz of flour, half a pint of milk, butter, or sugar. The lucky inmates of Doncaster workhouse received a tablespoon of treacle and a little ginger in their daily ration.

SMITH'S 'PROPER DIETARIES'

As a result of his observations, Smith proposed numerous improvements to the diets provided in workhouses, including recommendations as to the composition and cooking of food, as well as such matters as its distribution and serving. His declared guiding principle in devising his 'proper dietaries' was that 'the inmates of workhouses should be fed in a manner the most consistent with economy and the maintenance of growth, health, and strength.'

Prior to considering the food itself, Smith emphasised that its optimum use by workhouse inmates depended on a variety of other factors, such as: employment – a healthy appetite and digestion required regular exertion, preferably in the open air; cheerfulness –

Spoons from the Lambeth and Hungerford workhouses, imprinted with the name of the union to discourage theft.

encouraged through mental instruction, reading, religious exercises, outdoor activity, and helping with such duties as caring for the sick or vagrants; warmth – through the provision of a suitable amount of clothing and fires; agreeable and familiar foods – unusual foods are likely to not be eaten; rapid distribution – food should be served and eaten while hot. This could be improved by such measures as covering food in transit to the dining hall, serving soup etc at the dining tables, and replacing tin plates and pannikins with pottery plates. He also made the radical proposal that a knife, fork and spoon should be supplied to each inmate.

Smith then applied his medical mind to the cooking of food and recommended a number of changes to existing practices: when roasting meat, it should first be sealed in front of a hot fire to retain its juices; when boiling meat, the cooking should be adjusted depending on the dish. For making soup, the meat should be cooked slowly from the outset to extract the juices; otherwise it should first be plunged into boiling water to seal the juices in.

Bread should be well baked – too much moisture in a loaf makes it less digestible and prone to going mouldy; potatoes should sometimes be boiled and sometimes roasted. Roasted potatoes lose more in weight than boiled, but the loss is of water, so that a given weight of roast potatoes is more nutritious; peas should be cooked until quite soft, but not so much that they entirely break down; milk should not be boiled but simply made hot.

In compiling a new dietary plan, Smith took an equally rigorous approach, and based his choice of food items on four factors: the cost of each item, its nutritive elements as determined by chemical analysis, his own knowledge of the ordinary diet of the pauper classes, and how the different foods were digested. On these grounds, Smith produced lists of preferred foods under two headings: vegetable foods and animal foods.

In the category of vegetable foods, wheat flour was his preferred grain. He considered it superior to oats, barley and rye on the grounds of its better nutritional value, lower cost, flavour, versatility, and acceptability to all ages and classes. More specifically, Smith recommended the use of 'seconds' flour – the grade that still contained some bran and 'sharps' or husk particles – which was both cheap and nutritious. When it came to bread, workhouses were encouraged to bake their own as it saved money, provided employment for inmates, and avoided the adulteration that was still common amongst commercial suppliers. In addition to wheat, split peas were highly commended by Smith, although he recognised that their 'harsh and peculiar flavour' limited the frequency of their use. Rice, on the other hand, he dismissed as overpriced and having an insipid flavour. Amongst fresh vegetables, Smith extolled the virtues of the potato and advocated its cultivation using inmates' labour.

Under the heading of animal foods, beef came top of Smith's list: it was relatively cheap, had a good proportion of lean to fat, and was also the 'strongest' meat – in large part due to the amount of 'ozmazome' or meat juices it held, from which beef tea could be made. The recommended beef cuts were the round, thick-flank, brisket, and sticking-piece. The use of pork, on the other hand, had little to recommend it because of its high fat content. Fish, too, was also deprecated by Smith as having a nutritive value far below that of meat.

On the grounds of economy, Smith advised the use of skimmed milk in preference to 'new' or full-fat milk, as the latter was more expensive: the fat content of skimmed milk could be easily increased, he suggested, by adding in suet. Buttermilk could also form a useful part of the inmates' diet, as could cheese, although only in areas where it was already part of a labourer's normal diet. Eggs, cooked in puddings or lightly boiled, should only be used as part of the sick dietaries – Smith particularly commended the use of seagulls' eggs, where obtainable, as being large and cheap.

Based on these principles, Smith proposed a new set of dietary tables for the different classes of workhouse inmate. Those for able-bodied and aged/infirm men are shown below.

Meal	No. days weekly	Gruel pts	Milk gruel pts	Milk porridge pts	Bread oz	Milk oz	Meat oz	Potatoes oz	Meat pie oz	Suet pudding oz	Rice pudding pts	Broth pts	Soup pts	Cheese oz	Tea pts	Sugar oz	Butter oz
Able-bodied men																	
Breakfast	7	1½			6												
Supper	4	1½			6												
	3				8						1		1½				
Dinner	2				8						1		1½				
	1				4		16										
	2				6							1					
	2				4				10	1							
Aged and infirm men																	
Breakfast	7		1½		6												
Supper	3				6	2									1	½	½
	2		1½		6												
	2				6							¾	1½				
Dinner	4				4		3	10									
	1				3				16				½				
	1				5								1				
	1				4				10				1				

The able-bodied men's diet was calculated to provide 4,397 grains of carbon and 212 grains of nitrogen per week, while the aged and infirm men's diet provided 4,563 and 225 grains respectively. As well as producing the new menu plan, Smith provided 'formulae' – ingredients lists, nutritional value, and cooking hints – for each of his proposed menu dishes. Some examples are given below:

Gruel

For a pint (carbon 366 grains; nitrogen 13 grains)
Oatmeal 1½oz, suet ⅛oz, treacle ½oz, salt. Allspice by way of change.
1. The roughly ground oatmeal is to be preferred, and it must be well cooked.
2. The finely chopped suet should be added early and the treacle late in the cooking.
3. Add the milk after the oatmeal has been well cooked.

Potato Pie

To make 3¾lbs (per 1¼ lbs: carbon 1,227 grains; nitrogen 80 grains)
For crust. Flour 12oz lard or dripping, 4oz, water, 4¼oz, meat (beef and mutton, or beef and bacon mixed) 9oz, potatoes when peeled 30oz, onions 1½oz, pepper.
1. In order to keep the nutritive value of this food nearly uniform, let the consistence be stiff, and no more fluid be added to it during the cooking than is necessary to cook the ingredients properly.
2. When it is served, and after it has been weighed, add to each quantity a little hot meat liquor properly seasoned.
3. Take care that the crust is always made of a uniform thickness and dried in the baking to an uniform degree. Cook both the crust and the inside well.
4. Cook the meat a little, and season it before it is put into the pie, and cook it with a very gentle heat and slowly. If possible cook the meat in meat liquor, and make the pie with properly seasoned meat liquor and not with water.
5. Do not cut the potato into portions so small that the whole will be mashed down.
6. Take pains to season and flavour it well and to distribute the seasoning equally over every part of the pie.
7. Use shallow dishes, so that the share of each person shall include a portion of the crust, and all the contents of the pie underneath it.
8. Ascertain how many rations a dish will hold, and in dividing the pie it will thus be unnecessary to delay time by weighing each portion.
9. The crust should be made with dripping when possible – either that from the roast meat or a little skimmed off the meat liquor before vegetables have been added.

Smith's new dietaries did not present a major change in the types of food that were being served to workhouse inmates: the staple items remained bread, milk and gruel, supplemented by potatoes, broth, soup, cheese, pudding, and pie. What they attempted to do was to offer a scheme for all workhouses to provide a uniform and nutritionally adequate diet that reached its consumers in the best possible state for its utilization.

The new dietaries were not imposed upon Boards of Guardians, but provided for their information and advice, together with Smith's recommendations on the preparation and serving of food. However, unions were now required to submit recipes to the central authority when requesting dietary changes.

FURTHER DEVELOPMENTS UP TO 1900

The inertia and penny-pinching that characterised many Boards of Guardians meant that the new dietary advice did not lead to any immediate revolution in workhouse dining halls. However, over the next thirty years, significant changes did gradually begin to happen.

The overall amount of food provided to workhouse inmates increased in the last third of the nineteenth century. This was due to a number of different factors. Edward Smith's new dietaries, together with later pressure from the central authorities to improve children's diets, were partly responsible for this trend. Another factor was the increasing influence on workhouse diets from union medical officers. On the economic front, a decline in the price of imported American grain in the 1870s brought down the cost of bread, allowing larger portions to be provided at the same cost. A number of other basic foodstuffs either held their price or became cheaper during this period, for example there was an increase in the availability of products such as cheap tinned meat from Australia – supplemented, from 1880, by supplies of refrigerated meat. Finally, it was probably acknowledged that the large majority of inmates were now the elderly and infirm, for whom the workhouse was the only option and who would not be deterred by a frugal diet.

As well as quantity, some improvement in the quality of workhouse food also took place during this period. One factor contributing to this was the influence of the increasing numbers of female guardians – the first of these was elected in 1875 in Kensington, with 839 in office by 1895. In larger unions it also became more common for workhouse kitchens to have a paid trained cook, and also to have up-to-date equipment in their kitchens such as gas-fired ovens. The new legislation outlawing food adulteration was responsible for further improvements in food quality both inside and outside the workhouse.

As regards the workhouse dietary itself, one interesting development came in 1883 when more than a hundred unions were given permission to provide once-a-week fish dinners to their workhouse inmates for a trial period. Adults and children above nine years were allowed an 8oz portion, together with an allowance of bread and potatoes. The experiment appears to have broadly been judged a success, both in broadening the diet and also in saving money. However, some unions decided not to continue with the experiment because of the difficulty they experienced in cooking fish in large quantities.[57]

By the 1890s, unions were increasingly complaining about problems with the 'fixed ration system' where each inmate received a stipulated amount of food at each meal. This often caused waste where the amount supplied exceeded that which could be eaten by an individual – a not uncommon situation with children, the elderly, and the sick, who now constituted the majority of workhouse inmates. Uneaten food had to be thrown away and could not be re-served at a future meal. Fixed rations also caused delays at meal times where each inmate was served their individual regulation portion. Several unions experimented – without official approval – in serving bread in two portions: half the allotted amount at the start of the meal, and the remainder to those who requested it. At Chorlton, the adoption of this system made savings of up to 40 per cent in the amount of bread used. At Islington, the serving of bread in the form of 3oz rolls, and the placing of vegetables in self-service dishes on the dining tables was also shown to reduce waste. However, similar experiments at Camberwell's Gordon Road workhouse in 1896 led to a 'strike' by the able-bodied inmates who refused to begin eating their dinner without being served with their full bread ration at the outset.

This 1870 advertisement for Australian tinned meat products was aimed at institutions such as workhouses and hospitals.

Dietary experiments at Bethnal Green's Well Street workhouse briefly hit the headlines in 1897 when it was claimed that an elderly inmate had died of overeating. Workhouse officials were quick to rebut the story, even though overeating had indeed been given as the cause of death by the doctor in attendance. However, the dead man had a weak heart and could have died at any time from the least exertion. The extra food he had eaten had probably been given to him by a fellow inmate who was unable to finish his own prescribed portion.

As well as the waste, workhouse reformers also criticised the old dietaries as being unnecessarily monotonous. Even where a union wished to modify its dietary, the procedure and protracted correspondence involved did not encourage the guardians to undertake such changes.

THE 1900 DIETARY REVOLUTION

In 1897, the Local Government Board, which was now responsible for the poor-relief system, appointed a committee to examine workhouse dietary policy, including such matters as the fixed-ration system. At the end of its deliberations, the committee proposed that the Board should frame, with medical advice, 'a sufficient number of diets to meet the varying tastes of different localities, and to limit the choice of the guardians to the dietaries so framed.'

In 1900, the LGB carried out this suggestion and issued the Workhouse Regulation (Dietaries and Accounts) Order, which transformed the framework of workhouse diets established in the 1830s.

According to the Board, the changes in the Order were to remedy a number of problems with the existing dietary system, namely: the great waste of bread in workhouses, the unnecessary monotony of the workhouse diet, problems in feeding a fixed diet to children with widely varying appetites, and the complicated administrative arrangements in making changes to a union's dietary.

Initially, the order designated three basic forms of diet – the plain diet (for healthy able-bodied adults), the infirm diet (infirm, but otherwise healthy adults), and the children's diet (for those aged from three to fifteen). Based on this new scheme, workhouse inmates were now allocated to one of the following dietary classes:

Class 1	Men not employed in work. (Plain diet.)
Class 1a	Men employed in work. (As Class 1, but with a weekday lunch added.)
Class 2	Men not employed in work. (Infirm diet.)
Class 2a	Men employed in work. (As Class 1, but with a weekday lunch added.)
Class 2b	Feeble men. (Special infirm diet with a daily lunch added.)
Class 3	Women not employed in work. (Plain diet.)
Class 3a	Women employed in work. (As Class 1, but with a weekday lunch added.)
Class 4	Women not employed in work. (Infirm diet.)
Class 4a	Women employed in work. (As Class 1, but with a weekday lunch added.)
Class 4b	Feeble women. (Special infirm diet with an additional daily meal.)
Class 5	Children aged from three to seven. (With a weekday lunch added.)
Class 6	Children aged from eight to fifteen. (With a weekday lunch added.)

'Lunch' at this time would be a light mid-morning meal taken at around 10.30 a.m. The weekly pattern of meals provided for each of the classes was compiled by each union from a long list of 'rations' provided by the central authority. For example, for each weekday (i.e. Monday to Saturday) breakfast or supper, the plain diet offered eleven different combinations and amounts of bread, milk, cheese, porridge, and gruel. On Sunday, a choice of six breakfast/supper rations was available comprising bread plus either butter or margarine, and tea, coffee or cocoa. A typical plain diet dinner was boiled beef served with bread, dumplings, and potatoes or vegetables.

The daily infirm diet selection could be made from a list of twenty-one rations which provided such comforts as butter, margarine, jam, marmalade, treacle, plain cake, seed cake, tea, coffee, or cocoa. The list of twenty-five breakfast/supper rations available for the children's meals broadly followed the infirm diet, but with the occasional inclusion of cold boiled bacon, an egg, or bread and dripping. Dinner options included savoury mince, bread and potatoes or vegetables, followed by roley-poley pudding, rice or semolina.

After taking into account the different versions of the rations for males and females, for different age groups of children, and for the additional lunch meals, the total number of breakfast/supper rations listed in the new order numbered 146. If that wasn't complicated enough, the ration list on offer for dinners for all the various classes numbered 233. Added to that was a selection of thirteen dessert puddings that could be enjoyed by those on the infirm diet, plus a number of small variations in quantity for Classes 2b and 4b.

The complete list of rations available for the plain and infirm men's dinner diets is shown in the accompanying tables. Further instructions were issued alongside the new ration lists:

With the exception of boiled or roast beef meals, no two dinners should be repeated in the same week for a particular class.

Not more than one meal a week was to be selected from the rations marked ★ in the tables.

Not more than two meals a week were to be selected from the rations marked † in the tables.

Sufficient water was to be supplied at dinner with a separate mug for each person.

Salt was to be provided at all meals for all classes. Pepper, vinegar and mustard were to be provided at the discretion of the guardians.

In the spring and summer months, the standard dietary could be supplemented by seasonal additions of:

Stewed rhubarb, or other stewed fruit (up to one pint per head per week)

Onions (two ounces per week)

Watercress (two bunches per week)

Lettuce (four ounces per week)

To reduce wastage, each inmate was initially served only a proportion of their bread allowance, but could ask for more to make up their full allowance if they so wished.

Under the new system, children's portions were no longer required to be weighed out; instead, each child was served 'according to appetite'. Unserved children's food could be reused at a future meal on the same or the following day.

The new dietary provoked some complaints from Boards of Guardians, with requests for its implementation to be made optional. Some unions were concerned that it would result in a decrease in the quality of children's food, or lead to increase in costs, particularly where the extra meals mentioned in the new scheme were included. Others, who had already made recent changes to their dietary, were reluctant to change again. At Leicester, the guardians even expressed the opinion that the new menus would lead to a surge in the popularity of the workhouse and an increase in admissions. However, the Local Government Board refused to make any concessions, arguing that the flexibility offered in the new dietary and system of classification would enable unions to tailor their new dietary to meet all these objections.

To assist unions in their adoption of the new system of dietaries, and the much wider range of ingredients and dishes that it introduced, the Local Government Board commissioned a new thirty-two-page cookery book, *The Manual of Workhouse Cookery*, which was published in 1901. It contained recipes for all the dishes which were contained in the 1900 Order's schedule of rations. The distribution of the new cookery book to workhouse kitchens also aimed to ensure that all the dishes were prepared in a way that was simple, economical, and standard. The full text of the manual is reproduced at the end of this book.

Even with the large increase in the number of meal options, by modern standards, the 1900 dietary looks fairly stodgy and included relatively little fruit and green vegetables. However, for workhouse inmates it meant a significant improvement in the palatability of the food they received. Although gruel, bread, and cheese still featured in the new menus, inmates could now expect a hot, cooked dinner every day, including a dessert 'pudding' for the infirm.

In many ways, the 1900 workhouse dietary epitomises the type of food provided by many institutional kitchens in Britain for most of the twentieth century. For many older people, the typical menu options – boiled or roast meat with boiled potatoes, Irish stew, fish pie, or boiled fish, followed by suet pudding, semolina or sago – evoke strong (or even nostalgic!) memories of the school dinners they ate as a child.

1	Beef, boiled, 4½ oz. ; Bread, 4 oz. ; Potatoes or other Vegetables, 12 oz.
2	„ roast, 4½ oz. ; Bread, 4 oz. ; Potatoes or other Vegetables, 12 oz.
3	Mutton, boiled, 4½ oz. ; Bread, 4 oz. ; Potatoes or other Vegetables, 12 oz.
4	Pork, boiled, 4½ oz. ; Bread, 4 oz. ; Potatoes or other Vegetables, 12 oz.
5	Tinned Meat, 4½ oz. ; Bread, 4 oz. ; Potatoes or other Vegetables, 12 oz.
6	Beef, boiled, 3½ oz. ; Bread, 4 oz. ; Potatoes or other Vegetables, 6 oz. ; Suet Pudding or Dumpling, 4 oz.
7	Mutton, boiled, 3½ oz. ; Bread, 4 oz. ; Potatoes or other Vegetables, 6 oz. ; Suet Pudding or Dumpling, 4 oz.
8	Pork, boiled, 3½ oz. ; Bread, 4 oz. ; Potatoes or other Vegetables, 6 oz. ; Suet Pudding or Dumpling, 4 oz.
9	Beef, boiled, 4½ oz. ; Pease Pudding, 12 oz.
10	Mutton boiled, 4½ oz. ; Pease Pudding, 12 oz.
11	Pork, boiled, 4½ oz. ; Pease Pudding, 12 oz.
12	Bacon, boiled, 3 oz. ; Pease Pudding, 12 oz.
13	Beef, boiled, 4½ oz. ; Haricot Beans, 12 oz.
14	Mutton, boiled, 4½ oz. ; Haricot Beans, 12 oz.
15	Pork, boiled, 4½ oz. ; Haricot Beans, 12 oz.
16	Bacon, boiled, 3 oz. ; Haricot Beans, 12 oz.
17	„ boiled, 3 oz. ; Bread, 4 oz. ; Potatoes or other Vegetables, 12 oz.
18	Hashed Meat, 6 oz. ; Bread, 4 oz. ; Potatoes or other Vegetables, 12 oz.
19	Fish (wet), boiled or steamed, 10 oz. ; Bread, 4 oz. ; Potatoes or other Vegetables, 12 oz.
20	Fish (dry) boiled or steamed, 10 ozs. ; Bread, 4 oz. ; Potatoes or other Vegetables, 12 oz.
21	Fish (wet), fried, 10 oz. ; Bread, 4 oz. ; Potatoes or other Vegetables, 12 oz. (Sauce with boiled fish, ¼ gill per ration.)
22	Soup, Pea, 1½ pint ; Bread, 6 oz.
23	„ Lentil, 1½ pint ; Bread, 6 oz.
24	„ Haricot, 1½ pint ; Bread, 6 oz.
25	„ Barley, 1½ pint ; Bread, 6 oz.
26	Broth, 1 pint ; Bread, 8 oz. ; Cheese, 3 oz.
27	„ 1 pint ; Bread, 4 oz. ; Cheese, 2 oz. ; Suet Pudding, 8 oz.
28	„ 1 pint ; Bread, 4 oz. ; Cheese, 2 oz. ; Dumpling, 8 oz.
29	Meat Stew or Scouse, 1 pint ; Bread, 6 oz.
30	Irish Stew, 1 pint ; Bread, 6 oz.
31	Hotch Potch Stew, 1 pint ; Bread, 6 oz.
32	Meat Pie, 16 oz.
33	Potato Pie, 16 oz. ; Bread, 4 oz.
34	Sea Pie, 16 oz. ; Bread, 4 oz.
35	Meat Pudding, 16 oz. ; Potatoes or other Vegetables, 6 oz.
36	Suet Pudding, 16 oz.
37	Potatoes with Milk, 24 oz. ; Bread, 2 oz. ; Buttermilk, 1 pint.
38	„ „ 24 oz. ; Bread, 2 oz. ; Cheese, 2 oz.
39	Coffee, 1 pint ; Bread, 8 oz. ; Cheese, 3 oz.

Nos. 9–12: WINTER ONLY.

Nos. 22–23: WINTER ONLY. Nos. 24–25: SUMMER ONLY.

	A selection from Rations Nos. 1 to 39 in the preceding column, or from the following :—
40	Mutton, roast, 4½ oz. ; Bread, 4 oz. ; Potatoes or other Vegetables, 12 oz.
41	Pork, roast, 4½ oz. ; Bread, 4 oz. ; Potatoes or other Vegetables, 12 oz.
42	Collops, 5 oz. ; Bread, 4 oz. ; Potatoes or other Vegetables, 12 oz.
43	Savoury Mince, ½ pint ; Bread, 4 oz. ; Potatoes or other Vegetables, 12 oz.
44	Soup, Bouillon (Beef-broth), 1 pint ; Bread, 6 oz.
45	Fish Pie, 16 oz. ; Bread, 4 oz.
46	Egg, 1 ; Bread, 8 oz. ; Butter, ½ oz. ; Coffee, 1 pint.
47	„ 1 ; Bread, 8 oz. ; Margarine, ½ oz. ; Coffee, 1 pint.
48	„ 1 ; Bread, 8 oz. ; Butter, ½ oz. ; Cocoa, 1 pint.
49	„ 1 ; Bread, 8 oz. ; Margarine, ½ oz. ; Cocoa, 1 pint.
50	Beef, boiled, 3½ oz. ; Bread, 4 oz. ; Potatoes or other Vegetables, 6 oz.
51	Beef, roast, 3½ oz. ; Bread, 4 oz. ; Potatoes or other Vegetables, 6 oz.
52	Mutton, boiled, 3½ oz. ; Bread, 4 oz. ; Potatoes or other Vegetables, 6 oz.
53	Mutton, roast, 3½ oz. ; Bread, 4 oz. ; Potatoes or other Vegetables, 6 oz.
54	Pork, boiled, 3½ oz. ; Bread, 4 oz. ; Potatoes or other Vegetables, 6 oz.
55	Pork, roast, 3½ oz. ; Bread, 4 oz. ; Potatoes or other Vegetables, 6 oz.
56	Tinned Meat, 3½ oz. ; Bread, 4 oz. ; Potatoes or other Vegetables, 6 oz.
57	Hashed Meat, 4 oz. ; Bread, 4 oz. ; Potatoes or other Vegetables, 6 oz.
58	Savoury Mince, ½ pint ; Bread, 4 oz. ; Potatoes or other Vegetables, 6 oz.
59	Soup, Pea, 1 pint ; Bread, 4 oz.
60	„ Lentil, 1 pint ; Bread, 4 oz.
61	„ Haricot, 1 pint ; Bread, 4 oz.
62	„ Barley, 1 pint ; Bread, 4 oz.
63	„ Bouillon, 1 pint ; Bread, 4 oz.

Each of the foregoing (Nos. 50–63 inclusive) with one of the following Puddings, etc. (a.) to (m.), as selected by the Guardians to form one ration.

§ *Note.*—Not to be given with Nos. 59 to 63 (Soups).

(a.) Suet Pudding, 4 oz.
(b.) Roley-poley Pudding, 4 oz.
(c.) Golden Pudding, 4 oz.
(d.) Dry Fruit Pudding, 4 oz.
(e.) Bread Pudding, 4 oz.
(f.) Batter Pudding, 4 oz.
(g.) Dumpling, 4 oz.
(h.) Fresh Fruit Pudding, 6 oz.
(i.) Rice Pudding, 8 oz.
(j.) Sago Pudding, 8 oz.
(k.) Semolina Pudding, 8 oz.
§(l.) Rice Milk, ½ pint.
§(m.) Skim or Separated Milk, or Buttermilk, ½ pint.

Nos. 59–62: 59 WINTER ONLY ; 62 SUMMER ONLY.

Right: The corresponding list of rations for the men's 'infirm diet'.

eighteen

The End of the Workhouse

CHANGING TIMES

By the start of the twentieth century, change was in the air for the workhouse system. Two factors contributed to this. The first, already noted, was the election of a significant number of women as guardians – since the 1860s women had been active in improving workhouse conditions, particularly through bodies such as the Workhouse Visiting Society founded by Louisa Twining. The second, in 1892, was the lowering to £5 of the property rental value qualifying for guardian election, which enabled the election of working-class people as Board members. In that year's union elections at the Poplar in London, two new working-class guardians were elected to the Poplar Board: Will Crooks and George Lansbury. Will Crooks, who came from an impoverished family, had himself spent some time in the Poplar workhouse as a child and went on to become chairman of the Poplar Guardians, a member of Parliament and a vocal advocate of workhouse reform.

THE 1905 ROYAL COMMISSION

In December 1905, a Royal Commission was appointed to conduct a major review of the Poor Laws and the situation of the unemployed. Its remit was:

> To inquire: (1) Into the working of the laws relating to the relief of poor persons in the United Kingdom; (2) Into the various means which have been adopted outside of the Poor Laws for meeting distress arising from want of employment, particularly during periods of severe industrial depression; and to consider and report whether any, and if so what, modification of the Poor Laws or changes in their administration or fresh legislation for dealing with distress are advisable.

Over the next four years, it carried out the most extensive investigation since the Royal Commission of 1832. Its eighteen members included: C.S. Loch (secretary of the London Charity Organization Society), William Smart (professor of political economy at Glasgow University), Octavia Hill (campaigner for housing reform and co-founder of the National Trust), socialist reformers George Lansbury and Beatrice Webb, former guardians, Poor Law officials, and clergymen.

The Commission was famously split in its conclusions. A Majority Report, endorsed by fourteen of its members recommended the creation of a New Poor Law authority in each county or county borough, together with the replacement of workhouses by more specialized institutions catering for separate categories of inmate such as children, the old, the unemployed, and the mentally ill. A Minority Report, signed by four members (Beatrice Webb, George

Above: A women's day room at the
St Marylebone workhouse in about 1902.
Although the room is well furnished, the
floor is bare apart from a hearth rug.

Right: Will Crooks who, as the title of his
biography proclaims, went from workhouse
to Westminster.

Lansbury, Mr F. Chandler, and the Revd Russell Wakefield) was more radical and advocated the complete break-up of the Poor Law and the transfer of its functions to other authorities to provide care for various groups. The Minority Report's emphasis was on the prevention of destitution rather than its relief.

In 1911, George Lansbury wrote a pamphlet provocatively entitled *Smash up the Workhouse*, which argued that few – especially able-bodied – people should need to be in workhouses. For those who had no alternative, there should be a softening of the workhouse regime.

Although no new legislation directly resulted from the Commission's work, a number of significant pieces of social legislation took place in its wake. 1 January 1909 saw the introduction of the old-age pension for those aged seventy or more (5s a week for a single person, 7s 6d for a married couple). However, anyone who had been in receipt of poor relief in the previous twelve months was automatically disqualified from receiving the pension. In 1911, unemployment insurance and health insurance began in a limited form.

In 1913, a complete revision of workhouse rules and regulations took place – this was the first such exercise since the existing rule-book had been published as the Consolidated General Order in 1847. The new regulations were notable for having no mention of the 'workhouse' – the term 'Poor Law institution' was used instead. Likewise, 'paupers' were henceforth referred to as 'poor persons'. The new order also did away with the sevenfold system of classification that dated back to 1835; instead, Boards of Guardians were now able to devise whatever system of classification they felt appropriate. Finally, the new order stipulated that after 1915 no healthy children over the age of three were to reside in a workhouse for longer than six weeks.

FROM 1914 TO 1930

During the First World War, many Boards of Guardians offered workhouse premises for military use, mostly as hospitals (for example at Bristol, Oxford and Birmingham), but also for accommodating military personnel, prisoners of war (for example, Banbury and Congleton) and 'aliens' (for example Islington).

In 1919, the responsibility for poor relief passed from the Local Government Board to the Ministry of Health. The general depression in the years following the First World War, culminating in the miners' strike of 1926, put a tremendous strain on the poor-relief system with some unions effectively becoming bankrupt. In some areas, where colliery owners also had influence with local Boards of Guardians, there were allegations that relief was deliberately reduced to break the strike. Conversely, where miners and union officials dominated a Board, there were complaints that the rates were being used to supplement strike funds.

Neville Chamberlain, health minister in the 1925 Conservative government, believed that the Poor Law system needed reforming and in 1926 pushed through a Board of Guardians (Default) Act which enabled the dismissal of a Board of Guardians and its replacement with government officials. This was followed by a further Poor Law Act in 1927, and in 1928 Chamberlain introduced the Local Government Act, which would in many respects bring about many of the measures proposed by the Royal Commission's Report in 1909. Essentially, this would abolish the Boards of Guardians and transfer all their powers and responsibilities to local councils. These were required to submit administrative schemes to end 'poor relief' as such – 'as soon as circumstances permit' – and provide more specific 'public assistance' on the basis of other legislation such as the Public Health Act, the Education Act, and so on. The Local Government Act was passed on 27 March 1929 and came into effect on 1 April 1930 – a day which supposedly marked the end of the road for the 643 Boards of Guardians in England and Wales.

THE BOARDS OF GUARDIANS BOW OUT

On 31 March, 1930, on the eve of their abolition, the Halifax guardians held a dinner at the workhouse on Gibbet Street, to mark the end of the Board's existence. The occasion was hosted by clerk to the guardians, Arthur Thompson Longbotham, MBE, who was only the third person to occupy the post in the union's ninety-three-year history. The commemorative dinner menu included a resumé of the main events during that period and concluded:

> After 93 years of successful administration, the Guardians end their sphere of labour with a pauperism of 118 per 10,000 of the population, the lowest numbers in the West Riding of Yorkshire, and which contrast with 347 per 10,000 for the London Unions and 261 per 10,000 as the average for the whole Country. Their Institutions are at the highest point of efficiency and are entirely free from debt. 31st March, 1930. Exeunt omnes.

It is perhaps ironic that the food consumed by the Halifax Guardians largely consisted of items that many of their charges would never themselves taste.

On Tuesday 1 December, 1931, the last meeting of the Abingdon and Wallingford Guardians Committee took place at the Abingdon workhouse – now officially known as the Abingdon Poor Law Institution. The transfer of 'patients' from Abingdon to the Wallingford Institution was arranged to take place from 28 December onwards. The chairman of the guardians, Mr F. Cross, then spoke:

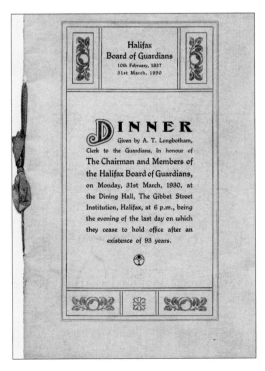

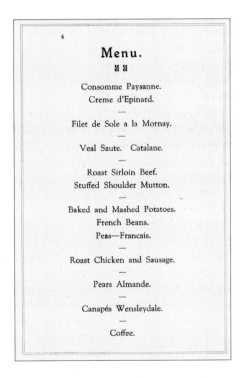

Above left: The cover of the commemorative menu produced by the Halifax Board of Guardians at their farewell dinner in 1930…

Above right: …and what they had to eat.

I think, perhaps, one or two words are due, seeing that this probably is the last time we shall meet here as the Abingdon Guardians Committee. Those who, directly and indirectly, have been responsible for the care and comfort of the sick who have been nursed here, and all those who have found a refuge from want and trouble will feel the passing of this institution after their labours here and the void it creates. Those who are moved from here will find themselves in fresh surroundings, but, I am sure, we not only hope, but believe that they will find a welcome and understanding from those who will have the care of them. (Cries of hear, hear.) There is one thing I am certain we want to do, and that is to pay a tribute to the officers of this institution and thank them for their services. Some of them we hope will be able to continue with us.

The inmates had a final Christmas dinner consisting of roast beef, roast pork, boiled potatoes and green vegetables, Christmas pudding, custard, beer and mineral water. On 1 Jan 1932, there were various presentations at a staff farewell social. The master of the Abingdon workhouse, Mr J.H. Smith, presented a silver salver to Dr Woodford, medical officer for the previous thirty-two years. The matron, Mrs Howard, presented a Westminster chimes striking clock to the master, and a silver salver and hot-water jug to Sister Hamblin. Songs were sung by Mrs Pickett, the master, and the gardener, and the rest of the evening was given over to dancing, the proceedings terminating with the singing of Auld Lang's Syne.

AFTER 1930

After 1930, some former workhouse sites were sold off and converted to other uses, such as factories, warehouses, schools, and houses. Some, like Abingdon, were soon flattened and replaced by a modern housing estate. However, many ex-workhouses carried on into the 1930s virtually unaltered. Objections from Boards of Guardians and councils meant that changes were sometimes very slow in taking place. Arguably, the 1929 Act did not succeed in abolishing the Poor Law – it merely reformed how it was administered and changed a few names. Poor law institutions became 'public assistance institutions' and were controlled by a committee of 'guardians'. However, physical conditions improved a little for the inmates, the majority of who continued to be the old, the mentally deficient, unmarried mothers, and vagrants.

The National Health Service Act of 1946 came into force on 5 July 1948. Even the sweeping changes that came with this had less impact than might be imagined. Former Public Assistance Institutions now came under the control of the Hospital Management Committees under Regional Hospital Boards, but many still carried the stigma from their workhouse days. Many of these new 'hospitals' also maintained 'Reception Centres for Wayfarers', i.e. casual wards for vagrants, until the 1960s.

In the 1970s and 1980s, many former workhouse buildings were demolished and the land sold off. Others were turned into office accommodation when modern hospital blocks were erected alongside, in what had formerly been the workhouse grounds.

The ultimate irony was the refurbishment of many former workhouse buildings as up-market residential accommodation whose residents were protected by high walls and electric gates. The former inmates of these establishments would no doubt be amazed at how much money their modern counterparts were prepared to pay to be locked behind the very walls which had once symbolised so much shame and degradation.

As for the food – visitors to Rhayader in central Wales may stumble across the old union workhouse in its present-day guise of a comfortable country house hotel, to which is attached the workhouse restaurant. Apparently, the menu does not include gruel.

nineteen

The 1901 Manual of Workhouse Cookery

THE NATIONAL TRAINING SCHOOL OF COOKERY

The task of devising the 1901 workhouse cookery manual was given to the National Training School of Cookery, the foremost cookery school of its day, which had been set up in London in 1873.

The driving force behind the School was Edith Clarke, who had become the establishment's second lady superintendent in 1875, a post she was to hold for forty-four years. In its early years, the school mainly taught basic household cookery to girls training to become domestic science teachers, together with more up-market courses for those from wealthier families. Clarke's interests quickly turned towards working-class women and how the standard of nutrition could be improved in poorer families. This she tackled by a campaign to introduce cookery lessons into London board schools – after much resistance, these began in 1878 at schools in Greenwich and Marylebone. She wrote a wide range of cookery books including *Plain Cookery Recipes* in 1883 and *High-Class Cookery Recipes* in 1885.

The school went from strength to strength and by 1902, it boasted HM King Edward VII as its patron and the Duke of Bedford as its president. The school's prospectus then offered:

A course for training cookery teachers in artisan, household, and advanced cookery, including gastronomy and the chemistry of food and cookery; classes in hygiene and human physiology; classes in household management for ladies and housekeepers; classes for ladies' maids in needlework, dressmaking and laundry; dishes cooked at the school on sale daily; teachers sent to all parts of the country for private lessons at moderate fees, and cooks sent out for dinner parties, ball suppers etc.

The school was therefore a natural choice when it came to devising a workhouse cookery manual. Although it did not bear her name, Edith Clarke was undoubtedly its author.

INGREDIENTS TABLES

In addition to the manual itself, copies of which were issued by the Local Government Board to each Board of Guardians in England and Wales, most workhouse kitchens would probably also have had a copy of *Tables for Calculating the Exact Quantities of Different Ingredients* published in 1901 by Local Government publishers, Shaw and Sons. The book was a handy ready reckoner for calculating the quantities of ingredients required to make, say, rice pudding for 350 inmates (65lbs 10oz rice, 10lbs 15oz each of sugar and fat, 175 pints of milk).

TABLES

FOR CALCULATING THE EXACT QUANTITIES

OF THE DIFFERENT INGREDIENTS

REQUIRED IN THE PREPARATION OF

1 TO 500 POUNDS OR PINTS

OF ANY OF THE COMPOSITE FOODS

SET FORTH IN THE

INGREDIENT TABLE

In Schedule A., Part III., of the Local Government Board's Workhouse

Regulation (Dietaries and Accounts) Order, 1900.

London:

SHAW & SONS, LOCAL GOVERNMENT PUBLISHERS,

6, 7, 8, & 9, FETTER LANE, E.C.

1901.

Left: The title page of the 1901 workhouse meals 'ready reckoner'.

TO MAKE	DRIPPING	MILK	FLOUR	TO MAKE	DRIPPING	MILK	FLOUR
pints	lbs. ozs.	qts. pts.	lbs. ozs.	pints	lbs. ozs.	qts. pts.	lbs. ozs.
1	0 1	0 0½	0 1½	56	3 8	14 0	5 4
2	0 2	0 1	0 3	57	3 9	14 0½	5 5½
3	0 3	0 1½	0 4½	58	3 10	14 1	5 7
4	0 4	1 0	0 6	59	3 11	14 1½	5 8½
5	0 5	1 0½	0 7½	60	3 12	15 0	5 10
6	0 6	1 1	0 9	61	3 13	15 0½	5 11½
7	0 7	1 1½	0 10½	62	3 14	15 1	5 13
8	0 8	2 0	0 12	63	3 15	15 1½	5 14½
9	0 9	2 0½	0 13½	64	4 0	16 0	6 0
10	0 10	2 1	0 15	65	4 1	16 0½	6 1½
11	0 11	2 1½	1 0½	66	4 2	16 1	6 3
12	0 12	3 0	1 2	67	4 3	16 1½	6 4½
13	0 13	3 0½	1 3½	68	4 4	17 0	6 6
14	0 14	3 1	1 5	69	4 5	17 0½	6 7½
15	0 15	3 1½	1 6½	70	4 6	17 1	6 9
16	1 0	4 0	1 8	71	4 7	17 1½	6 10½
17	1 1	4 0½	1 9½	72	4 8	18 0	6 12
18	1 2	4 1	1 11	73	4 9	18 0½	6 13½
19	1 3	4 1½	1 12½	74	4 10	18 1	6 15
20	1 4	5 0	1 14	75	4 11	18 1½	7 0½
21	1 5	5 0½	1 15½	76	4 12	19 0	7 2
22	1 6	5 1	2 1	77	4 13	19 0½	7 3½
23	1 7	5 1½	2 2½	78	4 14	19 1	7 5
24	1 8	6 0	2 4	79	4 15	19 1½	7 6½
25	1 9	6 0½	2 5½	80	5 0	20 0	7 8
26	1 10	6 1	2 7	81	5 1	20 0½	7 9½
27	1 11	6 1½	2 8½	82	5 2	20 1	7 11
28	1 12	7 0	2 10	83	5 3	20 1½	7 12½
29	1 13	7 0½	2 11½	84	5 4	21 0	7 14
30	1 14	7 1	2 13	85	5 5	21 0½	7 15½
31	1 15	7 1½	2 14½	86	5 6	21 1	8 1
32	2 0	8 0	3 0	87	5 7	21 1½	8 2½
33	2 1	8 0½	3 1½	88	5 8	22 0	8 4
34	2 2	8 1	3 3	89	5 9	22 0½	8 5½
35	2 3	8 1½	3 4½	90	5 10	22 1	8 7
36	2 4	9 0	3 6	91	5 11	22 1½	8 8½
37	2 5	9 0½	3 7½	92	5 12	23 0	8 10
38	2 6	9 1	3 9	93	5 13	23 0½	8 11½
39	2 7	9 1½	3 10½	94	5 14	23 1	8 13
40	2 8	10 0	3 12	95	5 15	23 1½	8 14½
41	2 9	10 0½	3 13½	96	6 0	24 0	9 0
42	2 10	10 1	3 15	97	6 1	24 0½	9 1½
43	2 11	10 1½	4 0½	98	6 2	24 1	9 3
44	2 12	11 0	4 2	99	6 3	24 1½	9 4½
45	2 13	11 0½	4 3½	100	6 4	25 0	9 6
46	2 14	11 1	4 5	125	7 13	31 0½	11 11½
47	2 15	11 1½	4 6½	150	9 6	37 1	14 1
48	3 0	12 0	4 8	175	10 15	43 1½	16 6½
49	3 1	12 0½	4 9½	200	12 8	50 0	18 12
50	3 2	12 1	4 11	250	15 10	62 1	23 7
51	3 3	12 1½	4 12½	300	18 12	75 0	28 2
52	3 4	13 0	4 14	350	21 14	87 1	32 13
53	3 5	13 0½	4 15½	400	25 0	100 0	37 8
54	3 6	13 1	5 1	450	28 2	112 1	42 3
55	3 7	13 1½	5 2½	500	31 4	125 0	46 14

SALT AND VINEGAR TO TASTE.   WATER OR FISH LIQUOR A SUFFICIENCY.

Right: The ingredients required for fish sauce for up to 500 people.

MANUAL

OF

WORKHOUSE COOKERY

RECIPES

PREPARED BY

THE NATIONAL TRAINING SCHOOL OF COOKERY

AND ISSUED TO BOARDS OF GUARDIANS BY THE

LOCAL GOVERNMENT BOARD

LONDON

PRINTED BY WILLIAM CLOWES AND SONS, LIMITED

STAMFORD STREET AND CHARING CROSS

FOR THE COMMITTEE OF THE NATIONAL TRAINING SCHOOL OF COOKERY

1901

MANUAL

OF

WORKHOUSE COOKERY

RECIPES

PREPARED BY

THE NATIONAL TRAINING SCHOOL OF COOKERY

AND ISSUED TO BOARDS OF GUARDIANS BY THE

LOCAL GOVERNMENT BOARD

LONDON

PRINTED BY WILLIAM CLOWES AND SONS, LIMITED

STAMFORD STREET AND CHARING CROSS

FOR THE COMMITTEE OF THE NATIONAL TRAINING SCHOOL OF COOKERY

1901

LONDON:
PRINTED BY WILLIAM CLOWES AND SONS, Limited,
STAMFORD STREET AND CHARING CROSS.

DIETARIES.

——◆◆——

MANUAL OF WORKHOUSE COOKERY.

_____

The Manual is mainly based on a special report furnished to the Local Government Board by the National Training School of Cookery.

_____

Elementary Rules of Cookery.

The following directions are of a simple kind, and the recipes so arranged as to make the preparation and cooking of the dishes easy. It is, however, assumed that those who have charge of the kitchens have had a fair amount of experience and sufficient practical knowledge of the principal rudiments of cooking to enable them to thoroughly understand the duties of the posts they occupy. It is most essential that persons, holding appointments as cooks in workhouses, etc., who have not yet mastered the elementary rules of the science of Cookery should be given opportunities for acquiring this most necessary knowledge.

Although the success of good Cookery does not entirely depend on book and rule, there are certain essential rules and regulations which must be carefully followed, if any uniformity in the result of cooking is to be obtained.

The following notes of instructions illustrate the essential principles of Cookery, and should therefore be carefully studied and carried out in practice.

Boiling or Steaming.

The best method of boiling meat and green vegetables * is to plunge the article to be cooked into boiling water (212° Fahr.), or in the case of steam into a heat equivalent to that of boiling water. This hardens the outside and retains the juices of the food. After the first five minutes the boiling heat must be reduced to the degree of slow or simmering heat (180–190° Fahr.), which is rather below that of boiling heat. If boiled too fast the outside of the meat is cooked whilst the interior is underdone, and if the fast boiling is prolonged the meat becomes indigestible and tough. Hard water is better than soft for boiling meats, etc. Boiling properly conducted loses less of the meat than roasting, and is therefore an economical method of cooking, provided that the meat liquor is turned into account; but although it is the simplest mode of cooking, it requires very great care. The most suitable joints of meat for boiling are : legs of mutton, shoulder of beef, round of beef, thick flank of beef, chuck, legs and shins of beef; clod and stickings of beef or neck of mutton are best used for stock, soups, also for stews and pies.

Baking and Roasting.

Roasting, though the most tasty, is the most expensive mode of cooking meat, as meat loses considerably in the process. Some of the loss evaporates in steam and some goes into the dripping-pan. The dripping from roast or baked meat is of most excellent flavour and should be carefully saved. When meat is roasted in the oven, *i.e.*, baked, the oven must be well ventilated, otherwise the meat thus cooked may be spoiled by the shut-up steam and odours given off from the meat. Roasting before the open fire is more expensive than roasting in a close oven, the loss in weight being greater. Whether meat is cooked in the oven or in front of the fire, it must be exposed to great heat for the first ten

(* Potatoes are best boiled or steamed in their skins and so served. "Vegetables should be well washed, but not soaked, in water (with some salt to remove insects). Green vegetables should have plenty of room ; when boiling, the pan should be uncovered and the contents occasionally skimmed, and the vegetables should not remain in the water an instant after they are cooked."—Buckmaster.)

minutes at least, in order to retain the juices by hardening the outside and also to brown the surface. After that the heat should be slackened. If roasting in front of the fire, draw the joint back a little; if in the oven, put the damper in a little way. The degree of oven heat required for roasting is from 300–320° Fahr., according to the kind of meat cooked. Of beef the following are the best joints for roasting : topside, round, buttock, mid-rib and fore-rib. Of mutton, the shoulders and legs.

Frying.

Frying is not an economical mode of cooking. Food can be fried in two ways, viz., dry frying or wet frying. For dry frying only very little fat is required, whilst for deep frying, which is practically boiling in fat, sufficient fat to well cover the article to be cooked must be used. For frying in general the fat must be very hot—not less than 350° Fahr.—before the article to be thus cooked is put in. When the fat is not hot enough the article to be fried will be spoiled, because the fat will soak in and render it unsightly, generally indigestible, and sodden.

Wet frying or deep frying is done in a deep pan. This method is largely adopted for cooking fish, but whatever is fried must be first coated.* When the fat is hot enough to fry, a faint blue smoke will rise from it. When the fat merely bubbles it is not ready for frying, and if immersed too soon the fish will look dirty and sodden and will not cook properly. The fish when properly fried should be of a nice golden brown colour. The fat should be strained after the frying is done; it can then be used over and over again.

Stewing.

This is the most economical method of cooking, and is strongly recommended for cooking the cheaper part of meat. Meat unsuitable for either roasting or boiling may by long and gentle stewing be rendered tender, nourishing, and palatable. There is very little waste in stewing, for all the juices that escape from the meat will go into the gravy or sauce served with it. It is also economical because it requires very little fuel, for after the

---

* Further directions as to this will be found on pages 17 and 18.

preliminary process of cooking the stewing can proceed at a low degree of heat.*   Actual boiling heat is scarcely ever required for stewing.

On Economy.

Punctuality, cleanliness and economy, are indispensable qualifications for every cook and officer in charge of a kitchen.   Bones and trimmings from roast, baked or boiled meats, must be saved and utilised for making stock.†   The fat which comes to the surface of the stock should be carefully removed before straining off the stock, and used for mixing with other fat which is being "rendered down" or clarified.   Dripping so prepared is most excellent for pastry, puddings, and for general cooking purposes. It is decidedly unwise to accept meat with a large proportion of fat, suet, etc., and then use it for rendering down, nor is it desirable to return such fat and get the butcher to make allowance.   It is far better to reject meat which is sent in too fat and to order suet, etc., under a separate heading and at a separate price.

The sale of fat is a sign of bad management, and Guardians would do well to order a daily Dripping Return and Account to be kept in each kitchen.

* ("The perfection of stewing depends upon the slow process by which the cooking is accomplished ; the temperature should never exceed 190° F."— Buckmaster.)

† (This must be done regularly and carefully *day by day*, no accumulation of trimmings or ingredients for the stock-pot can be permitted under any circumstances.)

RECIPES.

Clarified Fat.

Fat—cooked and uncooked.
Cold water to cover, or about $\frac{1}{2}$ gill to every pound of fat.

"Cut up the fat into pieces about half an inch square. Put into a pan, cover with cold water and bring to the boil. Skim carefully.

"Care must be taken that the fat does not burn. It must be kept over the fire until the pieces are slightly brown. Cool and strain. The slightest smell indicates over-cooking."

(From "Artizan Recipes," published by the National Training School of Cookery.)

For issue in lieu of butter, dripping from roast meat or that made from suet is preferable; that made from skimmings of the stock-pot is suitable for cooking purposes.

"100 lbs. ration-meat are found to produce as follows:—

Dripping.

Suet or surplus fat removed previous to cooking and clarified $3\frac{2}{16}$ lbs.
Fat skimmed during cooking and clarified   ..   ..   .. $\frac{11}{16}$,,
Fat skimmed from stock-pot and clarified   ..   ..   .. $1\frac{9}{16}$,,

Total .. $5\frac{6}{16}$,,

(Army Cookery Manual.)

Stock Broth.

Ingredients.

$1\frac{1}{2}$ oz. Bones.
$\frac{1}{2}$ oz. Carrots, Turnips and Onion.
Water, or Meat Liquor sufficient to produce 1 pint.
A few Peppercorns.
Salt and Pepper.   Bunch of Herbs.

Method.—Meat liquor or stock must be prepared in clean and suitable cooking-vessels (known as stock-pot). Any unserved gravy or meat juice, bones or gristle left over from boiled or roast meat may be put into the stock-pot.

Chop the bones into small pieces, put them into the cold water with a little salt, let it come to the boil, skim. If required at once, add the vegetables previously cleaned and sliced, also the herbs and peppercorns. If not required the same day, defer adding vegetables till next morning. Simmer from 3 to 4 hours. The stock is then ready for use. When the liquor is not used on the day on which it is prepared, it must be re-boiled first thing in the morning.

The stock-pot demands and will repay the most scrupulous care.

The following is taken from the "Manual of Military Cooking":—

"In order to ensure a constant change in the stock and that no bones remain longer than three days in the pot the following system should be adhered to :

The bones, vegetables, etc., should be placed in a net with a tally attached before being boiled, the bones of the second and third day should be similarly treated ; after the third day the bones boiled upon the first day should be removed, and similarly the bones of the subsequent days, the stock being continually replenished from day to day. The bones should always be removed from the stock before the vegetables and other ingredients are added. . . . Every effort should be made to reserve special boilers for making stock, in order that, if possible, the surplus portion of unused stock should be carried on from day to day. This process adds considerably to the strength of the soup made."

Vegetable Broth.

Ingredients.

1 pint Meat Liquor, or a sufficiency.
2 ozs. Fresh Vegetables—Cabbage, Carrot, Turnip, Onion, Leek, etc. (cut into dice).
$\frac{1}{2}$ oz. Dripping.   Salt and Pepper to taste.

Method.—Clean the vegetables and cut the cabbage and leek into fine shreds or dice. Mince finely the onion, carrot, and turnip, put all into a pot, add the dripping and cook over the fire for ten minutes. Then add the liquor, and boil for twenty minutes. Skim and season to taste. To make 1 pint of broth.

Bouillon (or Beef Broth).

Ingredients.

3 ozs. Raw Meat free from bone (Beef Stickings or similar quality).
5 ozs. Carrots, Turnips, Onions or Parsnips, and Cabbage.
Seasoning (Pepper, Salt and Herbs to taste).
1 pint Water, or a sufficiency.

Method.—Cut up the meat in large pieces, put it into the water, add seasoning and boil, skim, and let it simmer for one hour. Then add the vegetables (previously cleaned and cut up small) and herbs, and boil gently for another three hours. This will make 1 pint of bouillon, which can be served as a broth in place of beef tea, but must then be strained if required clear.

Pea Soup.

Ingredients.

3 ozs. Raw Meat (Beef Stickings or similar quality) without bones.
2 ozs. Bones and Gristle chopped small.
2 ozs. Split Peas.
Salt and Pepper to taste.
½ oz. Oatmeal.
1 oz. Carrot, Turnip and Onion.
Mixed Herbs to taste, i.e., Powdered Dried Parsley, Bayleaf, Sage, Marjoram, etc.
Water, a sufficiency.

Method.—Cut the meat into slices. Put the meat and bones in pot with cold water containing a little salt. Put the bones in a net and remove when soup is made. Heat up, skim ; when the pot boils, add cleaned vegetables, fresh and dry, also the peas, previously well washed, and cook for four hours to obtain 1 pint of soup. The meat to be served with the soup and fresh vegetables to be cut up very small. This is sufficient to make 1 pint of soup.

Lentil Soup.

Proceed as for pea soup, substituting 2 ozs. Lentils for peas.

Barley Soup.

Proceed as for pea soup, substituting 1 oz. Scotch barley for 2 ozs. peas.

Haricot Soup.

Ingredients.

3 ozs. Raw Meat without bones (Beef Stickings or similar quality) cut up small.
1 oz. Vegetables.
Dried Herbs and Salt and Pepper to taste.
2 ozs. Bones, cut up.
1 oz. Haricot Beans.
½ oz. Flour.
½ oz. Fat (Dripping).
Water, a sufficiency.

Method.—Put the meat and bones into a pot with cold water ; boil, skim, add vegetables and haricot beans previously well washed, cook slowly till reduced to one pint. Put the bones in a net, and remove when the stock is finished. Brown the flour in the dripping (a chestnut brown), dilute with some hot water and pour into the prepared stock. Stir till it boils, and cook for another twenty minutes. Season to taste. To make one pint of soup.

Meat Stew (or Scouse).

Ingredients.

5 ozs. Raw Beef free from bone (Stickings or similar quality).
1 oz. Flour.
½ oz. Dripping or Fat.
4 ozs. Potatoes.
4 ozs. Carrots and Turnips.
½ oz. Onions.
Pepper and Salt to taste.
Water to make 1 pint.

Method.—Cut up the meat and vegetables. Fry the flour in the fat till brown, stir in the water, add pepper and salt ; then put in the meat and vegetables. Simmer gently for two hours. To make 1 pint of stew.

Hotch-Potch Stew.

Ingredients.

5 ozs. Raw Beef free from bone (Stickings or similar quality).
¼ oz. Flour.
¼ oz. Peas (whole or split).
¼ oz. Scotch Barley.
4 ozs. Carrots or Turnips.
4 ozs. Cabbage.
1 oz. Onion.
Stock or Water sufficient to make 1 pint.
Seasoning – Pepper, Salt, Herbs to Taste.

Method.—Soak the peas overnight. Peel, or scrape clean, and cut the vegetables and onions into small squares. Scald the barley by pouring boiling water over it, allow to stand for a few minutes, then throw water away.

Add the meat, peas, barley, vegetables, and herbs to the stock or water, and simmer in a pan till the peas, barley, etc., are cooked.

Make the thickening by mixing flour, pepper, and salt with a little cold water.

Bring the meat and vegetables to a sharp boil, add the thickening, stir till it comes to the boil again, then simmer for half-an-hour.

(Adapted from Army Cookery Manual.)

Irish Stew.

Ingredients.

5 ozs. Raw Meat without bone, or 10 ozs. Neck of Mutton cut two ribs up, or Breast of Mutton.
Water, a sufficiency.
1 oz. Onions.
12 ozs. Potatoes.
Pepper and Salt to taste.

Method.—Cut up the meat, peel and slice the onions and potatoes ; stew the meat slowly for half-an-hour. Season with pepper and salt, then add the potatoes and onions, cover the pan well and cook for another hour. To make 1 pint of stew, exclusive of bones.

Meat Pudding.

Ingredients.

5 ozs. Raw Beef free from bone (Skirting or Clods and Stickings).
2 ozs. Beef Suet.
5 ozs. Flour.
Seasoning to taste.
1 gill of Water, or a sufficiency.

Method.—Cut up the meat, add seasoning. Chop the suet, mix in the flour with a little salt, and make a paste, adding the needful quantity of water. Line a basin which has been greased, place in the meat and pour water over it; cover with a lid of paste, tie a cloth over, and boil for 2 hours. To make 1 lb. of meat pudding.

Meat Pie.

Ingredients.

5 ozs. Raw Beef free from bone (Stickings or similar quality).
$\frac{3}{4}$ gill Water, or a sufficiency.
5 ozs. Flour.
Salt and Pepper to taste.
4 ozs. Potatoes.
$1\frac{1}{2}$ ozs. Dripping or Fat.

Method.—Cut up the meat in pieces, season with pepper and salt, put into a baking-tin, add water. Slice the potatoes and lay them on top of meat. Rub the dripping into the flour, make into a paste with cold water, lay the crust on top of the meat and potatoes, and bake two hours. This will make 1 lb.

Potato Pie.

Ingredients.

5 ozs. Raw Meat free from bone (Beef Skirting, Middle
        Pieces, Clods and Stickings).
1 oz. Dripping or Fat.   1 oz. Flour.
Pepper and Salt to taste. $\frac{1}{2}$ gill Meat Liquor.
8 ozs. Potatoes. $\frac{1}{2}$ oz. Onion.

Method.—Cut the meat up in pieces. Boil the potatoes, mash
with a fork; add dripping and flour, and make into a paste. Put
the meat into a dish, season with pepper, salt, onion, and meat
liquor, spread paste on top, and bake in the oven for one hour.
To make 1 lb.

Shepherd's Pie.

Ingredients.

4 ozs. Cold Meat free from bone and gristle.
$\frac{1}{2}$ oz. Fat.
12 ozs. Cold Potatoes.
$\frac{1}{2}$ oz. Onion, minced.
$\frac{1}{4}$ gill Gravy or Stock.
Pepper and Salt to taste.

Method.—Grease a tin, line it with potatoes which have been
mashed. Cut the meat up into dice, lay it in the tin, add gravy,
and season with onion, pepper, and salt. Cover this with potatoes,
put pieces of fat over the top. Cook for about half-an-hour until
hot and brown. This will make 1 lb.

Sea Pie.

Ingredients.

5 ozs. Raw Meat free from bone (Beef Stickings or similar quality).
$\frac{1}{4}$ oz. Fat.
Pepper, salt, sufficiency.
5 ozs. Carrots, Onions and Turnips.
$\frac{1}{4}$ oz. Flour.
Water, a sufficiency.

For Crust.

2 ozs. Flour.
Salt, a sufficiency.
¾ oz. Fat.
Cold Water, a sufficiency.

Method.—Melt the dripping in the pan, when hot put in the onion sliced ; fry golden brown, sprinkle in the flour, add water, and boil up. Add meat cut into pieces about one inch square, also vegetables cut into small dice. Simmer or steam gently for half-an-hour.

Make crust of flour, chopped suet, salt, and water. Roll out to size of the pan. Put carefully over the meat, and simmer or steam gently from 1½ to 2 hours. For serving, cut crust into portions, serve out the meat and vegetables, and place crust on top of each portion. To make 1 lb.

Pasties.

Ingredients.

4 ozs. Meat, Raw or Cooked, free from bone.
7 ozs. Flour.
½ oz. Onion.
2 ozs. Potatoes.
2 ozs. Dripping.
Salt and Pepper to taste.
Water, a sufficiency.

Method.—Cut the meat into small pieces, wash and peel the potatoes and cut them into dice ; chop the onion up finely ; mix them all together on a plate, with pepper and salt and two table-spoonfuls of cold water. Put the flour into a basin, rub the dripping into it, and add sufficient water to make it into a stiff paste. Flour a board, and put the paste on it ; roll it out about a quarter of an inch thick. Cut the pastry into pieces six or seven inches square, and place a little of the meat, potato, and onion in the centre of each ; fold the pastry over the meat. Place on a baking-sheet, and bake from half to three-quarters of an hour. This is sufficient to make four pasties of 4 ozs. each.

Cooked Meat Minced.

Pass the ration of cooked meat through mincer, and take care that it is served hot and with gravy.

Hashed Meat.

Ingredients.

12 ozs. Cooked or Tinned Meat free from bone.
2 ozs. Onion.
1 oz. Flour.
1 oz. Fat.
Stock or Water, a sufficiency.
Pepper and Salt to taste.

Method.—Chop the onions fine, and stew them with the flour and fat and a small quantity of stock or water, well stirred until the onion is cooked. Add the meat, cut across the grain into slices stir till quite hot and serve.* To make 1 lb.

Collops—Minced.

Ingredients.

1 lb. Raw Beef free from bone (Clods, Stickings, or similar quality).
½ oz. Onion.
1½ ozs. of Water, or a sufficiency.

Method.—Pass the meat through mincer, add water with pepper and salt to taste, also the chopped onions. Cook in a pan and serve hot. To make 1 lb.

Savoury Mince.

Ingredients.

½ lb. Cooked Meat (or 10 ozs. Raw Meat) free from bone.
1 oz. Onion.
Seasoning (Salt and Pepper) to taste.
2 ozs. Bread.
1 oz. Dripping.
½ pint Meat Liquor.

* ("Remember that the meat is already cooked and must only be warmed through."—Buckmaster.)

Method.—Cut up the meat in dice, soak the bread in meat liquor. Cut up the onion, fry in the dripping, add meat liquor and seasoning. Boil up, then add the meat and bread. Make hot through, and serve. To make 1 pint of mince.

Rice—plain boiled.

Ingredients.

3 ozs. Rice.
Water and Salt, a sufficiency to produce 1 lb.]

Method.—See that the water is boiling, then sprinkle in the rice (the latter should be first washed and drained). Allow it to boil fast for about twenty to twenty-five minutes.

Cooked Haricot Beans.

Ingredients.

8 ozs. Haricot Beans.
$\frac{1}{4}$ oz. Fat.
Pepper and Salt to taste.
Water, a sufficiency.

Method.—Wash the beans and steep them overnight in cold water. Place them in a saucepan with the fat and sufficient water and some salt. Boil two and a half hours or until tender. Serve hot and peppered. To make 1 lb.

Pease Pudding.

Ingredients.

$\frac{1}{2}$ lb. Split Peas.
$\frac{1}{4}$ oz. Fat.
Salt to taste.
Water, a sufficiency.

Wash the peas and steep them overnight, pour off the water, and tie up the peas tightly in a cloth (rinsed and floured). Boil in salted water (or meat liquor) or steam (until thoroughly cooked). Untie the pudding, mash the peas with the fat, season, and serve hot. Product, 1 lb.

Potatoes with Milk: (Tatws-Llaeth).

Ingredients.

10 ozs. Boiled Potatoes (hot or cold).
1 oz. Fat.
1 oz. Flour.
1 gill Milk.
Salt to taste.

Method.—Melt the fat and mix it with the flour in a stew-pan add gradually the milk, stirring with a wooden spoon ; season with salt and boil up. Then add the potatoes previously cut into slices or mashed. Stew for a quarter of an hour and serve hot with buttermilk. To make 1 lb.

The Same with Cheese.

If the dietary table allows a ration of cheese instead of buttermilk with the potatoes, the cheese may be chopped or otherwise finely divided and mixed with the potatoes, etc., prepared as directed above and browned in the oven.

DIRECTIONS FOR COOKING FISH.

Fried Fish.

Method suitable for plaice, cod, haddock, or skate. For small quantities :—

Wash and wipe the fish, dry it thoroughly, and cut up into even-sized pieces, each weighing about $\frac{1}{4}$ lb.

Prepare a batter and let it stand for some hours. Dip each piece of fish into batter so that it is completely covered, and drop into deep fat (clarified fat and dripping) ; the fat must be smoking hot. Fry for about five minutes, or until the fish has acquired a

c

nice light brown or golden brown. Drain well and serve. Do not attempt to fry too many pieces of fish at one time.

Note.—The fat used for frying must be moderately white, and there must be enough of it to well cover the fish to be fried in it. It should be strained at least once a week.

For large quantities : the following instructions communicated by the master of the Portsmouth Workhouse may be of service :—

"Wash and wipe the fish, dry it thoroughly, and cut into pieces of approximate ration-weight. Roll each piece in dry flour until thoroughly covered and drop into smoking hot fat. Fry until the fish has acquired a nice brown colour, then place the pieces on drainers in a large gas oven until served."

Fish fried in batter gains in weight by having batter baked on it.

Fish fried after being rolled in flour loses $\frac{1}{2}$ oz. in the lb.

Batter for Frying Fish, etc.

Ingredients.

$\frac{1}{4}$ lb. of Flour.
$1\frac{1}{2}$ gills Tepid Water.
$\frac{1}{2}$ oz. Fat.
$\frac{1}{2}$ teaspoonful Salt.

Method.—Melt the fat. Mix the flour and salt in a basin, add the fat and, by degrees, the water. Beat well, and let it stand for one hour or longer. This will make enough batter for frying two pounds of fish, or four portions of 8 ozs. each. If the batter is found too stiff add a little more water to it.

Boiled Fish.

COD, HADDOCK, HAKE, ETC.

Wash and wipe the fish, put it in a fish-kettle with strainer, and pour over enough warm water to well cover the fish. Add salt and vinegar in the proportion of one teaspoonful to one pint. Bring the fish slowly to the boil, then move on one side and let it cook slowly till tender. Fish must never be allowed to boil fast.

Fish-Sauce or White Sauce.

Ingredients.

1 oz. Dripping.
½ pint Milk.
1½ ozs. Flour.
Salt and Vinegar to taste.
½ pint Water or Fish Liquor.

(*To make "Fish-liquor"* :—Boil up bones and fins, 1 lb. to a quart of water; add a little salt; boil about 10 minutes; skim and strain.)

Method.—Melt the fat, stir in the flour, and let fry for a few minutes without browning, then add gradually the fish liquor (or water) and milk. Stir till it boils, add the vinegar and salt, and boil for ten minutes. The sauce is then ready. It should not be lumpy. To make 1 pint of sauce.

Fish Pie.

Ingredients.

5½ ozs. Raw or Cooked Fish (free from skin and bones).
¾ oz. Fat.
½ lb. Potatoes (cooked and mashed).
1 gill White Sauce.
Salt and Pepper to taste.

Method.—Cover the bottom of a greased pie-dish with a layer of mashed potatoes, upon this pour a layer of sauce, then put in layers of fish; season with pepper and salt. Cover with mashed potatoes, place a few small pieces of fat on top, and bake for twenty minutes. Product, 1 lb.

Dough for Dumplings and Cakes.

Ingredients.

½ quartern Flour (household or second).
½ oz. Yeast.
3 gills Water.
Salt, a sufficiency.

Method.—Put the flour into a basin, make a well in the centre. Mix the yeast with a little tepid water, and work in sufficient flour

C 2

to form a kind of batter. Allow it to stand in a warm place for about one hour. When the yeast, etc., has risen, add the remainder of water by degrees, beat the mixture thoroughly and work into a dough; use as directed. Product, $2\frac{1}{2}$ lbs.

Seed Cake.

Ingredients.

13 ozs. Dough.
2 ozs. Dripping.
2 ozs. Moist Sugar.
$\frac{1}{4}$ oz. Carraway Seeds.

Method.—Melt the dripping, add the moist sugar, and stir into the dough, mix in the carraway seeds, and allow to stand for at least half-an-hour. Three-parts fill a greased cake-tin with the prepared dough, set aside to rise and bake in a moderately-heated oven from forty to fifty minutes. Product, 1 lb.

Plain Cake.

Ingredients.

$7\frac{1}{2}$ ozs. Flour.
2 ozs. Moist Sugar.
$\frac{1}{4}$ oz. Baking Powder.
1 small pinch of Salt.
2 ozs. Dripping.
1 oz. Currants.
$\frac{1}{2}$ gill Milk.
$\frac{1}{2}$ gill Water, or a sufficiency.

Method.—Work the dripping and sugar in a basin till quite creamy, add the flour, a small pinch of salt, and the currants (previously cleaned). Stir in the milk gradually, and add the baking-powder last of all. Beat the whole well for a few minutes. Put the mixture in a well-greased cake-tin, and bake in a moderate oven for about forty-five minutes. Product, 1 lb.

Dumplings.

Ingredients.

11 ozs. Bread Dough.

Method.—Shape the dough into round balls, each weighing about 3 ozs.; drop them into boiling water, and let boil for twenty minutes. To make 1 lb.

Baked Batter Pudding.

Ingredients.

8 ozs. Flour.
1½ gills Milk.
1½ gills Water, or a sufficiency.
½ oz. Fat.
½ oz. Baking Powder.
Pepper and Salt to taste.

Method.—Mix the flour, pepper, salt and baking-powder well together; add the milk and water, and make a batter. Grease a baking-tin, run the batter into it about ½ inch deep. Place small pieces of fat on the top, and bake in a moderate oven. To make 1 lb.

Suet Pudding (Steamed).

Ingredients.

8 ozs. Flour.
½ teaspoonful Salt.
1½ gills Water, or a sufficiency.
2 ozs. Beef Suet.

Method.—Chop the suet, mix with the flour and salt, and make into a stiff dough with the water. Tie in a floured pudding-cloth, and boil or steam two hours, or until cooked. Serve with broth, gravy, or treacle. This will make 1 lb. This pudding is best steamed.

Roley-Poley Pudding.

(BOILED OR STEAMED.)

Ingredients.

8 ozs. Flour.
1½ gills Water.
2 ozs. Beef Suet.
Baking Powder and Salt, a sufficiency.
1½ ozs. Jam (or 2 ozs. Treacle).

Method.—Chop the suet; mix with the flour, baking-powder and salt, and roll the paste out on a floured board; spread the jam or treacle on the paste; wet the edges of the paste, and roll it up, pressing the edges together. Tie it up in a floured pudding-cloth previously dipped in boiling water, and boil or steam for two hours, or until cooked. To make 1 lb.

N.B.—If treacle or syrup is used, a portion of the flour should be reserved to thicken it before it is spread on the paste.

Golden Pudding.

Ingredients.

6 ozs. Flour.
2 ozs. Beef Fat or Dripping.
¼ teaspoonful Carbonate of Soda.
Salt, a sufficiency.
¼ lb. Treacle (or Golden Syrup).
½ gill Milk.
1 teaspoonful Ground Ginger.
1 gill Water, or a sufficiency.

Method.—Chop the suet, and mix with the flour, soda and ginger; add the treacle and milk, and mix all together. Pour into a greased basin, and steam for an hour and a half, or until cooked. To make 1 lb. of pudding.

Dry Fruit Pudding.

Ingredients.

7 ozs. Flour.
2 ozs. Fat.
1 gill Water, or a sufficiency.
2 ozs. Figs or Raisins, or Currants.
$\frac{1}{4}$ teaspoonful Salt.

Method.—Put the flour into a basin, add the salt. Chop the fruit and suet, add these to the flour. Mix with water, tie in a pudding-cloth, and boil three hours, or until cooked. To make 1 lb.

Fresh-Fruit Pudding.

Ingredients.

5 ozs. Flour.
1$\frac{1}{2}$ ozs. Fat.
$\frac{1}{4}$ teaspoonful Salt.
6 ozs. Fruit (including Rhubarb) in season at reasonable cost.
1 oz. Sugar.
1 gill Cold Water, or a sufficiency.
Small teaspoonful Baking Powder.

Method.—Put the flour into a basin, add the salt; chop the suet, add to the flour, and mix with some water into a stiff paste. Peel, prepare, and slice the fruit. Grease a basin, line with paste, fill with fruit, add water as may be requisite, put in the sugar, cover with a lid of paste, tie over with a cloth previously dipped in hot water, and boil 1$\frac{1}{2}$ hours, or until cooked. To make 1 lb.

Stewed Fruit.

Ingredients.

1 lb. Rhubarb or Fruit in season (at reasonable cost).
Sugar not exceeding 3 ozs.
Water, a sufficiency.

Method.—Suitably prepare the fruit, and stew with the sugar and a sufficiency of water until tender and well cooked. To make 1 pint of stewed fruit.

Bread Pudding (Steamed).

Ingredients.

4 ozs. Bread.
1 oz. Sugar.
1 teaspoonful Mixed Spice.
1 oz. Fat or Beef Suet.
1 oz. Currants or Raisins stoned and cleaned.
½ pint Milk.

Method.—Break up the bread into pieces and soak it in the milk ; if found too dry a little water may also be added. Chop the suet finely, clean the currants or raisins ; grease the basins or tins. Stir the spice, fruit and suet, into the bread mixture, and mix well. Fill the basins or tins with the mixture, cover with greased and floured cloth, tie down, and boil or steam for about 2½ hours, or until cooked. Sufficient to make 1 lb.

Bread Pudding (Baked).

Proceed as directed for steamed Bread Pudding, using the same ingredients.

Melt ½ ounce of dripping in a tin, put the mixture in the tin, spread it out, and bake for about ½ hour. Product, 12 ozs.

MILK PUDDINGS.

Rice Pudding.*

Ingredients.

3 ozs. Rice.*
½ oz. Sugar.
2 gills water, or a sufficiency.
Salt, a sufficiency.
½ oz. Fat.
½ pint Milk.

Method.—Wash and boil up the rice in half-pint of water ; grease a pie-dish and put in the rice, the milk, and sugar. Place

* (Semolina or Sago may be substituted by direction of the Guardians.)

the fat on top, divided in very small pieces. Bake in a slow oven for about an hour and a quarter, or stew until cooked. A pinch of salt should be mixed with the milk, etc. To make 1 lb. pudding.

Rice Milk.

Ingredients.

1 oz. Rice.
$\frac{1}{2}$ oz. Sugar.
$\frac{1}{4}$ oz. Fat.
1 pint Milk.
Salt, a sufficiency.

Method.—Proceed as for Rice Pudding. To make 1 pint.

Porridge (Sturrow. Sican-Gwyn).

Ingredients.

4 ozs. Oatmeal
Water and Salt, a sufficiency } To make 1 pint.

Method.—Add the oatmeal gradually to the boiling water with the salt; stir till it is thick and smooth enough, and boil for twenty minutes, or until cooked.

Gruel.

Ingredients.

2 ozs. Oatmeal
$\frac{1}{2}$ oz. Treacle
Water and Salt, a sufficiency } To make 1 pint.

Allspice to be used occasionally.

Method.—As for porridge.

Tea.

(For Adults.)

Ingredients.

$\frac{2}{10}$ oz. Tea.
2 ozs. Milk.
$\frac{1}{2}$ oz. Sugar.
Water to make 1 pint.

Method.—Tea made in large quantities is generally made in appropriately sized urns. In such cases the tea is introduced in a muslin bag or else in a strainer. As soon as the water actually boils drop in the tea, allow it to draw for not more than eight minutes. After this the bag or strainer of tea should be removed, or the liquor drawn off from the leaves and then kept hot till wanted. Milk and sugar are then added. The tea-urn or tea-pot must be thoroughly clean before use, and allowed to dry well after use before it is set aside.

Tea.

(For Children. Half Milk.)

Ingredients.

$\frac{2}{10}$ oz. Tea.
$\frac{1}{2}$ pint Milk.
$\frac{1}{2}$ oz. Sugar.
Water to make 1 pint.

Method.—As above.

Coffee.

Coffee should be prepared whole (berries), roasted, and should be finely ground in sufficient quantity for one day's consumption. One ounce of chicory is to be added to each quarter pound of coffee and well mixed.

Coffee.

(For Adults.)

Ingredients.

$\frac{4}{10}$ oz. Coffee, containing the above-named proportion of Chicory.
$\frac{1}{2}$ oz. Sugar.
3 ozs. Milk.
Water to make 1 pint.

Method.—Special care must be taken to see that the water is actually boiling before it is poured on to the coffee. The boiler should be rinsed with boiling water before the dry coffee is put in ; then pour the required quantity of boiling water gradually on to the coffee. Allow it to stand (heated) for some ten minutes before serving, so as to thoroughly extract its strength. When drawn off, the milk, which must be previously boiled, is then added with the sugar.

Coffee.

(For Children. Half Milk.)

Ingredients,

$\frac{4}{10}$ oz. Coffee with Chicory.
$\frac{1}{2}$ oz. Sugar.
$\frac{1}{2}$ pint Milk.
Water to make 1 pint.

Method.—As above.

Cocoa.

(For Adults.)

Ingredients.

$\frac{1}{2}$ oz. Cocoa.
3 ozs. Milk.
$\frac{4}{10}$ oz. Sugar.
Water to make 1 pint.

Method.—Pour the milk gradually on to the cocoa, and stir to a smooth paste ; add the water, stir till it boils, and allow to boil for at least ten minutes ; add the sugar shortly before serving.

Cocoa.

(For Children. Half Milk.)

Ingredients.

$\frac{1}{2}$ oz. Cocoa.
$\frac{1}{2}$ pint Milk.
$\frac{4}{10}$ oz. Sugar.
Water to make 1 pint.

Method.—As above.

SICK DIETS.

The following recipes are added for the convenience of medical officers of workhouses and infirmaries :—

Beef Tea.

Ingredients.

1 lb. Lean Beef (free from bone).
Salt to taste.
Water to make 1 pint.

Method.—Shred the meat finely, removing all fat and skin; put it in a double saucepan or jacketed pan with very little salt, pour cold water over it and let it soak for fifteen minutes, cover the pan and stew very gently for one and a half hours or longer, being careful not to allow the beef tea to boil. Skim, strain, if so directed by the Medical Officer, and serve

Beef Tea (quickly made).

Ingredients and procedure as above with or without the pre-liminary soaking, but after stewing for ten minutes, or longer if there be time, bring the contents of the pan to the simmering point and simmer slowly for ten minutes, but without allowing it to boil. Skim, strain, if so directed by the Medical Officer, and serve.

Raw Meat Juice.

Ingredients.

4 ozs. Lean Raw Beef, free from all fat and gristle.
Water, a sufficiency ; Salt to taste.

Method.—Mince the meat finely, sprinkle it with a little salt, add four ounces of cold water. Stir it well and allow to soak for one hour. Forcibly press the juice through a muslin. Serve alone or with milk as directed. The juice should be prepared twice daily and must be kept cold. To make one-fifth of a pint.

Mutton Broth.

Ingredients.

1 lb. Lean Mutton (Scrag end of Neck).
$\frac{1}{4}$ lb. Vegetables (Carrot, Turnip and Onion).
$\frac{1}{2}$ oz. Barley or Rice.
Water, a sufficiency.
Seasoning to taste.

Method.—Cut the meat into small pieces, removing the fat, and put it in the double saucepan or jacketed pan with the cold water ; let it soak. Chop the bones, place them in a net and cook them with the meat. When it boils add the salt and skim well. Cut the vegetables into dice ; wash the barley or rice and put it with the vegetables into the broth. Allow it to cook gently for two hours. To serve, take out the bones and apportion the meat equally. To make one pint.

Rabbit Broth.

Ingredients.

1 Rabbit.
3 pints Water.
1 oz. Pearl Barley.
2 ozs. Onion.
2 ozs. Carrot.
Seasoning to taste.

Cut the rabbit into small joints, put it to boil with the water (cold), skim as it boils ; then add the vegetables previously cleaned, cook slowly for one hour and a quarter, add the barley, cook for another fifteen minutes, season to taste, strain and serve. To make two pints and a half.

Flummery ("Uwd-a-Lleath," "Succan-a-Lleath," "Sowans").

Ingredients.

6 ozs. Unsifted Oatmeal.
Water sufficient to make 1 gallon.

Method.—Soak the meal in luke-warm water for twenty-four hours ; run or press the mixture through a fine hair sieve. Boil it until it becomes thick ; let it stand for fifteen minutes and serve with milk.

Barley Water.

Ingredients.

1 oz. Barley.
½ Lemon.
1 oz. Sugar.
Water sufficient to make 2 pints.

Method.—Put the barley, previously washed, into a saucepan with the water and the thin rind of lemon ; boil slowly for twenty minutes. Let it stand till cold, add the juice of lemon and the sugar, then strain and serve.

Lemonade.

Ingredients.

1 Lemon.
2 ozs. Sugar.
2 quarts Water.

Method.—Peel the lemon as thinly as possible and put it into a saucepan with the sugar and water, boil for about ten minutes, then add the juice of the lemon. Let it cool and strain.

Unless the lemon is peeled very thinly, the lemonade will become bitter.

Corn-Flour.

Ingredients.

1 oz. Cornflour.
1 oz. Sugar.
1 pint Milk.

Method.—Mix the cornflour smoothly with the milk. Boil for about ten minutes, stirring well the whole time. Add the sugar and serve. To make one pint.

Plain Jelly.

Ingredients.

2 ozs. Sugar.
1 oz. packet Gelatine.
Juice and Rind of 1 Lemon (or of 1 Orange).
1 pint Water.

Method.—Put all the above into a saucepan and whisk over the fire till almost, but not quite, boiling. Strain through a cloth, then pour into moulds to set.

INDEX.

LONDON : PRINTED BY WILLIAM CLOWES AND SONS, LIMITED,
STAMFORD STREET AND CHARING CROSS.

twenty

The Handbook of Cookery
for Irish Workhouses

In 1894, the Irish Local Government Board made a proposal to bring Irish workhouse dietaries into line with those operating in England, Wales and Scotland. By way of encouragement, it published some sample dietaries and ingredients lists that were then in use in the workhouses at Aylsham, Glossop, St Marylebone, Glasgow, Buchan and Inverness. Although there was little immediate response to this initiative, concerns continued to grow, particularly about the monotony of the food and wastage, especially bread. Finally, in 1910-11, the Irish LGB folowed the lead of their English counterparts a decade earlier. They compiled a long list of 'rations' from which unions could compile thier own dietary and at the same time published a new cookery manual to help workhouse cooks in Ireland adapt to the new dishes.

The book, *Handbook of Cookery for Irish Workhouses*, was subtitled 'Compiled from 'The Manual of Workhouse Cookery,' England;, 'The Manual of Military Cooking,' and other Authorities'. Somewhat longer than its English predecessor, the *Handbook* followed the same basic format, and many of same recipes. One innovation in the *Handbook* was the inclusion of two illustrations, describing the various joints obtained from a cow or sheep. Another addition in the *Irish Handbook* included advice on the operation of a 'stock-pot' where all meat bones, and other waste off-cuts were boiled, for up to five hours a day, to produce a liquor used in preparing soup or gravy. Bones in the stock-pot were used for up to two days then thrown away and replaced by fresh ones.

The extra recipes in the *Handbook* included a number of fish dishes such as fried mackerel, baked herrings, and boiled ling (otherwise known as Newfoundland dried fish). New vegetable dishes included colcannon (a mixture of potatoes and cabbage), and bacon and cabbage (the cabbage to be boiled for up to an hour). Nettles were also recommended as excellent springtime vegetables.

One dish that the *Handbook* did have in common with its English counterpart was the workhouse's signature dish, gruel. However, a slightly shorter second edition of the *Handbook* published in 1913 omitted this recipe – finally, a workhouse cookery book without gruel!

As it turned out, the *Handbook* was to have a fairly short shelf-life. Within a decade of its publication, the Irish War of Independence had resulted in the creation of the Irish Free State which did away with the Boards of Guardians and the workhouse system. During the ensuing Irish Civil War, a number of former workhouse buildings underwent military occupation and were damaged or burnt down. As was to be the case in England and Wales after 1930, many of the surviving buildings continued in use as hospitals or homes for the elderly or chronic invalids. The new institutions often inherited much from the workhouse era: the old buildings, existing inmates (now known as residents or patients), staff, and, no doubt, the odd workhouse cookbook.

HANDBOOK

OF

COOKERY

FOR

IRISH WORKHOUSES.

COMPILED FROM

"The Manual of Workhouse Cookery," England
"The Manual of Military Cooking,"
And other Authorities.

Issued to Boards of Guardians by
THE LOCAL GOVERNMENT BOARD FOR IRELAND.

DUBLIN:
PRINTED FOR HIS MAJESTY'S STATIONERY OFFICE
By ALEX. THOM & CO. (LIMITED), ABBEY-STREET.

And to be purchased, either directly or through any Bookseller, from
E. PONSONBY, LTD., 116 GRAFTON-STREET, DUBLIN; or
WYMAN AND SONS, (LIMITED), FETTER-LANE, E.C.; or
OLIVER & BOYD, TWEEDDALE COURT, EDINBURGH.

1911.
Price Threepence.

Left: The title page of the 1911 edition of the
Handbook of Irish Cookery.

The joints in beef and mutton.—Beef :—After slaughter the ox is chopped down, *i.e.*, divided into two sides. Each side is subsequently divided into two quarters, the divisions taking place between the twelfth and thirteenth ribs.

The usual custom is to "joint" the quarters as follows

In the forequarter :—

1. Clod or sticking piece—five joints of the cervical vertebræ

2. Chuck rib—three dorsal vertebræ, top ends of three ribs, bottom end of scapula, two cervical vertebræ—should be boned and stuffed, or may be baked and roasted whole. When stuffed, the bones should be made into gravy.

3. Middle rib—four dorsal vertebræ, top ends of four ribs, remainder of scapula. Can be cooked in a similar manner to the "chuck."

4. Fore rib—five dorsal vertebræ, top ends of five ribs Should be baked or roasted whole.

5. The Plate—lower ends of four ribs. May be boned and stuffed, or stewed, but should not be baked.

6. Brisket—Sternum and lower ends of eight ribs. Is best salted, but may be treated as the "plate."

7. Shoulder, or Leg of Mutton piece. Whole of the humerus, top of radius and ulna. Should be roasted, baked, or stewed.

8. Shin. Remainder of radius and ulna, less 4 inches which under terms of contract, must be removed from bottom end. Should be always used for soup or stew.

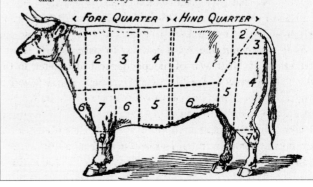

Right: The *Handbook's* culinary
atlas of the cow.

NETTLES.

Nettles are excellent vegetables in the spring. They should be boiled in plenty of boiling water with a little bread soda. When cooked, drain well, and chop them up as you would spinach, then place them in the dry boiler with some gravy or dripping, salt, and pepper. Stew for about 5 minutes and serve. There are various ways of cooking them, and they are a good substitute for other vegetables in soup.

The young leaf of the mangold wurzel is also excellent when cooked as above.

COLCANNON.

Ingredients.

12 ozs. potatoes.	½ oz. dripping.
6 ozs. cabbage.	Pepper and salt.

Method.

Boil the potatoes (peeled), and cabbage.

Mash the potatoes and mix with the finely chopped cabbage and the seasoning. Mix well with the melted dripping in pot. Put into a greased basin, make thoroughly hot in the oven, then turn out on a dish (1 lb.)

TO BOIL CABBAGE.
Method.

Take off all brown or faded leaves, remove the hard part of the stalk if the cabbage be old, and slit the stalk that it may cook more easily. Lay the cabbage in cold water with a little salt, for an hour. Must be cooked in plenty of fast boiling water with a tablespoonful of salt to every gallon, and a little bread soda. Boil quickly with the lid off, add a crust of bread to keep down smell. Time required depends upon their age—from half an hour to an hour.

Left: Stewed nettles and cabbage boiled for an hour – whoever said that workhouse food was unappetising?

HERRINGS FRIED.
Ingredients.

3 herrings,	1 tablespoonful of flour,
1 oz. fat,	Pepper and salt to taste.

Method.

Wash and scale herrings, split down back and remove bone, dry thoroughly, in a cloth. Mix flour with pepper and salt, pass herrings lightly through this mixture. Make fat quite hot in a frying pan, and fry the fish for 10 minutes. Drain in a dish before the fire.

FRIED MACKEREL.

Method.

Proceed as for herrings, splitting fish open down the back.

BAKED FRESH HERRINGS.

Method.

Take 1 dozen herrings, half with soft, half with hard roes. Empty, scrape and wash the fish well, and wipe with damp cloth to remove the scales ; split the bodies in halves, and remove the bones, heads, tails, and fins. Rub each half with pepper, salt, a very little mustard, and powdered allspice. Roll each half separately with tail end outward, and pack the rolls in a stone jar such as is used for table salt. Pound the soft roes and mix half a pint of vinegar and a little water, throw the liquid over the herrings. Put 6 bay leaves and 6 cloves on the top of the fish, and bake in a slow oven for about 1 hour.

BOILED LING OR NEWFOUNDLAND DRIED FISH.

Method.

Steep the ling overnight. Cut it to suitable size, and place it in a saucepan. Cover well with cold water, and bring to a boil, then let it simmer gently for half an hour.

Right: The *Handbook* was particularly strong on fish recipes.

Notes

1. Dickens and Tillotson, p. xv.
2. For Punishment of Sturdy Vagabonds and Beggars, 22 Henry VIII c. 12, 1536.
3. Eden Volume 3, Appendix 7.
4. Jackson.
5. Quoted in Pearl, p. 226.
6. Webb & Webb (1927) pp. 106-7.
7. Bellers.
8. Anon (1732), p. 53.
9. Ibid.
10. Hitchcock, p. 2.
11. Anon (1742), p. 1126.
12. Anon (1725), p. 5.
13. Cary, p. 10.
14. Anon (1832), p. 29.
15. Webb & Webb (1927), pp. 212-3.
16. Middleton Volume 2, p. 202.
17. Anon (1742), p. 1143.
18. Drummond and Wilbraham, p. 148.
19. Report of Royal Commission of Inquiry (1834) Appendix A, p. 532.
20. Ibid., p.275.
21. Anon (1903), p. 7.
22. Second Annual Report of the Poor Law Commissioners (1836), p. 314.
23. Drummond and Wilbraham, p. 235.
24. Report of Royal Commission of Inquiry (1834), p. 27.
25. Rich, p. 26.
26. Twentieth Annual Report of the Poor Law Board (1867-8), p. 46.
27. Royal Commission on the Poor Laws and Relief of Distress – Majority Report iv, p. 185.
28. Paupers in Workhouses, p. ii.
29. Majority Report. ii, p. 43.
30. Williams Statistical Appendix Sections B-C.
31. 1835 values from Johnston p. 131; 1991 values from COMA.
32. Haw, p. 109.
33. Third Annual Report of the Local Government Board (1874), pp. 248-61.
34. Lansbury, p. 136.
35. Roberts, p. 99.

36. Wythen Baxter, p. 439.
37. Preston-Thomas, p. 293.
38. Edwards, p. 16.
39. Smith (1866b), p. 52.
40. *The Lancet* (1865), Volume 86, pp. 73-4.
41. Ibid., pp. 298-300.
42. Reports by Poor Law Inspectors (1867-8), p. 385.
43. Return of Quantity of Spirits and Wine Consumed in Workhouses (1895).
44. Shaw, pp. 110-112.
45. Reid, pp. 66-7.
46. Rogers, p. 15.
47. Longmate (1974), p. 144.
48. Ribton-Turner, p. 277.
49. Fifth Annual Report of the Poor Law Commissioners (1839), p. 204.
50. Quoted in O'Connor, p. 129.
51. *The Lancet* (1847), Volume 49, p. 232.
52. Quoted in O'Connor, p. 137.
53. Fifth Annual Report of the Board of Supervision for the Relief of the Poor in Scotland (1850), pp. 2-14.
54. Mackay (1908), pp. 231-235.
55. Twelfth Annual Report of the Poor Law Commissioners (1846), p. 59.
56. Smith (1866a), p. 7.
57. Thirteenth Annual Report of the Local Government Board (1884), p.56.

Bibliography

RECIPE BOOKS

Cleland, E. (1759) *A New and Easy Method of Cookery*

Collingwood, F. and Woolams, J. (1797) *The Universal Cook, and City and Country Housekeeper*

Ellis, W. (1750) *The Country Housewife's Family Companion*

Glasse, H. (1747) *The Art of Cookery Made Plain and Easy*

Houghton, J. and Bradley, R. (1727) *A Collection for the Improvement of Husbandry and Trade Consisting of Many Valuable Materials Relating to Corn, Cattle, Coals, Hops, Wool, &c*

Nott, J. (1726) *The Cooks and Confectioners Dictionary: Or, the Accomplish'd Housewives Companion*

Shackleford, A. (1767) *The Modern Art of Cookery Improved or, Elegant, Cheap, and Easy Methods, of Preparing Most of the Dishes Now in Vogue*

BRITISH PARLIAMENTARY PAPERS

Abstract of Returns Made by the Overseers of the Poor (1777)

Annual Reports of the Poor Law Commissioners (1835-48)

Annual Reports of the Poor Law Board (1849-71)

Annual Reports of the Local Government Board (1872-1918)

Paupers in Workhouses (1861)

Report of the Royal Commission of Inquiry into the Administration and Practical Operation of the Poor Laws (1834)

Reports by Poor Law Inspectors on Workhouses in their Districts, in pursuance of Instructions, October 1866 (1867-8)

Return of Quantity of Spirits and Wine Consumed in Workhouses in England and Wales (1883, 1886, 1892, 1895)

Report of the Royal Commission on the Poor Laws and Relief of Distress (1909) – Majority Report and Minority Report

Smith, E. (1864) Report on the Food of the Poorer Labouring Classes in England (in Medical Officer of Privy Council: Sixth Report, 1863. pp. 216-329)

Smith, E. (1866a) Report to President of Poor Law Board by Doctor E. Smith, medical officer of Poor Law Board, on dietaries for inmates of workhouse

Smith, E. (1866b) Report to Poor Law Board on Metropolitan Workhouse Infirmaries and Sick-Wards

OTHER WORKS

Anon (1725) *An Account of Several Work-Houses for Employing and Maintaining the Poor, Setting Forth the Rules by Which They Are Governed*

Anon (1732) *An Account of Several Work-Houses...* (2nd edition)

Anon ['Christian Love Poor'] (1731) *The Workhouse Cruelty: Workhouses Turn'd Goals; and Goalers Executioners ... In the Parish of St. Giles's in the Fields, Etc*

Anon (1742) *A New and Compleat Survey of London, by a Citizen, and Native of London*

Anon (1847) 'M. Soyer's Irish Soup' (in *The Lancet*, vol. 49, pp. 232-33)

Anon (1903) *Hunslet Union New Workhouse and Infirmary* (Opening Souvenir Brochure)

Baxter, G.R.W. (1841) *The Book of the Bastiles*

Bellers, J. (1695) *Proposals for raising a College of Industry of all Useful Trades and Husbandry...*

Booth, W. (1890) *In Darkest England and the Way Out*

Burnett, J (1983) *Plenty and Want*

Cary, J. (1700) *An Account of the Proceedings of the Corporation of Bristol in Execution of the Act of Parliament for the Better Employing and Maintaining the Poor of That City*

COMA (1991) Dietary *Reference Values for Food Energy and Nutrients for the United Kingdom*

Dickens, C. and Tillotson, K. M. (1966) *Oliver Twist*

Drummond, J.C. and Wilbraham, A. (1939) *The Englishman's Food*

Eden, F.M.S. (1797) *The State of the Poor*

Edwards, G (1975) *The Road to Barlow Moor*

Gray, F. (1931) *The Tramp – His Meaning and Being*

Haw, G. (1911) *From Workhouse to Westminster: The Life Story of Will Crooks, M.P.*

Higgs, M. (1906) *Glimpses into the Abyss*

Hitchcock, T.V.E. ed. (1987) *Richard Hutton's Complaints Book: The Notebook of the Steward of the Quaker Workhouse at Clerkenwell 1711-1737*

Johnston, V.J. (1985) *Diet in Workhouses and Prisons, 1835-1895*

Lansbury, G. (1931) *My Life*

Leonard, E.M. (1900) *The Early History of English Poor Relief*

Longmate, N, (1968), *The Waterdrinkers*

Longmate, N. (1974) *The Workhouse*

London, J. (1903) *The People of the Abyss*

Mackay, G. (1908) *Management and Construction of Poorhouses and Almshouses*

Mackay, T. (1903) *A History of the English Poor Law (Volume III, 1834-1898)*

Middleton, C.T. (1778) *A New and Complete System of Geography*

O'Connor, J. (1995) *The Workhouses of Ireland*

Orwell, G. (1931) 'The Spike' (in *Adelphi*, vol.2, no.1)

Pearl, V. (1978) *Puritans and Poor Relief: the London Workhouse 1649-1660*

Place, A. (2004) *Pray Remember the Poor – the Poor Laws and Huddersfield*

Preston-Thomas, H. (1909) *The Work and Play of a Government Inspector*

Reid, A. (1994) *The Union Workhouse*

Ribton-Turner, C.J. (1887) *A History of Vagrants and Vagrancy, and Beggars and Begging*

Rich, B. (1614) *The Honestie of This Age*

Roberts, D. (1963) 'How Cruel Was the Victorian Poor Law?' (in *The Historical Journal*, vol. 6, pp.97-107)

Rogers, J. (1889) *Reminiscences of a Workhouse Medical Officer*

Slack, P. (1995) *The English Poor Law, 1531-1782*

Shaw, C. (1903) *When I was a Child*

Soyer, A. (1848) *Charitable cookery; or, The poor man's regenerator*

Smith, E (1870) *The Construction and Management of Workhouses*

Webb, S. and Webb, B.P. (1927) *English Poor Law History (Part I)*

Webb, S. and Webb, B.P. (1929) *English Poor Law History (Part II)*

Williams, K. (1981) *From Pauperism to Poverty*

WEBSITES

www.workhouses.org.uk

Name of Workhouse.	Inm'tes.	Men	Women.	Children.	Periodicals.	Newspapers.
ENGLAND.						
Ashton, near Manchester	776	330	284	162	None.	Odds and ends.
Blackburn	96	53	23	20	None,	None.
Bradford	500	300	200	...	Unsupplied.	Unsupplied.
Bromley, Kent	299	185	114	31	...	...
Bromsgrove	175	90	60	25	The *Quiver* occasionally.	None.
Brentford Workhouse, Isleworth	460	241	165	54	None.	Local.
Bury Union Workhouse...........	...	...	...	...	Have papers, &c.	Have library of 2,000 books.
Cheltenham	404	157	141	106	Too numerous to mention. There is a library.	Do.
Christ's Church.......................	130	35	35	40	None.	Fluctuating.
Coventry................................	349	157	128	64	1, the *Quiver*.	3 weekly, 3 or 4 daily.
Croydon	204	262	124	18	Well supplied.	Well supplied, except in the infirmary.
Derby	514	196	162	156	Fairly well.	30 per week.
Devonport	335	97	169	69	10 monthly.	None.
Dorchester	95	45	25	25	12 *Graphics* every fortnight.	Daily, one day old.
Dunmow, Essex	171	96	37	43	Irregular.	2 weekly.
Doddington, near Cambridge ...	137	60	33	44	*British Workman.*	Religious occasionally.
Dudley..................................	642	271	239	122	6 monthly.	5 weekly.
Eastville, Bristol	917	401	316	200	13 monthly.	20 weekly.
Epping Union	94	59	35	40	1 monthly.	2 daily.
Exeter—Union of St. Sodwell ...	319	154	101	14	Well supplied.	Well supplied, library 236 books.
— Union of St. Thomas	172	76	51	45	None to depend on.	Very seldom.
Gateshead	526	147	167	212	None.	4 weekly.
Great Yarmouth	500	200	200	100	Well supplied.	Well supplied, want books.
Guiltcross Union, Kenninghall, Thetford	99	...	...	35	None.	None except a few old sometimes.
Halifax..................................	458	251	156	51	Well supplied.	Well supplied.
Hull—Union of Sculcoates	719	Not divided.		170	Sufficient.	Sufficient; indeed, very good.
— Union of Hull, Corporation of the Poor......................	591	Not divided.		100	Inadequate.	Inadequate.
Hastings	225	83	81	61	Fairly well supplied.	Inmates buy the daily papers.
Howden, Yorks	65	30	18	17	None.	Occasionally.
Hampstead, West....................	262	128	114	20	No limit (?)	No limit (?)
Hexham Union	Not	mentioned.		...	Well supplied.	Well supplied.
Huddersfield	Not	given.	...	None.	5 monthly.	3 weekly, some 2 days old.
Kensington, St. Mary Abbots ...	810	300	480	30	Have a library.	Would be acceptable.
Leeds Union	469	186	133	150	In plenty.	Plenty.
Leek Union	141	59	36	46	Irregular.	Irregular.
Leicester...............................	634	...	...	...	Kyrie Society supplies.	Daily and weekly old papers.
Lewisham	1050	250	250	50	Occasional bundles.	1 local.
Liverpool, West Derby Union ...	2200	1000	1100	100	4 monthly.	None.
London—Hackney	1090	560	480	50	Well stocked library.	Require more.
— St. George's, Hanover-square	1532	1016	485	31	No regular supply.	8 daily, *Punch, Judy,* and *Fun* by lady visitors.
Manchester—Union of North Brierley	260	170	70	20	12 *British Workman* and *Children's Temperance.*	None.
Medway, near Rochester	607	246	264	167	6 monthly.	2 weekly.
Newcastle-on-Tyne	804	219	301	284	Have a library.	2 daily, 2 weekly.

What a typical workhouse inmate might be reading in 1890. At the time this list was compiled, most workhouses relied on charitable donations of books, magazines and newspapers. The supply varied widely, from 'none' at Blackburn to a library of over 2,000 books at nearby Bury.

Index

Note – *The Manual of Workhouse Cookery* includes its own recipe index (see page 181).

190

Other titles published by The History Press

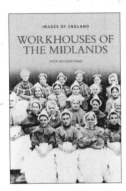

Workhouses of the Midlands
PETER HIGGINBOTHAM

With sections providing detailed histories of the establishments in each area, this book illustrates almost every facet of the evolution of the workhouse. Featuring more than 100 evocative images from across the Midlands, Derbyshire all the way through to Oxfordshire, *Workhouses of the Midlands* provides a unique insight into the regimented lifestyle of the workhouse and a history that should never be forgotten.

978 07524 4488 8

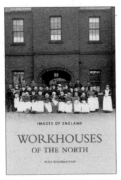

Workhouses of the North
PETER HIGGINBOTHAM

This book takes a look at both surviving and lost examples of workhouse buildings in the North of England, covering the old counties of Cumberland, Northumberland, Durham, Westmorland, Lancashire and Yorkshire. Family, local and social historians will all find it a source of useful reference and for the general reader it will provide an interesting account of an institution that few were sorry to see the end of.

978 07524 4001 9

Life in the Victorian & Edwardian Workhouse
MICHELLE HIGGS

This book establishes a true picture of what life was like in a workhouse, of why inmates entered them and of what they had to endure in their day-to-day routine. A comprehensive overview of the workhouse system gives a real and compelling insight into the social and moral reasons behind their growth in the Victorian era, while the kind of distinctions that were drawn between inmates are looked into, which, along with the social stigma of having been a workhouse inmate, tell us much about class attitudes of the time.

978 07524 4214 3

A Plain Cookery Book for the Working Classes
CHARLES ELMÉ FRANCATELLI

First published in 1852, Charles Elmé Francatelli's *Plain Cookbook for the Working Classes* features 241 recipes suitable for small budgets. From the simple art of boiling potatoes to the more advanced Pumpkin Porridge, each recipe is described in detail by Francatelli to ensure a delicious dish every meal time. With recipes ranging from Sheep's Head Broth to A Pudding made of Small Birds, Francatelli ably instructs even the most impoverished homemaker on how to prepare meals on a small budge

978 07524 4289 1

If you are interested in purchasing other books published by The History Press, or in case you have difficulty finding any History Press books in your local bookshop, you can also place orders directly through our website

www.thehistorypress.co.uk